# Asimov's *Foundation* and Philosophy

**Pop Culture and Philosophy®**

General Editor: George A. Reisch

**Volume 1** *Dave Chappelle and Philosophy: When Keeping It Wrong Gets Real* (2021) Edited by Mark Ralkowski

**Volume 2** *Neon Genesis Evangelion and Philosophy: That Syncing Feeling* (2022) Edited by Christian Cotton and Andrew M. Winters

**Volume 3** *The Ultimate Supernatural and Philosophy: Saving People, Killing Things, the Family Business* (2022) Edited by Richard Greene

**Volume 4** *Dark Souls and Philosophy* (2023) Edited by Nicolas Michaud

**Volume 5** *Pokémon and Philosophy* (2023) Edited by Nicolas Michaud

**Volume 6** *Queen and Philosophy: Guaranteed to Blow Your Mind* (2023) Edited by Jared Kemling and Randall E. Auxier

**Volume 7** *Punk Rock and Philosophy: Research and Destroy* (2022) Edited by Richard Greene and Joshua Heter

**Volume 8** *Better Call Saul and Philosophy: I Think Therefore I Scam* (2022) Edited by Joshua Heter and Brett Coppenger

**Volume 9** *Asimov's Foundation and Philosophy: Psychohistory and Its Discontents* (2023) Edited by Joshua Heter and Josef Thomas Simpson

**Volume 10** *Warren Zevon and Philosophy* (2023) Edited by John E. MacKinnon

**Volume 11** *The Godfather and Philosophy* (2023) Edited by Joshua Heter and Richard Greene

**Volume 12** *Anthony Bourdain and Philosophy* (2023) Edited by Scott Calef

**Volume 13** *Post-Punk and Philosophy* (2024) Edited by Joshua Heter and Richard Greene

**For full details of all Pop Culture and Philosophy® books, and all Open Universe® books, visit www.carusbooks.com**

Pop Culture and Philosophy®

# Asimov's *Foundation* and Philosophy

*Psychohistory and Its Discontents*

Edited by

JOSHUA HETER AND

JOSEF THOMAS SIMPSON

OPEN UNIVERSE
Chicago

Volume 9 in the series, Pop Culture and Philosophy®, edited by George A. Reisch

To find out more about Open Universe and Carus Books, visit our website at www.carusbooks.com.



Printed and bound in the United States of America. Printed on acid-free paper.

*Asimov's Foundation and Philosophy: Psychohistory and Its Discontents*

**ISBN: 978-1-63770-030-3**

This book is also available as an e-book (978-1-63770-031-0).

**Library of Congress Control Number: 2021941787**

# Contents

# In the Wrong Hands, It's a Weapon—in the Right Hands, Deliverance

This book has been centuries in the making. Well, sort of.

The city of Rome was founded in the eighth century B.C. and over a number of years, transformed into a bustling metropolis, eventually becoming the seat of the most powerful and far-reaching empire the world had ever seen. The Roman Empire lasted until 476 A.D. when the final emperor of Rome, Romulus Augustulus was deposed by the non-Roman Odoacer who then declared himself the leader of Italy. The Byzantine Empire—the remnants of the Roman Empire in the East—didn't fall until the fifteenth century A.D.

Perhaps unsurprisingly, the fall of Rome has been a topic which has received seemingly immeasurable attention from historians and political theorists. One of the more noteworthy works to come out of this longstanding fascination—impressive in both its size and scope—is the six-volume *The History of the Decline and Fall of the Roman Empire* by English historian Edward Gibbon, originally published from 1776 to 1789. Gibbon's aim was not only to chronicle the events which led to Rome's fall but also to explain why it happened and to raise the question of whether or not it could have been prevented.

In the early to mid-twentieth century, a young scientist and science-fiction writer would take Gibbon's *History* as his inspiration for a handful of short stories which would eventually grow into a series of novels that would become some of the most important science fiction of its time. Indeed, what may be more impressive than the expansive universe Isaac Asimov brought to life in his *Foundation* series is the impact the series has had, not just among future science-fiction writers, but among a number of academics and influential thinkers.

This brings us to the early part of the twenty-first century when a couple of over-educated science fiction fans, inspired by Asimov's books and a recently adapted television show, decided to put together a book analyzing the philosophical ideas and questions found within *Foundation*. After a bit of planning and preparation, the pair were fortunate enough to pull together a team of talented authors (made up of fellow over-educated philosophers and science fiction enthusiasts) to create the book you now hold in your hands.

Of course, thinking about this centuries-long chain of events invites us to consider at least two important philosophical questions central to *Foundation* via its most significant and unique world-building feature: psychohistory. Did the chain of events which began from the formation of a burgeoning me-tropolis in central Italy thousands of years ago and culminated with your reading of this book have to happen just as it did? Or, could things have turned out differently? And, given enough information at the genesis of this chain, how many of the subsequent events could have been predicted (with any substantial scientific rigor)?

In a roundabout way, this is simply to raise the question of whether or not all events are determined from the events which precede them. If they are, then it would seem to follow that the only thing hindering the accurate prediction of any particular event would be a lack of information on behalf of the predictor. But of course, if *all* events are determined, that would include any flawed predictions as well as any attempts to improve the prediction process in the future. And, if all events are determined, then our attempts to answer any of these questions (successful or not) will play out only in the way that they must.

As daunting as tackling these issues may be (not to mention the additional questions raised by some of the potential answers), they are hardly the only thoughtful philosophical questions raised by *Foundation* or addressed in this book. What obligations do we have to future generations (that do not yet exist!)? What is the proper way to think about the relationship between science and religion? Can science *itself* ever develop a religious quality? Under what conditions (if any) is lying or deception morally acceptable? What's the ethical way to program a robot?

Our hope is that in raising these questions, this book both challenges and entertains you or that you have at least *some* similar, positive experience with it. After all, your reading of this book is the culmination of thousands of years of history; it would be a real shame if all of it led to nothing more than your disappointment. That said, it would be a glaring omission on our part if we didn't also here include a word of caution for you moving forward with the book about raising (and attempting to answer) all of these philosophical questions. It's a warning not dissimilar from one given by Asimov himself:

Philosophy is never just ideas. In the wrong hands, it's a weapon. In the right hands, deliverance.

# I

# Foundation and Reason

***"Curiosity isn't a crime here."***

# 1
# Is Rationality an Illusion?

LEIB LITMAN AND MARK ZELCER

> Emotions, my dear Seldon, are a powerful engine of human action, far more powerful than human beings themselves realize, and you cannot know how much can be done with the merest touch . . .
>
> —ETO DEMERZEL

As science fiction goes, the *Foundation* series strikes readers as generally plausible: interplanetary colonization, super-sophisticated mathematical sociology, and blaster weapons are all believable enough as technological advances for the distant future.

One thing, however, that stands out as glaringly strange to the modern ear is all that mental manipulation. The ability of a mind to target another and manipulate its individual emotions directly and precisely is humanly implausible. In the book series, numerous characters do this without technology. Wanda Seldon is first; she has mentalic powers allowing her mind to directly coerce other minds. The Mule is considered a mutant because he was born with the power to mentally alter people's emotions, allegiances, and desires. Wanda uses her powers to recruit similarly gifted individuals for the second galactic empire; the Mule uses his to take over the galaxy, with disastrous consequences. There are many others.

Historically, many otherwise sensible scientists believed in what we now think of as occult mental powers, though few do nowadays. Yet beneath all the telepathy is something interesting. Sure, telepathy cannot change people's emotions, but emotions are manipulated all the time in more conventional ways and, surprisingly, most human decision making is dominated by emotional considerations. Emotions guide our reason, not the other way around. This is why Asimov does us a service by not having characters waste time trying to *convince* one another to do things. He merely enables many of his characters to adjust each others' emotions to suit their needs.

Philosophers often think we are in the business of convincing one another using reason, logic, and argument and we pay attention to characters' logical reasons for acting. For millennia we took rationality as the model for interacting with others and for making individual decisions. But that is not how humans really work. Emotions are primary. Accordingly, throughout the *Foundation* series, when big things need to be done, emotions are manipulated to accomplish them. Here we explore something that is taken for granted in the *Foundation* novels but is less appreciated by philosophers and non-philosophers alike: emotions control us far more than reason does and, as many have concluded, human rationality is often illusory.

## Manipulation of Emotion Is the Foundation of the Foundation

In *Prelude to Foundation* a sequence of characters makes what they take to be their own decisions in the service of aiding Hari Seldon's quest to develop psychohistory. Sunmaster Fourteen, the Emperor, and others, act on emotional impulses that they have been subtly manipulated into having by Eto Demerzel—really Robot Daneel Olivaw—to achieve his ends. Demerzel himself is secretly a twenty-thousand-year-old robot programmed to obey the three Laws of Robotics that protect *individual* humans, plus a "zeroth law," stating that a robot cannot allow harm to come to humanity *as a whole*. Demerzel was created specifically for this purpose.

In *Foundation and Empire*, we encounter the Mule, a mutant with the ability to influence emotions. He uses his mental power to emotionally 'convert' warship captains over to his side, take over the galaxy, and mess up the Seldon Plan to hasten the re-emergence of a peaceful Galactic Empire. As it happens, the Mule's whole planet—Gaia—has some interesting mental powers of its own.

In *Foundation's Edge*, Harla Branno, Stor Gendibal, and Janov Pelorat find themselves all drawn to Gaia, each for their own reasons—reasons so ostensibly rational that they convince other members of their government of their obviousness.

Pelorat goes to study history; Branno, from the First Foundation, wants to stop the Second Foundation; Gendibal, of the Second Foundation, wants to stop a threat from the First Foundation. (All Second Foundationers, remember, can mentally manipulate others.) And they all converge on Gaia as the result of the mostly psychological emotional manipulation of Bliss, a woman who seemingly has the same power to influence emotions as Demerzel. Many of the most significant plot moves throughout the series bypass rational argument and are accomplished by those with the ability to mentally manipulate others.

## How Emotion Affects Logic

Demerzel and others who are able to manipulate emotions evolved or were created with this mental ability because, in the Foundation, emotion is the ultimate ruler over human reason and action. After an emotion is amplified by someone, the influenced minds naturally and unconsciously confabulate rational explanations to justify those emotions—a psychological process that Ziva Kunda and others referred to as motivated reasoning. In the 1960s Eric Aronson outlined the cognitive mechanisms of motivated reasoning by considering the "logical" arguments that a smoker might use to rationalize the idea that smoking is not harmful.

Due to the ability of emotions to co-opt the reasoning process for its own ends, those able to influence emotion would leave people believing that their actions are products of their own rational deliberation. But while the targets of emotional manipulation in the Foundation are left believing that their decisions are based on their reason, their rational process is really following the orders of their emotional mind. What's going on?

## Hum(e)an Emotion and Reason

Plato is the first person we know of in Western thought to confront this issue. Plato believes that humans are endowed with a variety of opposing inner motivations. In the *Republic* (and again in different ways in the *Phaedrus* and *Timaeus*) he lays out a theory of a three-part human mind (what he called "soul"). Part is rational, part is concerned with our appetites for things like food and sex, and part is our drive to win and succeed. Some 2,200 years later this became a model for Freud's theory of the id, ego, and superego. For Plato, reason serves as the charioteer who must reign in and control the other two, which much like horses, pull in various directions at once. In a Platonically healthy person, reason is supreme and the emotions are subordinate to it; reason does, and ought to, lead the emotions.

The classical definition of a human being comes down to us from millennia of Aristotelians who, adapting Plato's basic idea, have claimed that man is a "rational animal." Man has an animal nature that involves his body with its physical needs, but he is also rational and capable of making rational decisions that can triumph over the impulse to satisfy one or another physical instinct.

Along similar lines, Descartes's *Meditations* sees humanity's essence as a "thinking thing." Man is essentially a creature that, with some qualification, performs cognitive tasks in accordance with reason.

Between Aristotle and Descartes however, Christianity spent the Middle Ages denying that man's nature is essentially rational. If man were innately rational he would be born virtuous, which he is not. Man, according to Christianity, is driven by sinful impulses to act on his carnal desires. It is only by wielding an arsenal of restraining countermeasures like faith, reason, prayer, the Church, and self-discipline, that he can rein in his authentically base self.

Well aware of the Aristotelian and Christian worldviews, the Scottish philosopher David Hume took the Christian account of man's passions and virtues, and secularized it. With Christianity, he keeps the passions, or emotions, in the center and relegates reason to their service. To think otherwise, he believes, is to misunderstand the respective roles of thought and emotion. Unlike Christianity, Hume is not concerned with our sinful nature, but our motivations for acting.

Hume is generally skeptical about the power of reason to guide us. No one is ultimately driven by reason, nor could they be. The second book of Hume's *A Treatise of Human Nature* is accordingly about the passions. This book deals with pride, lust, humility, love, hate, desire, aversion, fear, and hope. In a sense, it is a correction to puritanical Christian moral psychology that sees pride and other desires as sinful, and which need corralling by reason and conscience.

Hume writes so well, his assessment is worth quoting directly: "Nothing is more usual in philosophy, and even in common life, than to talk of the combat of passion and reason, to give the preference to reason, and assert that men are only so far virtuous as they conform themselves to its dictates." But this account, Hume concludes, is wrong. Instead "Reason is, and ought only to be, the slave of the passions, and can never pretend to any other office than to serve and obey them."

## The Beginning of Hari Seldon's Journey

> Seldon was breathing heavily, trying to see himself as a man driven by pride and not liking it.
>
> —on being told his mind had been "tampered with," in *Prelude to Foundation*, p 427.

Hume's conception of the emotions sets the stage for the entire *Foundation* saga. Initially, Seldon had no interest in developing psychohistory as an applied science. As is common among theoretically-oriented mathematicians, his only interest was to demonstrate that psychohistory was plausible in principle. Seldon changed his mind, however, after a lengthy conversation with Demerzel, in which Demerzel provided a seemingly compelling rationale as to why he should stay on Trantor and devote his life to psychohistory. As a result of that conversation, Demerzel convinced Seldon to completely uproot his life and not return to his home planet.

Much later in the story, after having deduced that Demerzel was a robot with powers to manipulate human emotion, Seldon began to doubt that it was Demerzel's *logic* that convinced him to stay on Trantor. Indeed, Seldon realized that by making such drastic changes to his life in such a short period of time, he was acting wholly out of character.

> I was easily convinced not to go home to Helicon and to make myself a wanderer over the face of Trantor . . . Looking back on it now, I see myself as *not* myself. I am not a person to be easily led, yet I was. More than that, I did not even think it strange that I was behaving so far out of character.

How was Demerzel able to make Seldon behave so contrary to his personality and convictions, all the while appearing to appeal to his reason? Demerzel revealed that he did so by subtly tapping into one of Seldon's primary emotions—his pride. It was Seldon's need to be recognized as the creator of psychohistory that ultimately drove him to join Demerzel and to leave his home planet behind. "You were proud of psychohistory as a concept, proud of having thought of it. You would not have minded for it to be a practical discipline. That would have further fed your pride . . . And I had but to strengthen it a touch and you were at once eager to work at psychohistory with an intensity that a moment before you would have scorned."

And so, it was revealed by Demerzel that the entire Foundation was created as a result of Hari Seldon's pride. It was not the conviction that psychohistory was worth working on that led Seldon to want to develop it. Instead, it was his pride, subtly amplified by Demerzel. Once the motivation was there, reason provided a plausible way to justify that motivation. This demonstrates a key Humean principle. Reason and our passions logically are not in conflict. Rather, our goals are set by our passions while reason, in the service of the passions, helps us realize them.

Pride is one of the key emotions Christianity historically considered sinful. Hume, however, did not see pride, or any other emotion, as good or bad, but rather as the primary engine of human mental life. For Hume, human cognition and action cannot be understood without the emotionally-driven motivation that brings them into being.

## Emotion's Role in the Development of Prejudice

The philosophical debate about the primacy of emotions over reason has had a profound influence on how we view individuals within a larger society. Societies are made up of individuals interacting with each other, often in complex ways. Sometimes those interactions are co-operative, at other times competitive. Often, people develop biased attitudes about various groups within society. These attitudes are often rationalized by logic and reason. But we can often ask whether the reasoning which justifies a particular bias is itself motivated by a deeper underlying emotion that is not in itself rooted in reason. To the extent that such an emotionally driven orientation is not available to consciousness it is referred to as an implicit bias.

It is this type of implicit bias that played a decisive role in the way Demerzel managed to put down the rebellion of Wye against the galactic emperor, Cleon I. Wye was ruled by an ancient dynasty that claimed to be the rightful ruler over the Galactic throne. For decades the mayor of Wye had been planning a rebellion to overthrow Cleon. But shortly before that rebellion took place the mayor of Wye transferred power to his daughter.

Wye was an egalitarian society where men and women lived in an atmosphere of overall equality. Despite Wye's sexual egalitarianism, the Mayor is discretely informed that she no longer has the support of her military. Her officers, who had pledged allegiance to her father, suddenly feel that they cannot serve her as she is a woman.

Normally in Wye no one would have given a second thought to a woman becoming mayor. But Demerzel, being able to read emotions, was aware that there was more below the surface. "Men are men—and the Wyan generals are almost all men. It does not actually take much to rouse resentment and latent fear of women in any man. It may be a biological matter that I, as a robot, cannot fully understand."

Demerzel then took advantage of this underlying latent fear and amplified it slightly. As a result, the generals changed their minds and abandoned a rebellion that they had been planning for decades. The change in course seemed perfectly logical to the generals. But to an outside observer this was impossible to comprehend. Emotionally driven decisions often only make sense to the emotionally affected person.

Dors and Seldon saw that what the generals had done was irrational and can only be understood by an appeal to irrational emotions.

> This is very interesting. Daughters have succeeded fathers—or mothers, for that matter—and held Mayoralties or other high offices on any number of occasions. There have even been reigning Empresses, as you undoubtedly know, and I can't recall that there was ever in Imperial history any serious question of serving under one. It makes one wonder why such a thing would now arise in Wye.

After considering that there is no compelling rational explanation for the rebellion, Seldon and Dors conclude that "it's so unnatural that it must be contrived and I imagine Hummin [Demerzel] is doing the contriving."

## The Unconscious Nature of Emotional Influence

The primacy of emotions is aptly captured by one of Demerzel's metaphors in response to Seldon's refusal to believe that his pride had anything to do with his interest in psychohistory. To that, Demerzel responded "You are perfectly aware that it is neither admirable nor useful to be driven by pride, so you try to subdue that drive, but you might as well disapprove of yourself powered by your heartbeat."

In Demerzel's world, emotional motivation is an engine of the mind much the same as the heart drives circulation. And much like the heart, emotions operate outside of conscious control and do not require a person's awareness of their existence. It is precisely because emotions often affect human judgment outside of awareness that philosophers, historically, had trouble pinning down their effect on reason.

In order for emotion to affect reason, it has to operate outside of awareness. In the Foundation, most of the characters are oblivious to the fact that they are being influenced. If people were aware that their reason was being influenced by emotion they would quickly course-correct. Emotion would then be in conflict with reason, as opposed to Hume's position that it *drives* reason.

The necessarily unconscious nature of emotion's influence on reason speaks to another philosophical debate—one that examines whether all mental states are conscious or whether mental states can also be unconscious. John Locke famously argued that there is no such thing as a non-conscious mental state. As Daniel Dennett put it, to a Lockean, the notion of unconscious thought is "incoherent, self-contradictory nonsense" (*The Mind's I*, p, 11).

The idea that all thought has to be conscious has seen a lot of pushback in twentieth-century philosophy and psychology. In the Foundation, emotions are unconscious mental states, capable of affecting people's reasoning outside of awareness. In the Wye rebellion, Demerzel tapped into the *latent* resentment and fear of the generals. The key philosophical idea here—which stands against Locke's position—is that fear and resentment can be latent. A latent emotion is one that exists below the surface of awareness. Yet, these latent emotions are real mental representations. They have intentionality; they are about something. Although unconscious, they are real mental states. And they are able to influence reasoning.

Philosophers have tried to reconcile Locke's view with the idea that there are unconscious mental states, with mixed results. Regardless, however, of how unconscious emotions are represented in the mind, there is no debate about the ability of unconscious emotions—and more broadly, other unconscious mental states—to profoundly influence reason, logic, and behavior. While the philosophical debate about the underlying nature of unconscious representation continues, there is now wide consensus about the ability of unconscious cognition to influence thought.

## Is Emotional Influence Like an Optical Illusion?

Optical illusions are fun. But they also reveal something important about the human mind. We have all seen illusions where objects appear bigger than they actually are. Sometimes objects appear to move when they are actually standing still. Other illusions make objects appear in a completely different color. What is most fascinating about optical illusions is that our perception does not change even after we know that we are looking at an illusion. The orange square in the famous Cube Illusion appears orange even after we are fully aware that it is actually gray (Purves and Lotto, p. 34). The human mind is incapable of exercising control over its conscious perceptual experience. How we perceive the world is not up to us. Perceptual experience is determined by the machinery of mind, operating outside of our control. But what about emotion and its effect on reason?

In the Foundation, emotional control over reason operates analogous to an optical illusion. A person sees the world the same way, even after realizing that they are being manipulated. When Demerzel tells Hari that he won't ever be able to speak about Demerzel's true nature, the characters know they are being manipulated, yet stay under their emotion's influence and still seem to believe they made reasonable decisions.

*Foundation and Empire* contains some remarkable passages in which Pritcher talks about the fact that he is now loyal to the Mule, whereas he once was not, with full cognizance of the fact that the Mule made him this way and the second before he would have been prepared to fight to the death to defeat the Mule. In *Second Foundation* he has a discussion with the Mule about the nature of his own loyalty. To which the Mule says "it is impossible for you to realize what your feelings would be if free to form themselves along the lines of your natural motivation. The human mind resents control."

According to Asimov, it is impossible for people to imagine what their thoughts would be if they were not under the influence of unconscious emotional motivations. But this raises deep questions—questions of the kind which philosophers call 'epistemic'. Are emotions, in other words, able to deceive us into thinking that we are being rational without us being able to rationally reflect on the interrogative thought process? This is how Asimov sees human nature in the *Foundation* series.

## Who Is Your Inner Demerzel?

Asimov's writing style in the *Foundation* series makes it more obvious than real life does, that people can appear to act in their self-interest and rationally think about what they want, but are ultimately the product of their emotional lives. Often these emotional lives are manipulated from the outside. Sometimes they are manipulated by the neurotransmitters that flow through our brains, sometimes via carefully crafted political messages calculated to pull at our heartstrings.

Throughout the *Foundation* series Asimov does a masterful job spelling things out for us, often hiding all the relevant details about who is pulling which strings, until the "big reveal" supplies the missing details. But in the real world, in our minds, in your mind, in the minds of humans, the same thing happens only there is no one to point out who or what dictates our emotional lives. Sometimes it is our hormones, maybe our relationships, personality, or pride. But make no mistake, emotions pull our strings, not rational deliberation.

Demerzel is a projection of the real biochemical and social forces that influence us in our daily life. We all have an inner Demerzel, something that moves our emotional dials and makes us do what we do. Our actions and their reasons are a significant part of what makes us who we are. For that reason, so many philosophers have thought about the nature of human beings in terms of the interaction between emotion and reason, and the often-unconscious forces that influence our conscious experience and rationality. And, perhaps, the ultimate lesson of the Foundation is for each of us to ask—who is our own, personal, inner Demerzel?

## From Whence Comes the Savior?

The goal of psychohistory is to save the Galaxy from itself. This is taken as a moral goal though we sidestepped the question of whether the means used to accomplish it are ethical. Emotional manipulation of this sort is not very familiar ethical ground. We tend to see it happen in propaganda, marketing, and even in our daily interactions. But the directness in which the Foundation's characters can do it is less defensible than exposing them to commercial jingles. Hume's theory of ethics is grounded, very deliberately, in the emotion of empathy and not in any science of reason. Reason cannot be a source for ethics and empathy cannot tell us whether or not it is ethical to mentally coerce another.

But Demerzel's creators clearly were utilitarian in their calculations. Whether or not they were doing the right thing by manipulating emotions resembles the question a modern well-meaning politician has: explain why some policy is in the public interest or just appeal to their constituents' emotions. Demerzel's creators had no moral qualms about their action.

Sparing the Galaxy thousands of years of chaos is worth this kind of manipulation. They knew that the only way to save humanity from itself is to play with emotions in the right way.

Humans will anyway always think they are acting rationally even if their emotions are really driving the train that their reason is riding on. Designing robots to do this required deep insight into the human condition. They had to know that the robots were fundamentally different from the humans they were trying to save. We don't know whether the gambit was ultimately successful or whether human emotions were really their downfall after all. But, in the Foundation, giving robots the right tools may be the best hope humanity has.

# 2
# Socrates's City and Seldon's Galaxy

NATHANIEL GOLDBERG

He's put on trial for being a threat to the state. He fails to convince his accusers of his innocence. As a result, he faces exile or even death.

This is a fitting description of the fictional psychohistorian Hari Seldon, a hero of Isaac Asimov's *Foundation* novels and their Apple TV+ adaptation. It *also* describes the factual ancient Greek philosopher Socrates, the basis for the hero of his student Plato's dialogues. Seldon is not Socrates, of course. Plato's Socrates is based on the historical individual. And Asimov almost certainly didn't base Seldon on either. Beyond this, both the Socrates from history and the Socrates from Plato's dialogues choose death, while Seldon chooses exile—though they all apparently do so happily.

Still, other similarities between Plato's Socrates and Asimov's Seldon abound. Most striking is how both are portrayed in their author's most famous work: Plato's *Republic* and Asimov's original *Foundation Trilogy*.

In Plato's *Republic*, Socrates constructs (in theory) an ideal city resistant to decay. The city has three groups of citizens: Guardians, Auxiliaries, and Producers. Guardians rule by applying knowledge of the abstract reality of Socrates's Forms. And the city's greatest threat is an individual as gifted as a Guardian but with unchecked desires, such as the potentially tyrannical Thrasymachus.

In Asimov's *Foundation Trilogy*, Seldon constructs (in practice) an ideal galaxy resistant to decay. The galaxy has three groups of citizens: Second Foundationers, First Foundationers, and everyone else. Second Foundationers rule by applying knowledge of the abstract mathematics of Seldon's psychohistory and the rest of the Seldon Plan. And the galaxy's greatest threat is an individual as gifted as a Second Foundationer but with unchecked desires, such as the actually tyrannical Mule.

Asimov didn't base Seldon's galaxy on Socrates's city any more than he based Seldon on Socrates. Regardless, similarities between them have gone almost entirely unnoticed. (The only exceptions are myself and Paul Krugman, in his introduction to a special edition of the *Foundation Trilogy*.) Comparing Seldon's galaxy with Socrates's city, however, sheds light on both.

## Socrates's City

Plato wrote the *Republic* around 380 B.C.E. It concerns how to understand justice. Toward that end, Plato has Socrates construct a theoretical city with three groups of citizens.

Most citizens are Producers. Governed by appetite and desire, Producers produce goods and are in turn their chief consumers. Some citizens are Auxiliaries. Governed by spirit and fortitude, Auxiliaries are the driving force defending the city from internal and external threat. Finally, a few citizens are Guardians. Governed by intellect and wisdom, Guardians rule the city. That's because only they have knowledge of the Forms—perfect abstract ideals—which are objective truths of how things really are.

Socrates represents the Forms with his Allegory of the Cave:

> Imagine human beings living in an underground, cavelike dwelling . . . Light is provided by a fire burning far above and behind them. Between the prisoners and the fire, there is an elevated road along [which] a low wall has been built—like the screen in front of people that is provided by puppeteers, and above which they show their puppets. . . . There are people alongside the wall carrying multifarious artifacts that project above it. (Plato, *Republic,* 514a–516c)

These human beings are prisoners. Rather than seeing things how they really are, they see only "the shadows that the fire casts on the wall of the cave in front of them" (*Republic*, 515a)—shadows caused by the second set of people and their artifacts. Those artifacts represent a false reality.

But not everyone remains imprisoned in a cavelike dwelling. Some emerge to see the originals that the artifacts are based on. Eventually, they come to realize that just as the fire sheds light on the false reality inside the cave, the sun sheds light on the true reality outside it (*Republic*, 516a). Those outside the cave see things as they really are, analogous to the Forms, by light of the radiant sun. This remains only an allegory, however. Because the Forms are abstract, Guardians' minds, rather than their eyes, are ultimately attuned to them.

Guardians rule because only they come to know objective reality. Regardless, all three groups require one another. Guardians establish order by applying knowledge of the Forms to the city. They require Auxiliaries to enforce that order, since intellect requires spirit to defend against internal and external threats. Producers require both Guardians and Auxiliaries to jointly establish and enforce that order, since they can do neither. And both Guardians and Auxiliaries require Producers to satisfy their own more circumscribed appetitive needs. Indeed, Socrates explains, the ideal city is one in which Guardians provide the mental framework by ruling, Auxiliaries the physical framework by defending, and Producers the raw materials and goods. So configured, Socrates concludes, the city is resistant to "decay."

Finally, the most dangerous person to rule the city would have an intellect and spirit that rivaled the Guardians' and Auxiliaries', but was ruled instead by their appetite. Such an individual is exemplified in the dialogue by Thrasymachus, a potential tyrant rejecting the existence of the Forms. For him, there is no 'objective' reality of how best to rule. Instead, the name of the game is to force his false reality onto others. During the course of the dialogue, Thrasymachus tries to co-opt the intellectual Socrates's spirited interlocutors Glaucon and Adeimantus to satisfy his own appetite for control. After Thrasymachus attacks Socrates, Glaucon and Adeimantus assume his side of the argument (Plato, *Republic*, 357a) until Socrates wins them over near the dialogue's close (608c).

## Seldon's Galaxy

Asimov wrote what would become the *Foundation Trilogy* as a series of short stories from 1942 to 1950. He edited and published them as a trilogy of novels—*Foundation*, *Foundation and Empire*, and *Second Foundation*—in 1951, 1952, and 1953, respectively. The *Foundation Trilogy* concerns how best to reduce a "thirty thousand year period of misery and anarchy" between the now-falling First Galactic Empire "before a unified government," a Second Galactic Empire, "would arise once more" (*Foundation Trilogy*, 2012, p. 507). To that end, Asimov has Seldon construct an actual political order with "two Foundations at 'opposite ends of the Galaxy' . . . designed so that in one short millennium events would knit and mesh so as to force out of them a stronger, more permanent, more benevolent Second Empire" (p. 258).

Like Socrates's city, Seldon's galaxy has three groups of citizens. Most citizens are neither First nor Second Foundationers. They instead produce and provide raw materials and, their appetite fulfilled, are in turn the chief consumers of their finished goods. Some citizens are First Foundationers. Spirited proselytizers (pp. 89–145), traders (pp. 147–250, 261–341), and allies (pp. 261–341). First Foundationers face generational crises with solutions forced on them by historical trends, making them the driving force defending the galaxy from those thirty thousand years of misery and anarchy. While First Foundationers are portrayed as expansionist and Auxiliaries are not, each is ultimately defending its larger political unit—Seldon's galaxy and Socrates's city—from internal and external threat. Even if First Foundationers appear expansionist in their particular sphere of influence, the Seldon Plan operates on the galaxy as a whole. The Second Galactic Empire being coextensive with the First, there is no ultimate expansion. Finally, a few citizens are Second Foundationers. Intellectuals, Second Foundationers rule from behind the scenes because only they have full knowledge of the Seldon Plan.

The Plan has two parts. One part is the Plan's initial conditions, namely, establishing the First Foundation on the remote, resource-poor planet Terminus. The other part is using the abstract mathematics of psychohistory to predict subsequent galactic events based on those initial conditions. Second Foundationers also ensure the survival of the Plan when those predictions prove wrong. Seldon "left the Second Foundation behind him to maintain, improve, and extend his work," and so Second Foundationers are "Seldon's group" (p. 746). Seldon is in effect the Second Foundation's founding member and its first leader or "speaker."

Seldon and other Second Foundationers represent the Plan similarly to how Socrates represents the Forms. Second Foundationers agree that most people's reality exists "Down—down—," as if in a cave. For

> all the suffering that humanity ever knew can be traced to the one fact that no man in the history of the Galaxy, until Hari Seldon, and very few men thereafter, could understand one another. Every human being lived behind an impenetrable wall. (pp. 605–06)

Everyone before Seldon and most after were imprisoned in a cavelike dwelling. Rather than understanding how people really are, they lived behind an impenetrable wall of a false reality. Seldon emerged from behind the wall to understand objective truths of human behavior. He then incorporated those truths into the Plan—its initial conditions, psychohistory's mathematical equations, and their calculated consequences—which he represented with the Prime Radiant.

A subsequent First Speaker activates the Prime Radiant in the presence of a Second Foundation acolyte:

> the room was in darkness. But only for a moment, since with a gradually livening flush, the two long walls of the room glowed to life. First, a pearly white, unrelieved, then a trace of faint darkness here and there, and finally, the fine neatly printed equations in black, with an occasional red hairline that wavered through the darker forest like a staggering rillet. (p. 608)

The equations represent the abstract mathematics of psychohistory. The First Speaker explains:

> "Come, my boy, step here before the wall. You will not cast a shadow . . ."
>
> They stood together in the light. . . .
>
> The First Speaker laughed softly, "You will find the Prime Radiant to be attuned to your mind." (pp. 608–09)

After Seldon, other Second Foundationers also emerge from the darkness to understand objective truths of human beings that psychohistory and the rest of the Plan shed light on. They see human beings as they really are. As such, they "will not cast a shadow" on the abstract psychohistorical equations in the form of the light of the Prime Radiant. This also remains only an allegory, however. Because the Plan is abstract, Second Foundationers' minds, rather than their eyes, are ultimately "attuned to" it.

Second Foundationers rule because only they come to know objective reality. Regardless, all three groups also require one another. Second Foundationers establish order by applying knowledge of the Plan to the galaxy. They require First Foundationers to enforce that order, since intellect requires spirit to defend against internal and external threats. The rest of the galaxy requires both First and Second Foundationers to jointly establish and enforce that order, since they can do neither. And both First and Second Foundationers require the rest of the galaxy to satisfy their own more circumscribed appetitive needs. Indeed, given the raw materials that the rest of the galaxy produces and provides, “the First Foundation supplies the physical framework of a single political unit, and the Second Foundation supplies the mental framework of a ready-made ruling class” (p. 613). So configured, Seldon concludes, the galaxy is resistant to “decay” (p. 507).

Finally, the most dangerous person to rule the galaxy would have a spirit and intellect that rivaled the First and Second Foundationers’, but was ruled instead by his appetite. Such an individual is exemplified in the trilogy by the Mule, an actual tyrant rejecting the Seldon Plan. For him, there may be no ‘objective’ reality of how best to rule. Instead, the name of the game is to force his false reality onto others. During the course of the trilogy, the Mule tries to co-opt spirited First Foundationers and to destroy Second Foundationers to satisfy his own appetite for control (pp. 345–585).

## Applying Knowledge through Deception

Socrates and Seldon therefore each construct a political entity with intellectual, spirited, and appetitive parts. Each highest part rules by applying abstract knowledge of objective reality. Each political entity is resistant to decay. And each entity’s greatest threat is an individual whose appetite co-opts their intellect and spirit, allowing them to force their false reality onto others.

As if all this isn’t striking enough, there’s another, deeply ironic similarity between Socrates’s city and Seldon’s galaxy. Both Guardians and Second Foundationers apply their knowledge through deception.

There are many examples of deception throughout the *Republic* and *Foundation Trilogy*. The most prominent in the *Republic* is that Guardians deceive people into thinking that everyone is born of the same mother Earth and that at birth Guardians have gold added to their souls, Auxiliaries silver, and Producers iron and bronze (414c–415a). Guardians reinforce this deception as needed by changing political groupings of children and punishing those acting contrary to their group.

One of the two most prominent examples of deception in the *Foundation Trilogy* is that Seldon (and other Second Foundationers) deceives people into thinking that the First Foundation’s purpose is to compile a repository of all knowledge, the *Encyclopedia Galactica*. This motivates the settlement of Terminus by First Foundationers. First Foundationers and the rest of the galaxy continue believing this until fifty years after the establishment of the First Foundation, when the late-

Seldon's hologram, preprogrammed to convey messages at specific dates, reveals the First Foundation's true purpose to serve as the nucleus of a new empire (*Foundation Trilogy*, pp. 26–85).

The other most prominent example of deception occurs when Second Foundationers deceive people into thinking that First Foundationers destroyed the Second Foundation. The deception is meant to reset the Seldon Plan, because by stopping the Mule the Second Foundation revealed its influence too soon. First Foundationers and the rest of the galaxy continue believing in the Second Foundation's destruction until closer to the end of the one-thousand-year gap between empires (pp. 737–47).

Another, almost certainly coincidental, similarity between the *Republic* and *Foundation Trilogy* is that Socrates explains that souls have a "thousand-year journey" (*Republic*, 292d) between reincarnations, while, as just mentioned, Seldon explains that his Plan allows the galaxy to have a thousand-year gap between empires. A further, almost certainly *non*-coincidental, similarity is between what Socrates says in the *Apology*, one of Plato's earlier dialogues, and what the Second Foundation's First Speaker says to the same acolyte above. Socrates says that he is wise because he is aware of his ignorance (*Apology*, 21d). The First Speaker says the inverse: "The most hopelessly stupid man is he who is not aware that he is wise" (*Foundation Trilogy*, p. 607).

## Noble Lies

It's deeply ironic that both Socrates and Seldon think that the best way to govern based on objective reality is to deceive people into believing a false one. That's not only ironic, though. It's also uncomfortable. After Guardians emerge from their cavelike dwelling into the light of the radiant sun, Socrates has them descend back down to cast shadows against the wall. After Second Foundationers emerge from their cavelike dwelling into the light of the Prime Radiant, Seldon has them descend back down to do the same.

Socrates, at least, recognizes the irony and discomfort. He tries to ease the discomfort by claiming that the deception is a "noble falsehood" (*Republic*, 414b), also translated as "noble lie." It's a *lie* because it's untrue and told to deceive. Socrates thinks that it's *noble* because it establishes and enforces his city's political order, which he thinks is good. Seldon and other Second Foundationers' deceptions could also be called "noble lies." They're also untrue and told to deceive. Seldon and these others presumably also think that they're *noble* because the first establishes the galaxy's political order and the second enforces it, which they also think are good.

Yet is it noble for Guardians to lie that everyone is born of the same mother Earth and had metals corresponding to their social group added to their souls? And is it noble for Seldon and other Second Foundationers to lie about the First Foundation's purpose and about the First's having destroyed the Second?

That depends on what "noble" means. Socrates apparently has in mind something like morally proper or upright. Are these lies like that? This is a hard question. People have been reading the *Republic* for centuries—and *Foundation* stories for nearly a century—because great works of philosophy and science fiction ask hard questions.

We can, however, make progress on answering them by considering three assumptions that Socrates and Seldon both make that need to be true for their lies to be noble:

1. There *are* objective truths about how things and people really are. Since Guardians and Second Foundationers allegedly must lie to apply knowledge of objective truths, without these truths there'd be no justification for lying.
2. Guardians and Second Foundationers can *come to know* those objective truths. Since Guardians and Second Foundationers, again, allegedly must lie to apply knowledge of objective truths, without this knowledge there'd likewise be no justification for lying.
3. *Only* Guardians and Second Foundationers can come to know those objective truths. If that's because there *are* no objective truths (case 1) or no one can *come to know* them (case 2), then either way there'd be no justification for lying. If that's because *everyone* can come to know those truths—there's nothing special about being a Guardian or a Second Foundationer—then there'd once more be no justification for lying, since everyone could be told those objective truths outright. (Goldberg, "Political Myths")

## Not as Easy as 1, 2, and 3

Consider where things stand. Socrates and Seldon each believe that Guardians and Second Foundationers, respectively, should apply objective truths. Each believes that doing so requires telling noble lies. And that in turn requires that 1, 2, and 3 all be true. Except figuring out whether 1, 2, and 3 are true isn't easy!

Still, there's reason to think 1 false. Throughout history, people have always claimed particular beliefs as objective truths—until, that is, they didn't. The sun circles the earth was taken as an objective truth until Galileo argued that the earth circles the sun. That was taken as an objective truth until Kepler argued that the earth doesn't so much circle the sun as it moves in an ellipse. Kepler took that as an objective truth based on Newton's theory of classical mechanics. Einstein also took it (more or less) as an objective truth but based instead on his own theory of general relativity. And a lot of people think that general relativity itself can't be an objective truth, because it's inconsistent with another fundamental theory in science, quantum mechanics. Are there any 'objective truths' at all?

One possibility is that there simply aren't. So-called 'knowledge' is really just what we currently believe. And that changes with time. So 1 is false.

Another possibility is that there are objective truths. Experts just can't come to know them. That's why we keep getting them wrong. They're simply beyond our reach, even for Guardians and Second Foundationers. So 2 is false.

Now, if either 1 or 2 is false, then Socrates's and Seldon's lies aren't noble. Worse, there's also reason to think that 3 is false, that is, that it's not the case that only Guardians and Second Foundationers can come to know objective truths. That could be because there are no objective truths, as per 1. Because Guardians and Second Foundationers can't come to know those truths, as per 2. Or, a third possibility, because *everyone* can come to know those truths.

That everyone can do so might seem doubtful. Not everyone's an expert, after all. In Socrates's city and Seldon's galaxy, not everyone is a Guardian or a Second Foundationer, respectively. Yet isn't it suspicious that Socrates and Seldon claim that Guardians and Second Foundationers are the only ones who can come to know objective truths, when they'd each put themselves in that privileged group of people? Socrates certainly didn't fancy himself an Auxiliary or a Producer, and Seldon just was a Second Foundationer. That's certainly convenient. They'd be in charge! Indeed, isn't it just as convenient for them as it would be when tyrants construct political systems with themselves in charge? Thrasymachus and the Mule wanted to rule. Neither fancies himself anything but the leader. So how can we be sure that Socrates and Seldon aren't more like Thrasymachus and the Mule than they care to admit?

## A Cave within a Cave

None of this shows that 1, 2, or 3 is actually false. It does however give us reason to doubt whether they are true. And that should make us cautious in believing that Socrates's and Seldon's lies are really noble.

Then again, whether or not Socrates's city and Seldon's galaxy have noble lies in them may be the wrong question to ask. Socrates and Seldon are merely characters within stories that Plato and Asimov tell. They don't necessarily speak for their author's own views. In fact, when Socrates tells others about the Allegory of the Cave, and when a subsequent Second Foundationer tells his acolyte about Seldon's Prime Radiant, Plato and Asimov are in effect telling a story *within* a story. Plato's and Asimov's views are twice removed. But then, by *reading* a story within a story, we're in effect in a cave within a cave. Plato's Socrates and Asimov's Seldon are deceiving others. How can we be sure that Plato and Asimov aren't deceiving us?

There are two ways to take this. One is to throw up our hands in defeat. It seems as if we can't ever get at objective truths this way. Another is to take this deeper level of irony as shedding light on a deeper kind of truth. There may or may not be objective truths. Further, even if there are, all, some or none of us may or may not be able to come to know them. Still, it's good that Plato and Asimov have Socrates and Seldon question their own realities, even if they skirt the line between their own versions of objectivity and falsehood in the process. It's likewise good that we should question ours, even if we skirt the same. Doing so sheds light on our lives. It gets us to think about what is and what isn't, and whether knowing (or at least believing) one can help us know (or at least believe) the other. And there's no better way to do that than by engaging with various Socrateses and Seldons within philosophy and science fiction.[1]

[1] Thanks go to Joel G. McKinnon for rekindling my interest in Asimov with his fantastic Seldon Crisis podcast, to all the students in my Philosophy and Science Fiction class for their remarkable insights, and to the editors of this volume for their invaluable feedback.

# 3
# How Symbolic Logic Saved the Foundation

JOSHUA TEPLEY

> You see, there is a branch of human knowledge known as symbolic logic, which can be used to prune away all sorts of clogging deadwood that clutters up human language.
>
> —SALVOR HARDIN, Mayor of Terminus City

There are many heroes in Isaac Asimov's *Foundation* series: Hari Seldon, Salvor Hardin, Hober Mallow, and Bayta Darell—to name just a few. But in addition to these, there is one true hero of the Foundation that has received no recognition whatsoever. This hero is not a person, an animal, or even a machine. Rather, it's an abstract object. The hero I have in mind is *symbolic logic*.

What is symbolic logic? Is it real or fictional? And how exactly is it a hero of the Foundation?

## The First Seldon Crisis

Symbolic logic makes its appearance in "Foundation," the first installment in Asimov's *Foundation* series. "Foundation" tells the story of the very first Seldon crisis, which takes place fifty years after the birth of the Foundation. The crisis arises when the Kingdom of Anacreon, which borders Terminus (the planet on which the Foundation is located), threatens to annex the planet, parcel up its land into estates, and grant these estates to its nobility. The Board of Trustees of the Encyclopedia Committee, headed by Lewis Pirenne, isn't worried: its five members trust the Empire to protect the Foundation from the Kingdom of Anacreon. But the first Mayor of Terminus City, Salvor Hardin, is dubious. He believes that the Empire is too distant and powerless to do anything.

The Foundation receives an envoy from the Empire, an ostentatious diplomat named Lord Dorwin, who memorably drops his "r's" when he speaks in the style then fashionable among the imperial elite. He *apparently* assures the Board that the Empire will defend the Foundation in the upcoming conflict, and he cites as evidence of this a treaty he has just signed with the Kingdom of Anacreon. The Board is pacified, but Hardin is not.

In an effort to convince the Board that its confidence in the Empire is misplaced, Hardin has the treaty between the Empire and the Kingdom of Anacreon translated into symbolic logic and then analyzed. He shows the translation and its analysis to the Board of Trustees. The upshot is that "something like ninety percent of the treaty boiled right out of the analysis as being meaningless, and what we end up with can be described in the following interesting manner: Obligations of Anacreon to the Empire: *None*! Power of the Empire over Anacreon: *None*!" (*Foundation*, 1991, pp. 81–82). The Board, whose members are familiar enough with symbolic logic to follow the analysis, is forced to agree with Hardin's conclusions.

But what of Lord Dorwin's personal assurances that the Empire would protect the Foundation? It turns out that there *were* no such assurances. Hardin admits to the Board that he has taken the liberty of recording all of Lord Dorwin's comments during his visit to the Foundation and had these translated into symbolic logic, too. After "eliminating meaningless statements, vague gibberish, useless qualifications," the analysis revealed that there was "nothing left. Everything canceled out" (p. 83). As Hardin puts it to the Board: "Lord Dorwin, gentlemen, in five days of discussion *didn't* say one *damned thing*, and he said it so you never noticed. *There* are the assurances you had from your precious Empire." Once again, the Board is forced to agree.

Nevertheless, the Board refuses to take action. Instead, it pins its hopes on the Seldon time capsule, which is scheduled to deliver a message in two months' time. The Board believes that Seldon's message will provide the magic bullet needed to defend the Foundation against Anacreon.

Unfortunately, the time capsule contains no such message. Rather, Hardin's pre-recorded holographic projection drops the bombshell that the encyclopedia project is a sham, a mere ploy to get the Foundation established in the first place. Seldon's hologram goes on to explain that the Foundation is now, by Seldon's own design, effectively cut off from the Empire and must find its own way through the impending crisis without any outside assistance.

Thankfully, Salvor Hardin, who had long since lost all confidence in the Board's ability to lead, planned a bloodless coup to go into effect while the time capsule was delivering its message. Hardin's coup goes off without a hitch, and he—the Mayor of Terminus—is now in charge. The story ends with a cliffhanger, and how Hardin succeeds in repelling the Kingdom of Anacreon is left for the next installment.

## Is Symbolic Logic a Hero?

Some readers might be skeptical about my claim that symbolic logic is a "hero" of the Foundation. After all, while Hardin's translations of the Empire-Anacreon Treaty and Lord Dorwin's statements into symbolic logic do convince the Board that the Empire won't come to the Foundation's rescue, they don't move the Board to take action. The Board simply puts its hopes in something else—the Seldon time capsule.

Nevertheless, I think that symbolic logic deserves some credit for solving this Seldon crisis. First, the symbolic logic translations convinced Hardin of the Empire's unwillingness to intervene and emboldened him to plan his bloodless coup. If it hadn't been for these translations, Hardin might not have taken such a drastic step. Second, disabusing the Board of its belief that the Empire would protect the Foundation was necessary in order to get the Board to accept Hardin's leadership after the coup. If the Board had remained convinced of the Empire's fidelity to the Foundation, then it probably wouldn't have taken Hardin's rebellion and its own loss of power so easily or peacefully.

Of course, the idea of *any* heroes in a world ruled by psychohistory is hard to understand. If the science of psychohistory can do what Seldon claims it can, then large-scale changes in human history are beyond the influence of any particular human beings. If psychohistory works, then the Foundation would have survived the Kingdom of Anacreon's assault no matter what Salvor Hardin did. So, why does he deserve any credit for his actions? How can he be a hero if the same end result would have happened no matter what? This puzzle of psychohistory is beyond the scope of this chapter to solve. Suffice it to say that insofar as there are any heroes in the Foundation series, symbolic logic deserves to be counted among their number.

## John W. Campbell, Jr.

Why did Asimov include a reference to symbolic logic in "Foundation"? It never appears anywhere else in his *Foundation* series, so why does it appear in this particular story? How did Asimov learn about symbolic logic in the first place?

One hypothesis is that Asimov learned about symbolic logic in graduate school. Asimov wrote "Foundation" in 1941, while he was getting his PhD in Chemistry at Columbia University. The late 1930s and early 1940s were the heyday of Logical Positivism when many scientists and philosophers were convinced that science, with the help of symbolic logic, was going to give us answers to all meaningful questions. Logical Positivism was so popular in academic circles at the time that the faculty at Columbia University would certainly have been aware of it. Hence, Asimov could have learned about symbolic logic through his graduate studies.

This story sounds plausible, but it isn't true. We know from a 1979 interview with Asimov that he knew nothing of symbolic logic when he started writing "Foundation." The idea came from John W. Campbell, Jr. who had commissioned the story for his magazine *Astounding Science Fiction*. As Asimov explains:

> . . . psychohistory originated in a discussion between myself and Campbell . . . And I think Campbell must have been reading about symbolic logic at the time. There is some reference to symbolic logic in the first story and that was more or less forced on me by John Campbell; it didn't come naturally to me, because I knew nothing about symbolic logic. And he felt in our discussion that symbolic logic, further developed, would so clear up the mysteries of the human mind as to leave human actions predictable. The reason human beings are so unpredictable was we didn't really know what they were saying and thinking because language is generally used obscurely. So what we needed was something that would unobscured the language and leave everything clear. (Gunn, *Isaac Asimov*, pp. 254–55)

John W. Campbell, Jr. is one of the most important figures in the history of science fiction. As editor of *Astounding Science Fiction* (later renamed *Analog: Science Fiction and Fact*) from 1937 to 1971, he is credited with shaping the modern genre into 'hard' science fiction, and he discovered and cultivated the talents of a number of giants in the field, including Isaac Asimov and Robert A. Heinlein. Although he and Asimov didn't see eye to eye on many issues, including politics and parapsychology, Asimov always credited Campbell for his own establishment in the field and referred to him with the utmost gratitude and respect.

So, it seems clear that symbolic logic found its way into "Foundation" because Asimov was a young and impressionable science-fiction writer beholden to an older and overbearing magazine editor. That may seem disappointing, but there is a silver lining: according to the interview with Asimov quoted above, it was Campbell's interest in symbolic logic that gave the two of them the idea for psychohistory in the first place. As Asimov admits, "it was John Campbell who really started psychohistory with symbolic logic" (p. 255).

So, without Campbell's interest in symbolic logic, and his overbearing personality, perhaps there would be no *Foundation* series in the first place—or at least not the same *Foundation* series we have now, in which psychohistory takes center stage. Symbolic logic, regardless of its ignoble reason for appearing in Asimov's story, is a hero in more ways than one: in the story, it saves the Foundation from the Kingdom of Anacreon; and in the real world, it was the inspiration for the idea of psychohistory, the guiding thread of the Foundation series.

## What Is Logic?

While everyone is familiar with the words 'logic' and 'logical', most people would be hard pressed to say what exactly logic is. Thankfully, there's a straightforward answer: logic is the study of arguments. But what are *arguments*?

In everyday language, an argument is a disagreement or a dispute. That's *not* what "argument" means in philosophy. In philosophy, an argument is *any group of two or more statements, one of which is supposed to be supported by the others*. The statement which is supposed to be supported by the others is called the "conclusion," and the statements which are supposed to support the conclusion are called "premises." Thus, every argument consists of one or more premises and a single conclusion. Here's a simple example:

**Argument A**

(1) Lewis Pirenne is a Trustee of the Encyclopedia Committee.
(2) All Trustees of the Encyclopedia Committee are scientists.
(C) Therefore, Lewis Pirenne is a scientist.

This is an example of a *deductive* argument, since the truth of its premises guarantee the truth of its conclusion. Not all arguments are deductive. In some arguments, the premises are meant to make the conclusion likely or probable. These are called *inductive* arguments. (We could turn this argument into an inductive one by changing "all" to "most" in the second premise.) Logic covers both kinds of arguments, but we'll now focus on deductive arguments.

The premises of a deductive argument are *supposed to* guarantee the truth of its conclusion. But not everything does what it's supposed to do. Philosophers use some technical terminology to talk about good deductive arguments. Arguments with premises that do, in fact, guarantee the truth of their conclusions are called 'valid' arguments. It's important not to confuse this with the meaning of 'valid' in ordinary language, which means 'worth taking seriously' or 'containing a grain of truth'. In logic, a valid argument is simply one with the right logical structure—namely, one in which the truth of its premises guarantees the truth of its conclusion.

Valid arguments need not have true premises. (The above argument is valid even if some Trustees of the Encyclopedia Committee are *not* scientists.) Valid arguments with only true premises are called 'sound' arguments. Given the definition of validity, any valid argument with true premises must have a true conclusion. So, the conclusion of a sound argument must be true.

Sound arguments are the gold standard in philosophy: they're what philosophers are striving to achieve when they offer arguments for something—that God exists, that the mind is just the brain, or that free will is merely an illusion. And the way to criticize or push back against an argument in philosophy is to show either that it's invalid or that it has one or more false premises. Any deductive argument that has either one of these flaws is a bad argument and must be either repaired or rejected.

## What Is Symbolic Logic?

Symbolic logic is the use of symbols in order to show that arguments in ordinary language are valid or invalid. For example, suppose someone offers the following argument:

**Argument B**

(1) If the Empire defends the Foundation, then it is not the case that the Kingdom of Anacreon will attack the Foundation.
(2) If the Kingdom of Anacreon attacks the Foundation, then the Foundation will fall.
(3) It is not the case that the Empire defends the Foundation.
(C) Therefore, the Foundation will fall.

Is this argument valid? The answer isn't immediately obvious.

What logicians have discovered is that it's possible to replace parts of natural language with symbols, and then develop formal systems in order to determine the validity (or invalidity) of arguments based on these symbols. For example, in *propositional logic* (also known as sentential logic or statement logic), we replace any complete sentence with its own capital letter and then replace the logical term 'and' with the symbol ∧, 'or' with the symbol ∨, 'if . . . then' with the symbol →, and 'it is not the case that' with the symbol ~. After doing so, the argument above becomes:

**Argument B***

(1) A → ~B
(2) B → C
(3) ~A
(C) C

Translating arguments from natural language into symbols is just the first step in determining their validity (or invalidity) in symbolic logic. The second step is applying some set of rules to that translation. These rules are "mechanical" in the sense that they can, in principle, be followed by a computer. In other words, applying these rules doesn't require any creativity or room for interpretation. Using such rules, it can be shown that the argument above is *invalid*. It would take too much space to walk you through this proof. But rest assured that if you took the time to learn these rules, as the scientists leading the Foundation have done, then you would see clearly that this is the case.

The mechanical application of these rules to symbolized arguments, which leaves no room for disagreement, is one of the main values of symbolic logic: once a group of sentences is translated into symbols, there is no room for disagreement over the logical relationships between them. And this is precisely why symbolic logic is so effective in the story: Salvor Hardin is able to prove to the Board of Trustees that the treaty with Anacreon is worthless because its members know the rules of symbolic logic and are able to follow his derivations.

## Predicate Logic

The symbolic translation given in the previous section is an instance of *propositional logic*, in which the basic units are complete sentences and the logical symbols are limited to connectives (and, or, only if, and not) and parentheses. Propositional logic is a powerful tool, but it doesn't hold a candle to *predicate logic*. Predicate logic allows us to introduce logical symbols *within* a sentence, which makes this logic much more powerful.

To see what I mean, consider the following argument:

**Argument C**

(1) Salvor Hardin is Mayor of Terminus City.
(2) Lewis Pirenne is not Mayor of Terminus City.
(C) Therefore, Salvor Hardin is not Lewis Pirenne.

Translated into propositional logic, this argument becomes:

**Argument C***

(1) P
(2) Q
(C) R

The rules of propositional logic don't justify this inference. According to these rules, this is an *invalid* argument. But surely this argument *is* valid.

The key is introducing symbols for proper names (like "Salvor Hardin" and "Lewis Pirenne") and predicates (like "is mayor of Terminus"). In predicate logic, proper names are represented by lowercase letters (a, b, c, d, etc.), and predicates are represented by uppercase letters (F, G, H, etc.). The logical connectives within a sentence are the same as those between sentences, as used in propositional logic, but we need to introduce one more in order to symbolize this particular argument: namely, "=" for "is," when "is" is used to express numerical identity. Using "M" to stand for "is Mayor of Terminus City," "h" to stand for "Salvor Hardin," and "p" to stand for "Lewis Pirenne," this argument becomes:

**Argument C****

(1) Mh
(2) ~Mp
(C) ~(h=p)

Once again, there's not enough space to walk you through the proof showing this argument is valid. But it is valid, and anybody familiar with the rules of standard predicate logic will have to agree.

The symbols we've introduced so far allow us to translate statements about individuals—like Salvor Hardin and Lewis Pirenne. But many statements are about multiple things. For example, we might say that "all mayors are ambitious" or "some emperors are corrupt." In order to express statements like these in predicate logic, we need two more kinds of symbols: quantifies are variables.

There are two quantifiers in predicate logic: *everything* and *something*, and the symbols for these are the upside-down A (∀) and backwards E (∃). Quantifiers can't function alone. They are always used in combination with variables, which are represented by italicized lower-case letters, usually starting with $x$ ($x$, $y$, $z$, etc.). The variable tied to a specific quantifier is listed immediately after that quantifier, and any other instance of that variable appearing within the same sentence is said to be "bound" by that quantifier. Take the following statement:

Everyone living in Terminus City knows somebody who knows Salvor Hardin.

Using "T$x$" to stand for "$x$ lives in Terminus City," "K$xy$" to stand for "$x$ knows $y$," and "h" to stand for "Salvor Hardin," this statement can be translated into predicate logic as follows:

$$(1) \quad \forall x\, \exists y\, (\mathrm{T}x \rightarrow (\mathrm{K}xy \wedge \mathrm{K}y\mathrm{h})).$$

How to translate sentences of ordinary language into statements of predicate logic is not always obvious. But like with everything else, practice makes perfect. The more time one spends with predicate logic, the easier these translations get. And even though generating symbolic translations can be tricky, once you have those translations, determining the logical inferences based on them is just as mechanical and straightforward as it is for propositional logic. And that is the point of predicate logic: to make logical inferences between statements clear, unambiguous, and obvious to everyone who knows this logical language.

## The Empire-Anacreon Treaty

According to Hardin, his logical analysis of the treaty between the Empire and the Kingdom of Anacreon has two major flaws: much of it turns out to be meaningless, and the rest of it fails to imply that the Empire and Anacreon have any substantive obligations to each other. In order to see how a translation into symbolic light might reveal such things, consider the following excerpt from the treaty (which is purely hypothetical, since Asimov includes no text from the treaty in his story):

> Whereas the Empire is the Empire, be it resolved that it controls whichever star systems it controls . . . Given its longstanding

> relationship with the Empire, Anacreon hereby renders unto the Empire that which it owes the Empire . . . Anacreon shall not annex any star system which, according to this treaty, belongs to the Empire. . . .

To start, notice that the first sentence is vacuous: it's certainly true that the Empire is the Empire and that it controls whichever star systems it controls, but these statements are *trivially* true. They could not possibly be false! Logicians call such statements "tautologies," and translating the first sentence of this treaty into symbolic logic allows us to demonstrate this. Using "e" to stand for "the Empire," "S*x*" to stand for "*x* is a star system," and "C*xy*" to stand for "*x* controls *y*," this sentence can be translated into predicate logic is as follows:

$$(2)\quad e{=}e \wedge \forall x\,((Sx \wedge Cex) \rightarrow Cex).$$

Using the inference rules of predicate logic, it can be shown that the denial of this statement is a contradiction, from which it follows that this statement is a tautology. If the Empire-Anacreon Treaty contains a number of tautologies, then these parts of the treaty are, in a sense, "meaningless"—not because they lack cognitive content, but because they don't make substantive claims.

The second sentence of this hypothetical treaty has two different problems. The first clause, which acknowledges Anacreon's longstanding relationship with the Empire, is not, strictly speaking, a tautology. It is not trivially true in the sense that it couldn't possibly be false. But it is trivially true in another sense: it states a simple empirical fact from which nothing substantive follows. Yes, Anacreon and the Empire have a long history. So what? Symbolic logic can be used to drive this point home. Using "a" to stand for "Anacreon," "e" to stand for "the Empire," and "R*xy*" to stand for "*x* has a longstanding relationship with *y*," this clause can be translated as follows:

$$(3)\quad Rae.$$

What follows from this statement, according to the rules of predicate logic? Not much. We can infer that the Empire exists and that Anacreon also exists. We can also infer this statement itself (since everything logically implies itself) and any tautology we like (since tautologies are logically implied by everything). But that's it. So, unless this statement appears elsewhere in the treaty, as part of another statement, then it's also meaningless—again, not in the sense that it is nonsensical, but in the sense that nothing substantive can be derived from it.

The main clause of this sentence has a different problem: the statement "Anacreon hereby renders unto the Empire that which it owes the Empire" is neither a tautology nor a simple empirical fact. It makes a substantive claim that could have meaningful implications. The problem is that this statement doesn't by itself imply that Anacreon renders anything unto the Empire. In order for it to imply that, the treaty would have to state somewhere else that there is something which Anacreon owes the Empire. This, too, can be shown using predicate logic. Using "a" to stand for "Anacreon," "e" to stand for "the Empire," "R$xyz$" to stand for "$x$ renders $y$ unto $z$," and "O$xyz$" to stand for "$x$ owes y to $z$," this sentence can be translated into predicate logic as:

$$(4) \quad \forall x\,(\mathrm{O}ax\mathrm{e} \rightarrow \mathrm{R}ax\mathrm{e}).$$

From the inference rules of predicate logic, it cannot be inferred that Anacreon renders anything unto the Empire—that is, $x$ (Ra$x$e)—unless the treaty states elsewhere that there is something which it owes the empire—that is, $x$ (Oa$x$e). In other words, unless the latter (or something which logically implies it) appears somewhere in the treaty, this statement has no substantive implications.

Finally, consider the third sentence of this make-believe treaty: "Anacreon shall not annex any star system which, according to this treaty, belongs to the Empire." This statement is certainly meaningful, and it might seem to imply that Terminus is protected by the treaty. After all, Terminus does belong to the Empire, doesn't it? The problem is the clause "according to this treaty." If Terminus is not mentioned elsewhere in the treaty as belonging to the Empire, then it doesn't follow from the treaty that Anacreon is forbidden from annexing it! This, too, can be shown using predicate logic. Using "a" to stand for "Anacreon," "e" to stand for "the Empire," "S$x$" to stand for "$x$ is a star system," "B$xy$" to stand for "$x$ belongs to $y$," and "A$xy$" to stand for "$x$ shall not annex $y$," this sentence can be translated into predicate logic as follows:

$$(5) \quad \forall x\,((\mathrm{S}x \wedge \mathrm{B}x\mathrm{e}) \rightarrow \mathrm{Aa}x).$$

It cannot be inferred from this, using the inference rules of predicate logic, that Anacreon shall not annex Terminus (that is, using “t” to stand for “Terminus,” “Aat”) unless the treaty says elsewhere that Terminus is a star system that belongs to the Empire (that is, “St $\wedge$ Bte”).

These examples have been simple, and purposefully so. But they do illustrate three ways in which predicate logic could be used to show the weakness of the Empire-Anacreon treaty. First, predicate logic can show that the treaty contains tautologies, which are true but trivially so because they cannot possibly be false. Second, predicate logic can show that simple assertions, such as empirical ones, don’t by themselves have any substantive implications. And third, predicate logic can show that non-trivial conditional assertions don’t have any substantive implications unless the antecedent (first part) of those conditionals are independently asserted.

# II

# Foundation and History

*"History is the ultimate weapon, because it harnesses time itself."*

# 4

# Demons, Game Shows, and Baguettes

SYLVIA WENMACKERS

*Foundation* is based on a fictional branch of science called psychohistory, which assigns probabilities to future events. The story touches upon old philosophical questions. How much of our history was inescapable? And how much influence can we have on the future?

We may also wonder about the inevitability of psychohistory itself. In the world of *Foundation*, would this method have been developed if Hari Seldon hadn't existed? Perhaps this is indeed the case.

## From Heavenly Mathematics to Universal Science

In ancient times, before there was any light pollution, people watched the skies on unclouded nights. They noticed that the relative positions of the stars are fixed. Depending on their culture, they grouped them into different figures and gave these constellations different names, but they all observed that the stars appear to revolve around the Earth, just like the Sun does, and that the constellations follow a seasonal pattern. Seafaring folk used the stars to navigate at night, and for centuries the heavenly motions provided the most reliable method to tell the time.

People also noticed that some objects in the skies didn't move with the same periodicity as the Sun and the so-called fixed stars. Women noticed that the monthly phases of the Moon resembled their own bodily cycles. But there were also 'wandering stars' that followed erratic paths, which we now know as planets. Since the Sun, the Moon, the planets, and the fixed stars seemed to move of their own accord, like animals and people do, they were believed to be animated and even divine beings. People believed these celestial beings influenced the life of humans. This led to a desire to describe and predict their motions, to get a peek into their own fates. So, the history of astrology, which involves fortune-telling based on planetary positions, and astronomy, which is the science of celestial objects, are intimately linked (Selin, *Astronomy across Cultures*).

Ancient Greek natural philosophers asked of which substance everything was made. They made various proposals. Plato adopted the theory that everything on Earth consisted of combinations of four elements: earth, water, air, and fire. Aristotle added a fifth element, the aether. He believed that the Moon and the higher heavens consisted of this aether, to which he ascribed a natural tendency for circular motion. Like Plato, he believed that mathematics could describe and predict these perfect, heavenly motions.

According to a later commentator, Plato asked the astronomers which uniform and orderly movements we must assume to explain the apparent, chaotic motion of the planets. Plato also suggested an answer: their motion can be explained by combinations of circular motions, centered on the spherical Earth. Starting from Plato's suggestion, multiple generations of mathematicians and astronomers developed an Earth-centered model for the motion of the planets. In second-century Egypt (then part of the Roman empire), this culminated in the work of Claudius Ptolemy, who synthesized and improved all known astronomy.

The Aristotelean and Ptolemaic worldview, based on an Earth-centered universe, remained influential for more than a thousand years: first in the Hellenistic world, then in the Islamic world, and later in Europe. Following Aristotle, medieval scholars thought that the natural world around us was radically different from the heavens. In particular, they believed that the predictable regularities of the heavens were nowhere to be found on Earth.

Then, Copernicus showed how the Sun, not the Earth, could be seen as the center of the universe. And the heavenly scope of mathematics changed profoundly around the seventeenth century, when natural philosophers such as Galileo Galilei and Isaac Newton formulated mathematical laws that apply to objects on Earth as well as in the heavens. Against the background of Aristotle's sharp distinction between the sublunary sphere (everything below the Moon) and the heavens above it, Newton's proposal for a law of universal gravitation was a revolutionary idea! The same law that holds for an apple falling towards the Earth, also applies to the Moon that revolves around the Earth, as well as to the Earth and the planets that orbit the Sun. This had been unthinkable for over a thousand years, but now seemed to make sense.

So, by the end of the seventeenth century mathematics descended from the heavens and showed it was equally powerful on Earth. This opened the gates for a mathematical description and prediction of a wide range of phenomena in the physical sciences. Gradually, the idea of predicting everything that happens around us, including biological processes and human behavior, emerged as a natural next step in the ad-vancement of science.

## Laplace's Demon

It took some time to digest the implications of Newton's new and powerful approach to science. Pierre-Simon de Laplace was an early-nineteenth-century physicist and philosopher, who was well-versed in Newtonian mechanics and its applications to astronomy. He explained the Newtonian worldview using a thought experiment about a vast intelligence, now known as Laplace's demon.

> An intelligence knowing all the forces acting in nature at a given instant, as well as the momentary positions of all things in the universe, would be able to comprehend in one single formula the motions of the largest bodies as well as the lightest atoms in the world, provided that its intellect were sufficiently powerful to subject all data to analysis; to it nothing would be uncertain, the future as well as the past would be present to its eyes. (*A Philosophical Essay on Probabilities*)

Laplace's thought experiment highlights an important assumption underneath the Newtonian worldview: determinism. In a deterministic universe, an exact specification of the world at a given time allows computing the situation at all other times, past and future—in principle, at least. In reality, we aren't able to predict the past and future perfectly, because we don't know the exact position and velocity of all particles at a given time, because we don't have the memory to store so much information, and because we lack the computational power to predict events faster than they unfold.

Despite our limitations, we can use Newtonian mechanics to accurately predict the motion of planets in our solar system or the movements of cannonballs or missiles on Earth. We must take into account measurement errors and the fact that initial errors lead to bigger errors in predicted values over time. Laplace was well-aware of these problems: he evoked his super-human intelligence, for whom "nothing would be uncertain," precisely to highlight our human limitations. To deal with such problems, Laplace developed new methods in probability theory, which he viewed as our best way to handle incomplete information.

A Laplacian demon in a deterministic world would be a perfect predictor with no use for probability theory. For us humans, however, probability theory provides a way to deal with the gaps in our knowledge and the resulting uncertainty in our extrapolations. In this respect, *Foundation*'s science remains well within the nineteenth-century boundaries to human knowledge: "Hari Seldon knew that his psychohistory could predict only probabilities, and not certainties. There was always a margin of error, and as time passed that margin increases in geometric progression" (*Foundation and Empire*, 1952, Part 2).

## A Paradoxical Game Show

Suppose you're chosen to participate in a game show. During the TV show you'll be faced with two boxes: one opaque box that may contain either one million dollars or nothing at all, and one transparent box that contains a thousand dollars. You'll have to make a choice between two options: either you take home the contents of both boxes or you merely take the contents of the opaque box.

Now, why would you even consider settling for just one box? Well, the contents of the opaque box—one million dollars or nothing at all—is determined before you enter the studio with the help of some very good forecaster of human behaviour. (For understandable reasons, the production team is unwilling to give more details about who or what this is.) If the forecaster predicted that you would be greedy and take both boxes, the TV company put nothing in the opaque box. If the forecaster predicted that you would only take the opaque box, however, they've put in one million dollars.

You're told all this beforehand and you've been pondering what to do ever since. Now, you're standing under the hot spotlights, faced with the two boxes. You hear the presenter say: "The choice is yours." The studio goes quiet, all you hear is your heart pounding in your chest. Everyone awaits your answer. So, what will you say?

Will you take the opaque box, to get one million dollars? But if the forecaster got it wrong, you'll miss out on the thousand dollars that you can see in the other box. And shouldn't you take both boxes anyway? After all, the content of the opaque box is already fixed, so you take home whatever it contains, plus another thousand dollars if you ask for both boxes. And yet, a nagging voice in the back of your mind tells you: but if the forecaster predicted that, there will be nothing in the opaque box.

This scenario is known as Newcomb's Paradox and there is no agreed upon answer to it. The feeling of participating in this game show comes close to what it must be like to live in a society governed by Seldon's Plan: it keeps you second-guessing whether your actions can really be free if they've been predicted long ago. It keeps you looking for ways to break the rules, by doing something surprising, to escape the grasp of the prediction. Additional rules are imposed to prevent people from breaking the system.

Newcomb's paradox additionally stipulates that you aren't allowed to outsource your decision to a randomizer such as a coin toss. In the *Foundation*, a "necessary assumption is that the human conglomerate be itself unaware of psychohistoric analysis in order that its reactions be truly random" (*Foundation*, 1951, Part 1). It's generally assumed that a Laplacian demon cannot be part of the universe it is supposed to predict. Otherwise, knowledge of predicted events can be used to alter those events, thereby nullifying the prediction. From an external perspective, that response may perhaps be predicted—but this suffices to show that the supposed Laplacian demon inside the world failed to be one. In other words, perfectly accurate and complete predictors can only operate outside of the system about which they make predictions. Similarly, the findings of psychohistory would easily collapse once they're exposed. Therefore, they must be kept a secret.

## Predicting the Solar System

Newtonian mechanics is deterministic, which means that in principle the course of events is perfectly predictable, at least for an external observer. Yet, determinism doesn't automatically lead to predictability in practice. The late-nineteenth-century mathematician and philosopher of science Henri Poincaré was among the first to study dynamical systems, in which small changes in initial conditions may blow up to gigantic differences in the long run. Since the 1970s, these are known as chaotic systems.

Poincaré was working on a problem that had already troubled Newton: the stability of the solar system. Newton had found the law for universal gravitation, which describes the force that governs the structure of our solar system. However,

Newton had been unable to prove that the orbits of planets are stable over long periods of time. In fact, he had postulated that God intervenes every now and then to correct the orbits, so that the solar system stays intact. Laplace believed he had made real progress in proving stability without the need for divine intervention. However, the later work by Poincaré showed why Newton, Laplace, and others couldn't have succeeded.

Poincaré worked on the three-body problem (say, the Sun, Earth, and Moon) with the goal of finding stable solutions. However, he found that three masses with Newtonian gravity are in general not stable—a finding which is central to the plot of a science-fiction novel, *The Three-Body Problem*, by Liu Cixin. Except for very special configurations, their orbits are usually not repeating. Instead, they're what we now call chaotic. By definition, a chaotic system is deterministic, so its present state in principle entails all past and future states. However, tiny differences in the initial positions and velocities (below a given detection limit) give rise to enormous differences and seemingly erratic behavior in the long run, thereby blocking practical predictability.

A typical example of a chaotic system in nature is the weather: although our atmosphere is governed by deterministic laws, practical predictability is limited to a few days into the future and quickly deteriorates over longer timespans. This is called the butterfly effect, which suggests that the flapping of a butterfly's wings in Brazil could set off a tornado in Texas. (My science-fiction story "Path Correction" zooms in on the implications of chaos for an individual's life, in contrast to psychohistory's large groups.) Likewise, our solar system itself is chaotic, albeit with a very long period of near-stability (in the order of ten million years).

## Improbable Baguettes

The reason offered for the required secrecy of psychohistoric predictions is "in order that its reactions be truly random" but how could randomness help prediction? We've just seen that Poincaré was among the first to notice that determinism doesn't always imply practical predictability. Perhaps more surprisingly, the opposite is true as well: indeterminism doesn't always imply practical unpredictability. Collectively, chance events give rise to some of the most stable and predictable patterns.

Poincaré had a keen insight into such chance patterns. Allegedly, he used this knowledge to expose his baker for fraud.

Whether based on true events or entirely fictional, it's an instructive tale. Poincaré suspected that his Parisian baker was selling baguettes that were below the state-mandated standard weight. To check this, he weighed each loaf of bread he bought there and plotted the distribution of the weights. It formed a bell-shaped curve, with the peak of the curve below the mandated weight. Poincaré reported to the authorities that the baguettes were too light on average, and the baker was put on notice.

Nevertheless, Poincaré kept up with weighing the baguettes. The average weight now equaled the standard, but the weight distribution was no longer symmetric. Instead of a bell-shape, the curve looked as though the left-hand side, towards lower weights, had been cut off. Poincaré again informed the authorities, who confirmed his suspicion: while the baker was still using too little dough, he sold the above-average baguettes to Poincaré.

Whether fiction or fact, this story shows how a basket of baguettes with random variations in weights produces a predictable pattern: an unbiased bell-shaped distribution. Moreover, the biased selection by the baker in the second part of the story leaves traces in the final distribution. Similar techniques are useful to detect voter fraud or to check tampering with lottery results. For this to work, the pool of data must be large enough. This brings us to another key assumption in psychohistory: "that the human conglomerate being dealt with is sufficiently large for valid statistical treatment" (*Foundation*, 1951, Part I).

## From Social Atomism to Mob Science

The main assumption of psychohistory, even more important than secrecy, is this: "Psychohistory dealt not with man, but with man-masses. It was the science of mobs; mobs in their billions. It could forecast reactions to stimuli with something of the accuracy that a lesser science could bring to the forecast of a rebound of a billiard ball. The reaction of one man could be forecast by no known mathematics; the reaction of a billion is something else again" (*Foundation and Empire*, 1952, Prologue). This condition is repeated throughout the *Foundation* novels. For instance: "Without pretending to predict the actions of individual humans, it formulated definite laws capable of mathematical analysis and extrapolation to govern and predict the mass action of human groups (*Foundation and Empire*, 1952, Part I).

This aspect of psychohistory is firmly rooted in a nineteenth-century branch of physics: statistical mechanics.

It studies collections of particles of which the positions and velocities aren't known exactly, but their probability distributions are. As a result, the particles exhibit lawlike behavior at the collective level, much like Poincaré's baguettes collectively betrayed their baker's fraud.

Another watershed occurred when the nineteenth-century astronomer and sociologist Adolphe Quetelet realized that—much like particles and baguettes—people can be characterized by statistical distributions, too. Approaches such as Quetelet's are sometimes called 'social atomism'. Like statistical mechanics, it uses two levels of description: the level of individual particles or persons (of which not all properties are known exactly) and the collective level of groups of colliding atoms (say, a gas) or groups of interacting people—in other words, a society.

Like the weights of baguettes that vary due to small deviations in the amounts of dough, physical characteristics of humans such as length and weight also vary due to a combination of genetic and environmental factors. Quetelet noticed that the distribution of human characteristics often follows a bell-shaped curve, which is the same distribution as that of Poincaré's baguettes and also of measurement errors in astronomy. An astronomer himself, Quetelet knew that each astronomical measurement can be thought of as the result of a constant value plus or minus a random error term. So, the true value can be approximated by averaging over many measurements. This led Quetelet to the idea of 'the average man'.

Quetelet's average man is a hypothetical, ideal individual with fixed characteristics exactly equal to the average of those of a large group of men. We now consider this to be a problematic notion, which carries a normative judgment of people with 'abnormal', 'deviant', or 'non-ideal' properties. Unfortunately, such ideas are common in the history of statistics, a branch of applied science that was developed conjointly with heredity and sociology. For instance, Quetelet was certainly influenced by Francis Galton, another nineteenth-century statistician and sociologist who coined the term 'eugenics'.

Quetelet also found a typical relation between the length and weight of people in a population: the body-mass index or BMI. He proposed this index to determine the health of a population. To his credit, in this case he didn't invoke the notion of an ideal, average man. In fact, he warned against using the BMI to characterize the health of individuals, since it only applied to populations—a warning that has been violated ever since.

Physical characteristics of people are one thing, their behavior is a totally different matter! Quetelet did aim to develop a field of research he called social physics: he hoped to predict crime rates using data on various social factors and using the methods of statistics. The nineteenth-century philosopher Auguste Comte was very critical of the statistical approach to sociology but Quetelet's methodology became dominant. Nowadays, the use of statistical methods is well-established in all the social sciences. Moreover, the dream of predicting crime and recidivism from statistical data still guides the development of AI models in policing and law, while the problem of bias in historical records is far from solved.

## The Specter of Statistical Determinism

One of the criticisms raised against Quetelet's social physics was that it seems at odds with human freedom. Although the incompatibility isn't as strong as with a Laplacian demon that can predict human behaviour at the individual level, a similar tension remains. For instance, Quetelet noticed that numbers of births and deaths as well as crime rates are very reproducible from year to year and can therefore be predicted with a terrifying exactness.

The resulting notion of 'statistical determinism' makes us wonder how much an individual can really change the course of history. The nineteenth-century historian Thomas Buckle thought such stable statistics are entirely incompatible with human free will. He believed in a kind of historical determinism that resembles the core of Seldon's Plan: "The laws of history are as absolute as the laws of physics, and if the probabilities of error are greater, it is only because history does not deal with as many humans as physics does atoms, so that individual variations count for more" (*Foundation and Empire*, 1952, Part 2).

Statistical determinism invites further reflection not merely on Salvor Hardin or the Mule, but also on how free Seldon could have been in coming up with psychohistory and in designing his Plan in the first place. If historical determinism equally applies to the course of science, then it seems that if Seldon hadn't come up with psychohistory, eventually someone else would have. We've seen some reasons to believe so. After all, many of the core ideas—from the applicability to mathematics in our sublunar realm, over the predictability of large collections of random events, to the applicability of statistics to human characteristics—were already developed before or during the nineteenth century.

## Present and Future Psychohistory

Another reason to think that Seldon's theory was in some sense inevitable can be found by looking at the progress in the actual mathematical modelling of group behavior that has occurred since Asimov's novels were published. Chaos theory was further developed in the 1970s. Moreover, the very methods from statistical physics that inspired Asimov to speculate about psychohistory have indeed been applied to understand sociological phenomena.

Research fields such as sociophysics, opinion dynamics, and econophysics study how properties of individual people and their small-scale interactions give rise to large-scale phenomena, such as segregation, consensus formation or polarization, and price fluctuations. They do this by modeling interacting artificial agents in a simulated society (Hart and Case, "The Parable of the Polygons").

These fields are still in flux, for they are part of science and science is never complete. What Asimov wrote about psychohistory captures an important lesson from the philosophy of science:

> The Seldon Plan is neither complete nor correct. Instead, it is merely the best that could be done at the time. Over a dozen generations of men have pored over these equations, worked at them, taken them apart to the last decimal place, and put them together again. They've done more than that. They've watched nearly four hundred years pass and against the predictions and equations, they've checked reality, and they have learned. (*Second Foundation*, 1953, Part 2)

A lot has happened since people first looked up at the heavens, asking where its patterns come from and wondering if they can be used to tell our own fates. Naive attempts have been discarded and better methods found.

Centuries have passed, and we sure have learned a lot. Imagine what more we will learn in the next millennia before Seldon appears.[1]

---

[1] I'm grateful to my husband and fellow science-fiction fan, Danny Vanpoucke, for his feedback on an earlier version of this chapter.

# 5

# Psychohistory by Any Other Name

CHRISTOPHER PETERSEN

In the *Foundation* series, the mathematician and scientist Hari Seldon predicts not only the destruction of Trantor, seat of the Galactic Empire, but the eventual fall of the Empire itself. Tragically, it is a fall that is all but inevitable. However, this doesn't mean that nothing can be done, as Seldon explains at his trial:

> I do not say now that we can prevent the fall. But it is not yet too late to shorten the interregnum which will follow. It is possible, gentlemen, to reduce the duration of the anarchy to a single millennium, if my group is allowed to act now. We are at a delicate moment in history. (*Foundation Trilogy*, 2010, p. 29)

Seldon goes on to point out that it should be possible to deflect this "onrushing mass of events" just a little, enough to significantly reduce the amount of human misery to come. Seldon also proposes establishing a project for creating a "Galactic Encyclopedia" so as to safeguard from destruction all the knowledge that humans have accumulated since such knowledge will be indispensable for restoring the Empire when that (very far away) time comes. Understandably baffled, Seldon's inquisitors ask on what basis he can be so confident in his prediction. Seldon replies:

> On the basis of the mathematics of psychohistory . . . it is a prediction which is made by mathematics . . . the fall of Empire, gentlemen, is a massive thing . . . it is dictated by a rising bureaucracy, a receding initiative, a freezing of caste, a damning of curiosity—a hundred other factors. It has been going on, as I have said, for centuries, and it is too majestic and massive a movement to stop. (pp. 25, 28)

Here Seldon references the method that has enabled him to make such a prediction: "psychohistory." What exactly is this method? On the subject of psychohistory, a partial definition from the *Encyclopedia Galactica* reads "that branch of mathematics which deals with the reactions of human conglomerates to fixed social and economic stimuli" (p. 17). More specifically, the method of psychohistory involves taking information concerning such stimuli and using various mathematical and statistical tools to predict the course of human history; in this case the future of the Galactic Empire.

Some readers may notice that the factors listed by Seldon above are akin to some of the reasons invoked by historians to explain the decline and fall of empires, the classic example being the demise of the Roman Empire. Famously, Edward Gibbon in his magisterial six-volume classic *The Decline and Fall of the Roman Empire* was the first to comprehensively examine such factors. It is no secret that when Asimov first came up with the idea for the *Foundation* series he had been reading Gibbon's work (for the second time!) and was inspired to do something like it but on a galactic scale.

And this is in part why Asimov named the crucial method used in *Foundation* "psycho*history*." Later, though, he expressed regret about the label saying:

> Actually, it was a poor word and did not represent what I truly meant. I should have called it 'psychosociology' (a word which the O.E.D. lists as having first been used in 1928). However, I was so intent on history, thanks to Gibbon, that I could think of nothing but psychohistory. (*Gold*, p. 187)

Now it's understandable that Asimov later came to think that the label was not a good one given the ultimate descriptions of psychohistory in the *Foundation* series itself as involving a kind of fusion between thermodynamics and human psychology. But "psychosociology" does not seem much of an improvement or any more accurate. In any case, there are good reasons for keeping the term psychohistory as the name for the method used in *Foundation*.

## The Gibbon Connection

One important reason for retaining the label of 'psychohistory' is to maintain the connection with Gibbon's *Decline and Fall* mentioned before. The interview above might give you the impression that the influence of Gibbon's work on Asimov was superficial. But this is not the case. Look again at some of the cited factors in Seldon's reply to his inquisitors. Some of these are factors that Gibbon explicitly refers to in his analysis of the fall of the Roman Empire.

Beyond these similarities, it's clear that *Foundation* also mimics some of the same beats involved in the fall of the Roman Empire as put forward by Gibbon. One of these beats is worth highlighting but before doing so it is important to note that in *Foundation*, the method of psychohistory has the power to go beyond just making general predictions about the future of the Empire. In fact, Seldon uses psychohistory to make a number of *specific* predictions as well, which come to be known as the "Seldon Plan." The Seldon Plan is a guide of sorts for the Foundation concerning several crises that it is highly likely to confront in its future. The example here has to do with the second crisis.

This second crisis that is faced by the Foundation which by this point has been established at a place in the dying Empire called Terminus (whose more than able mayor is Salvor Hardin) concerns how to deal with the immediate threat of war and annexation by one of the "barbaric kingdoms," namely, Anacreon. The solution to this crisis had already been long in the making, involving the gradual transformation of the Foundation's science into a religion (complete with rituals and a priestly class) that then wove itself deeply into the fabric of the Four Kingdoms—so deeply that the acting leader of Anacreon when faced with the prospect of a mob led religious rebellion had no choice but to stand down. Thus, religion as an instrument of foreign policy enabled the Foundation, still very much in its infancy, to ward off a barbarian invasion. In similar fashion, (though not exactly the same), Gibbon in his account of the barbarian invasions of Rome emphasizes religion (really, superstition) as an instrument for transforming the various barbarian groups into a semi-civilized people such that civilization is able to survive the collapse of Rome. This is important because it helped to forge a kind of continuity between the world of Late Antiquity and what would become modern Europe. As Gibbon says:

> The perpetual correspondence of the Latin clergy, the frequent pilgrimages to Rome and Jerusalem, and the growing authority of the Popes, cemented the union of the Christian republic: and gradually produced the similar manners, and common jurisprudence, which have distinguished, from the rest of mankind, the independent, and even hostile, nations of modern Europe. (*Decline and Fall*, p. 433)

So while religion, particularly the Christian religion, was a major reason for the decline of Rome in Gibbon's account, religion was also crucial, at least in its superstitious form, for allowing some elements of civilization to survive. And thus for Rome (according to Gibbon) and Seldon, religion offered a solution to their respective crises.

The strong connections between *Decline and Fall* and *Foundation* constitute one of *Foundation*'s virtues and might be reason alone for sticking with calling the method of *Foundation* 'psychohistory', but more can be said.

## Psychohistory as Philosophy of History

For the method of psychohistory to be as powerful as possible, surely the more data fed into the equations the better, yes? And such would no doubt include historical data. So while the model is not making predictions exclusively via history and human psychology, and thus is a misleading label in this sense, nonetheless there is a role that history is playing here, specifically there is a particular kind of *philosophy* of history that must be a key assumption for any model utilizing the method of psychohistory. This assumption is that history can be understood as a *scientific* discipline in two vital ways: 1. that the past is subject to mathematical treatment and 2. That the past, when properly mathematized, can be used to predict the future.

Philosophy of history is certainly not a prevalent specialization among philosophers today. This is in part due to a wariness with a particular kind of philosophy of history that held sway for some time, namely, what is known as "substantive" or "speculative" philosophy of history. This version of philosophy of history is typically quite metaphysically extravagant and teleological, meaning that history is thought to have some ultimate purpose or end to which it is heading. This would be true of any version of Christian apocalypticism or something like Georg Hegel's view of human history as "Reason" working itself out towards some clearly defined end. In fact, the belief that history has some kind of greater *meaning* is a common one among non-philosophers (though not among most professional historians) and during times of great change or upheaval such a view often finds its way back into public discourse. It is fairly obvious, especially given Asimov's humanism, that such a philosophy of history is not at the heart of the method of psychohistory.

Nonetheless, there is another tradition of philosophy of history that is more amenable to our purposes. This version is, appropriately enough, called "critical philosophy of history" since it aims to think critically about the discipline of history, examining such matters as the methodology of historians, determining what are good methods historians can or should use and what to count as historical evidence (or more ambitiously what to count as historical knowledge). The common theme here is figuring out how to make history a *better* discipline. One answer to this has been to try and make history more *scientific*.

The first attempts to make history more scientific were due to a few Enlightenment thinkers such as Montesquieu, John Robertson, David Hume, and of course Edward Gibbon. Prior to the works of these gentlemen, most thinkers approached the past with an extremely skeptical attitude, despairing that one could ever 'know' anything about history. The following remarks by Samuel Johnson is representative of this attitude:

> We must consider how very little history there is; I mean real authentic history. That certain kings reigned, and certain battles were fought, we can depend upon as true; but all the colouring, all the philosophy of history is conjecture. (Quoted in the "Introduction to the Everyman Edition" of *Decline and Fall*, p. lviii)

For most people during this time there seemed to be only two options: either that history was all theologically determined (and thus the identification of human causes in history a meaningless exercise) or that very little of the past could be known. Fortunately, Gibbon's massive achievement showcased for many the possibilities of sustained historical inquiry and the real possibility of acquiring knowledge about the past.

Subsequently, throughout the development of history as a discipline, attempts to make history into something more scientific have waxed and waned, two examples being Marxism and the quantitative methods of the 1960s. Historians have typically resisted such attempts which is why many of these never caught on. This is where matters remain today: most academic historians are happy to think of history as a purely humanistic discipline rather than a science.

## Cliodynamics, the New Psychohistory?

Nevertheless, there has been a recent, concerted effort to make history into more of a science. One example is the work of Peter Turchin, an evolutionary biologist who likes to describe his turn to history as a kind of midlife crisis: "Instead of divorcing my wife and marrying a graduate student. I divorced my biology and married history" (Quoted by Marc Parry). Turchin calls his version of psychohistory "cliodynamics."

Turchin goes on to say that the motivation of his turn to history was twofold: 1. he felt that all the major questions in his field, population dynamics, had been answered and 2. he became fed up with what he saw as a lack of rigor in history often citing the supposed two hundred or so explanations for the fall of Rome as an example. Such a situation, claims Turchin, is as "risible as if, in physics, phlogiston theory and thermodynamics coexisted on equal terms." Turchin's fix for such perceived sloppiness is to take what he has learned in population dynamics, especially concerning its mathematical models, and apply them to large scale historical change. Despite this damning charge against history broadly conceived, Turchin is careful to note that what he is proposing should be understood as different from history proper. Instead, it is an exercise in "theoretical historical social science" deserving of its own name: "cliodynamics" from "Clio, the muse of history, and dynamics, the study of temporally varying processes and the search for causal mechanisms." And yet contrary to the claim to be doing something different than history proper, Turchin elsewhere is explicit that the goal of cliodynamics is to turn history into an "analytical" and "predictive" science. The success of such an endeavor depends on the adoption of two practices from the natural sciences:

> Cliodynamics borrows heavily from two disciplines in the natural sciences. The focus on groups rather than individuals is akin to the approach of statistical mechanics, which integrates over motions of a myriad of particles to predict such properties of the ensemble as temperature or pressure.

And

> Cliodynamics owes an even greater debt to the discipline of nonlinear dynamics. Human societies and states can be modeled as dynamic systems, consisting of parts that interact with each other . . . the key concept here is dynamic feedback. A change in the state of one component of the system has an effect on another, but the change in the second might in turn affect—feedback on—the first. (*War and Peace and War*, p. 10)

This is pretty close to what Asimov had in mind for psychohistory. In the interview quoted above, Asimov went on to explain the methodological basis for psychohistory:

> I modeled my concept of psychohistory on the kinetic theory of gases . . . The molecules making up gases moved in an absolutely random fashion in any direction in three dimensions and in a wide range of speeds. Nevertheless, one could fairly describe what those motions would be *on the average* and work out the gas laws from those average motions with an enormous degree of precision. (*Gold*, p. 188)

This should make clear the similarities between psychohistory and cliodynamics. Even better, in his book *War and Peace and War*, Turchin starts off by acknowledging the close relationship between cliodynamics and psychohistory concluding that while for some the "verdict has been that any scientific history must remain science fiction rather than a real science", cliodynamics is a research program that aims to undermine such a verdict (pp. 2, 3).

So far the bulk of Turchin's work has been applying this method to the rise and fall of empires. Turchin's and others' conclusions are that once all the historical data (ranging from all over the globe) is crunched and put through the proper mathematical machinery, a sure pattern emerges (at least for decline and fall scenarios):

> The very stability and internal peace that strong empires impose contain within them the seeds of future chaos. Stability and internal peace bring prosperity, and prosperity causes population increase. Demographic growth leads to overpopulation, overpopulation causes lower wages, higher land rents, and falling per capita incomes for the commoners. At first, low wages and high rents bring unparalleled wealth to the upper classes, but as their numbers and appetites grow, they also begin to suffer from falling incomes. Declining standards of life breed discontent and strife. The elites turn to the state for employment and additional income, and drive up its expenditures at the same time that the tax revenues decline because of the growing misery of the population. When the state's finances collapse, it loses the control of the army and police. Freed from all restraints, strife among the elites escalates into civil war, while the discontent among the poor explodes into popular rebellion. (pp. 7, 8)

The basic idea here is that rapid demographic growth coupled with prosperity eventually leads to "elite overproduction" and "gross inequality." If, says Turchin, we see these markers then we can make a reasonable prediction that unrest and political instability are probably on their way.

Turchin himself stresses that caution is always warranted when engaging in predictions of any kind. Furthermore, any such predictions are always probabilistic and not wholly deterministic. Of course, this is also how psychohistorical predictions work, as Seldon's own figures never amounted to one hundred percent (though admittedly something like 99.999999 percent is a kind of *de facto* determinism).

One major reason for caution is the fact that it is impossible to anticipate truly unique or contingent events. And this is in part what the figure of the "Mule" represents in the *Foundation* series, a true anomaly that the psychohistorical equations could not directly predict. Asimov was writing before the advent of chaos theory which emphasizes the fragility of a system due to initial sensitivity conditions. Inspired by Tolstoy's famous essay on history at the end of *War and Peace*, Turchin likewise points out a factor that he thinks could upset cliodynamical equations. Turchin believes that freewill is an important (and real) capacity that humans have and that, from time to time, it can make a difference in history. Nevertheless, he concludes, this is such a rare event that for all practical purposes such variables can be left out of our predictive models, in a similar fashion to when physicists help themselves to simpliefied models when ignoring air resistance in ballistics.

Many, especially practicing historians, have taken umbrage to such a view of history that recalls previous attempts to mold the discipline into something along the physical and biological sciences. The complexities of human society, they insist, will ensure that history can never become a predictive science. Certainly, some of this resistance is motivated by a desire to safeguard the autonomy of history as a discipline, especially in an age when the humanities are falling more and more out of favor (at least this is the perception among humanities professors) with a corresponding rise in favor for the STEM fields. Such resistance is understandable given the ephemeral nature of the various grand theories concerning history that have been proposed, most of which have left historians quite skeptical towards anything that looks like such.

Many historians also worry about creeping determinism in such models that they see as largely inconsistent with their emphasis on the contingency of human history. Most academic historians see history as "a complex stew of chance, individual foibles and one-of-a-kind situations that no broad-brush of history will ever capture" (Laura Spinney) and thus are leery of any attempt to undermine such contingent features.

Also, there are other reasons to be skeptical of the promise of something like cliodynamics. For one, it's not clear that old-fashion historical reasoning could not have led to the same conclusions as the patterns identified above by Turchin for empires (in fact they have, as far back as Gibbon even). In such a situation, it looks as if cliodynamics can help to confirm such conclusions already reached by historians, a hugely important thing to be sure, but not itself bringing any significant historical insight of its own let alone produce any helpful predictions.

Moreover, in this example, Turchin is very much leaning on a Malthusian understanding of demographic growth, an interpretation that became outmoded as soon as humans (beginning with the West) developed the capacity to handle burgeoning demographic growth (famines are no longer a problem, at least in most of the world). Such a model may work fine in predominately agrarian and pre-industrial societies. And thus it remains an open question just how much predictive power this particular model concerning the rise and fall of nations or empires possesses for the present age.

In any case, cliodynamics suggests the potential usefulness of history as a predictive tool. Hopefully, it also in turn illuminates the particular kind of philosophy of history that must be foundational to the method of psychohistory if it is to make use of historical data in its predictions. Yet if we were to follow Asimov and abandon the label of psychohistory, this interesting perspective on the nature of history would be lost.

We don't have to follow Asimov's later opinion that the term 'psychohistory' should be abandoned, even though other models, such as sociological and thermodynamic ones, do shed light on how psychohistory is actually used in the *Foundation* series.

1

# 6
# The Foundations of Psychohistory

JOHN P. IRISH

> Nature has implanted in our breasts a lively impulse to extend the narrow span of our existence, by the knowledge of the events that have happened on the soil which we inhabit, of the characters and action of those men for whom our descent, as individuals or as a people, is probably derived.
>
> —EDWARD GIBBON, *An Address on English History*

Edward Gibbon's influence on the writing of Asimov's *Foundation* is well documented. Gibbon's grand and historical narrative of the rise and fall of Rome gave Asimov the idea for his series.

"I was quite frank in my intention of using Edward Gibbon's *Decline and Fall of the Roman Empire* as my model and as a basic guide for plot ideas," Asimov writes, "but I needed something that would make science fiction out of it" (*Gold*, p. 180). Asimov introduces many important philosophical themes throughout the series, but one of the most interesting, the one that makes "science fiction out of it," is his concept of psychohistory. However, the concept of psychohistory was not unique to Asimov's novels; the idea is rooted in earlier writings of the the seventeenth and eighteenth centuries.

## Seldon and Psychohistory

In the first story of Asimov's series, "The Psychohistorians," Hari Seldon is detained and ultimately punished for the crime of political treason. He is found guilty of predicting the downfall of the Galactic Empire, resulting in thirty thousand years of a Dark Age. This Dark Age would result in the loss of thousands of years of intellectual knowledge.

> **Seldon:** I have said, and I say again, that Trantor will lie in ruins within the next three centuries.
>
> **Commission's Advocate:** You do not consider your statement a disloyal one?
>
> **Seldon:** No, sir. Scientific truth is beyond loyalty and disloyalty.
>
> **Commission's Advocate:** You are sure that your statement represents scientific truth?
>
> **Seldon:** I am.
>
> **Commission's Advocate:** On what basis?
>
> **Seldon:** On the basis of the mathematics of psychohistory. (*Foundation*, 2004, pp. 31–32)

Asimov, in an interview years later, went on to explain precisely what psychohistory was and how he came up with the concept:

> At the time I started these stories, I was taking physical chemistry at school, and I knew that because the individual molecules of a gas move quite erratically and randomly, nobody can predict the direction of a single molecule at any particular time. The randomness of their motion works out to the point where you can predict the total behavior of the gas very accurately, using the gas laws. . . . It seemed to me that if we did have a galactic empire, there would be so many human beings—quintillions of them—that perhaps you might be able to predict very accurately how societies would behave, even though you couldn't predict how individuals composing those societies would behave. . . . Throughout the entire trilogy, then, there are the opposing forces of individual desire and that dead hand of social inevitability ("A Conversation with Isaac Asimov," p. 70).

The idea of applying the methods of the natural sciences to the social sciences was not new. For hundreds of years, natural philosophers, scientists, and mathematicians had been thinking of ways to apply the principles and methodologies of the natural sciences to the social sciences. This idea, however, found its most fierce debate during the seventeenth and eighteenth centuries in Western Europe.

## Descartes and Anti-Historical Skepticism

The French philosopher René Descartes (1596–1650) is generally considered the founding father of modern philosophy. Although he published essentially nothing on politics, history, or ethics, he did have a profound impact on the study of philosophy of history. Descartes's goal was to build a new method of scientific and philosophical investigation, one which would be constructed on the certainty of mathematical knowledge. This new method, Descartes believed, could be applied to all fields of study, including the social sciences.

Descartes began by accepting only things that appeared to him as "clear and distinct." "I will admit as true," he begins, "only what has been deduced from indubitable common notions so evidently that it is fit to be considered as mathematical demonstration" (*Philosophical Writings* I, p. 247). From there, like the geometrician building proofs, he began deducing other proofs which followed from these fundamental concepts. Here we see the connection between Seldon's psychohistory and the new Cartesian (following Descartes) method: both believed that mathematics could provide a universal model for understanding all aspects of knowledge.

This emphasis upon mathematics as the building blocks for all knowledge was not just relegated to the natural sciences:

> I came to see that the exclusive concern of mathematics is with questions of order or measure, and that it is irrelevant whether the measure in question involves numbers, shapes, stars, sounds, or any other object whatever. This made me realize that there must be a general science which explains all the points that can be raised concerning order and measure, irrespective of the subject matter. (*Philosophical Writings,* I, p. 19)

Descartes believed that he had discovered a universal key to the formal study of all systems and fields of knowledge. Seldon's psychohistory is the science-fiction manifestation of that Cartesian approach. The use of mathematics and history to organize, categorize, and predict large-scale human behavior patterns was the essence of the philosophical and epistemological foundations behind psychohistory.

Descartes and his new method were promoted by philosophers known as rationalists. These philosophers believed in the power of reason to generate knowledge purely on *a priori* grounds, that is, independent of experience. Those philosophers who opposed Descartes and the rationalists are known as empiricists. The empiricists believed that knowledge came from observation (or experience through the senses) and reason. This philosophical debate would have significant ramifications for the study of history.

Descartes's attempt to clear away all previous knowledge led some philosophers to question the study of the past. They argued that the methodology of those attempting to study history seemed to narrow rather than enlarge the mind. Human reason, not inherited knowledge, was sovereign. The Cartesian new method (this anti-historical skepticism) called into question the relations of the past and the value of historical knowledge.

## Gibbon and the Empirical Study of History

Several thinkers challenged Descartes and his rationalistic approach to this new methodology. One of these individuals was Edward Gibbon (1737–1794). It was Gibbon's *magnum opus*, *The Decline and Fall of the Roman Empire*, which gave Asimov motivation to conceive the *Foundation* series in the first place. As a philosophical historian, Gibbon was forced to deal with the issues posed by the rationalists like Descartes. Gibbon both inherited and rejected Cartesian ideas about the new method, at least with how it would be applied to history writing.

Despite Descartes's anti-history skepticism, some believed that the study of the past still provided valuable information and necessary building blocks for knowledge. One of the early empiricists who challenged the Cartesian method was the English philosopher John Locke. Locke (1632–1704) is one of the most influential philosophers of the Enlightenment. One of Locke's most significant contributions to the study of history was his rejection of the Cartesian new method. Locke believed that sense experience and reason were the foundations upon which knowledge is built. Locke further believed that most of our knowledge was only probabilistic; these two ideas set him at odds with the rationalists.

The ideas of Locke heavily influenced Gibbon. Gibbon frequently references the influence that Locke's writings had on his intellectual development: "Locke's *Treatise of Government* instructed me in the knowledge of Whig principles, . . . I carefully went through the *Essay on Human Understanding* . . . and more than once I have been led . . . into a deep and instructive train of thinking" (*Memoirs* IV, pp. 99–100).

Gibbon knew early on that he wanted to be a historian. His first published work, *Essay on the Study of Literature* (1761), was a vigorous defense of the study of history, the classics, and the humanities. Gibbon set out to defend the study of history against the contempt he felt characterized the attitude of Descartes and other rationalists toward the social sciences. "At present Natural Philosophy and Mathematics are seated on the throne, from which they view their sisters prostrated before them, enchained to their chariot, or at best employed to decorate their triumphal procession. Perhaps their fall may not be far off" (*Literature*, p. 3). Gibbon's defense was an attack on the Cartesian scorn for the past. In discarding the past, Gibbon believed, the new method ran the risk of rejecting much of what humanity could still learn from the philosophical study of history.

Philosophers of history faced two general criticisms implied in the Cartesian new method: first, the sources themselves might be fake or inconsistent with each other, thus calling into question the certainty, upon which evaluations can be made; and second, the inherent biases which often plague historians' research and assessments. Both of these criticisms served to call into doubt the historian's assessments. Gibbon dealt with both of these concerns in his first published essay.

First, as to the credibility of historical documents, documents purported to be authentic may very well be fakes. The historian's job is to compare documents against each other, carefully scrutinize what they used, and call out the falsifications of documents when they're discovered. "Criticism, in my view, is the art of judging writing and writers; what they said, how well they said it . . . History opens up an immense field devoted to the examination and criticism of facts" (*Essay on Literature*, p. 13).

As Locke had explained, "Rational Knowledge, is the perception of the certain Agreement, or Disagreement of any two Ideas, by the intervention of one or more other Ideas" (*Essay*, 4.17). Historical facts are not the enemy of certain knowledge, as Descartes and the rationalists insisted; instead, it is the job of the philosopher of history to compare these historical facts against each other. The historian's goal is "not to grasp a demonstration but to compare the weight of conflicting probabilities" (*Essay on Literature*, p. 16). Gibbon believed in the value of the cumulative wisdom of the ages—but always keeping a critical eye toward Lockean historical consistency, accuracy, and verifiability.

Second, another source of doubt about the validity of claims to historical knowledge was the bias of historians. This often led historians to become advocates for ideology instead of objective observers. Critical scrutiny and the desire for objective truth were goals worthy of all historical study. "Someone who writes for all men," Gibbon argued, "must draw only on sources common to all men, in their hearts and in the spectacle of nature. Pride alone can lead him to overstep these limits. . . . Not only the author's character but that of his work will have an influence on the way it is carried out" (*Essay on Literature*, pp. 8–9). Critical historians desire objective truth, independent of personal biases. For Gibbon, the use and abuse of historical evidence were something philosophers of history should take seriously; that responsibility required both the use of proper evidence and the proper use of evidence.

## Ancients versus Moderns (Lord Dorwin versus Salvor Hardin)

The debate over the value of historical evidence was a topic of great concern for philosophers of history like Gibbon. During the eighteenth century, that debate found a home in what was known as the "Ancients versus the Moderns." For the "Ancients" (of which Gibbon was one), it was essential to recognize and appreciate the cumulative culture of our past (especially the respect which should be afforded to the Greeks and Romans). For the "Moderns," however, their contempt for the past and the preference for their own culture implied the superiority of modern writers over those of the past. It was the job of the intellectual, the moderns argued, to cast aside all remnants of the past (including historical documents) in favor of the present.

According to Gibbon, all documents were valid, as they potentially provided empirical evidence for epistemological certainty. "Let us conserve everything preciously. From the meanest facts a Montesquieu will unravel relations unknown to the vulgar. . . . Their hope is that genius and felicitous efforts will detect properties hitherto concealed" (p. 26). The importance of preserving and employing all facts and historical evidence for the critical historian cannot be underestimated. These bits and pieces serve as the raw data, the empirical evidence, needed to construct the historical narrative essential for their jobs. "No author is forgotten, not even the one farthest removed from his current labors: perhaps it is there the critic will encounter a beam of light that will confirm his discoveries or challenge his hypothesis" (p. 13). You never know where historical evidence might take you; for Gibbon, the exciting part was in the exploration and the discovery.

Gibbon's concern for discarding historical information, as promoted by Descartes and the new method, was that this approach could lead to irreparable harm to the critical historian. Unlike anything found in nature, theoretical fields like mathematics, or even in aesthetics, historical information would be impossible to retrieve once destroyed. "For the losses of history" argued Gibbon, "are indeed irretrievable: when the productions of fancy or science have been swept away, new poets may invent, and new philosophers may reason; but if the inscription of a single fact be once obliterated, it can never be restored by the united efforts of genius and industry" (*An Address*, p. 462). Descartes and his fellow rationalists, represented by the "Moderns," were dangerous adversaries for the philosopher of history; actions resulting from their viewpoint could result in irreparable harm.

Asimov was aware of the issues surrounding this historical debate as it showed up in Part II of *Foundation*, in the story of "The Encyclopedists." In an exchange between Lord Dorwin and Salvor Hardin, over which sources were most valuable to the archeologist, the two captured the essence of the different sides perfectly:

> "Then why rely on him? Why not go to Arcturus and study the remains for yourself?"
>
> Lord Dorwin raised his eyebrows and took a pinch of snuff hurriedly. "Why, whateveah foah, my deah fellow?"
>
> "To get the information first-hand, of course."
>
> "But wheah's the necessity? It seems an uncommonly wound-about and hopelessly wigmawholish method of getting anywheahs. Look heah, now, I've got the wuhks of all the old mastahs—the gweat ahchaeologists of the past. I wigh them against each othah—balance the disagweements—analyze the conflicting statements—decide which is pwobably cowwect—and come to a conclusion. That is the scientific method. At least"—patronizingly—"as I see it. How insuffewably cwude it would be to go to Ahctuwus, oah to Sol, foah instance, and blundah about, when the old mastahs have covahed the gwound so much moa effectually than we could possibly hope to do."
>
> Hardin murmured politely, "I see." (*Foundation*, p. 76)

In Gibbon's view, the epistemic value of these primary texts was fundamentally important. The debate between the "Ancients and the Moderns" represented a fundamental disagreement over the value of historical information and who could judge the epistemic value of that information. The value of historical evidence aside, the philosopher of history does much more than assemble this raw data; history "opens up an immense field devoted to the examination and criticism of facts" (*Essay on Literature*, p. 13).

The philosopher of history is no mere compiler of facts; instead, their job is to explore the causes of the past: "These great men will not be confused with mere compilers" (*Essay on

*Literature*, p. 6). Historians penetrate the depths of the past. They don't just assemble historical evidence; they probe and assess, then make judgments about that past. "He weighs, combines, doubts, decides. Being exact and impartial he yields only to reason, or to authority, which is the reason of facts" (p. 13). They are storytellers, weaving creative narratives of who we were, who we are, and who we will become. One of the fundamental differences between the scientist and the historian is that "sciences consist of knowledge alone. Their principles are speculative truths, not maxims of conduct. . . . [Historians] make the proposition familiar, apply it justly, and use it as a guide in one's studies and a torch in one's direction" (p. 16). History guides and directs us. Finally, for Gibbon, historians never presuppose that what they are achieving is an absolute certainty, like Descartes and the rationalist; instead, they delve into probabilities: "he never presents his conjectures as truth, his inductions as facts, his probabilities as demonstrations" (p. 13).

## Gibbon's Looking Backward and Seldon's Looking Forward

Asimov eventually questioned the feasibility of psychohistory. "As mathematicians began to be interested in the details of what is now called 'chaos', it seemed to me that human history might prove to be essentially 'chaotic' so that there could be no psychohistory" (*Gold*, p. 187). This concern eventually found its way into Asimov's prequels to the series. In *Prelude to Foundation*, Asimov has a young Seldon argue that psychohistory could be nothing beyond a theoretical and mathematical construct: "It was merely a mathematical demonstration. It made a point of interest to mathematicians, but there was no thought in my mind of its being useful in any way" (*Prelude to Foundation* , pp. 14–15).

Seldon even further questions the fundamental differences between the two fields: "mathematics is an orderly thing of human invention. One thing follows from another. There are definitions and axioms, all of which are known. . . . History is different. It is the unconscious working out of the deeds and thoughts of quadrillions of human beings. Historians must pick and choose" (*Prelude to Foundation*, p. 100). Despite Asimov's belief—or disbelief—in the ultimate mathematical predictability of human behavior, the idea itself has proven to be a great source of intellectual debate among philosophers. These are fundamental to the discipline.

Edward Gibbon's *The Decline and Fall of the Roman Empire* is one man's vision of the past and the downfall of a great civilization. Gibbon believed that the writing of history could serve as a valuable exercise in understanding where we have come from and where we are going. Hari Seldon's projection of the decline of the Galactic Empire is one man's vision of the future and the downfall of a great civilization. Both believe the evolution of history is destructive. But where Gibbon and Seldon disagree is the value and the very nature of that historical knowledge. According to Gibbon, historical knowledge can be didactic, serving as a model for future generations to remember and avoid similar mistakes for the future. The predictive model that Seldon has developed is wholly objective and devoid of ethical considerations. "It is a prediction," as Seldon argues, "which is made by mathematics. I pass no moral judgments" (*Foundation*, p. 36). As Gibbon sees it, the very nature of history is moral. However, despite some differences between Gibbon and Seldon's vision and methodology of history, both believe their history begins and ends with humanity.

Philosophers of history will continue to debate the nature of historical knowledge. These questions will also continue to be explored in science-fiction popular culture. Asimov's *Foundation* series is a grand adventure, but more importantly, it's an experiment in a thought process. What is the nature of our knowledge of the past? What can humans do to avoid their fate? Do we have the ability to alter our future through the study of our past? Gibbon thought so, and so have many other philosophical historians.

# 7
# History as Creativity

ELAD MAGOMEDOV

Among all the intriguing concepts that serve as keystones in Asimov's *Foundation* series, the most important one, from which all others emerge, is the concept of psychohistory.

Using an equation that takes as its variables the social and economic circumstances in which a social conglomerate is involved, psychohistory is capable of predicting future events with a certain degree of probability. Hari Seldon's reliance on psychohistory allowed him to maneuver the galactic history into a concrete outcome: the emergence of a second Empire as a consequence of the Foundation's ability to overcome a series of existential crises which it should face as soon as its freedom of action is limited to one possibility (*Foundation*, pp. 82–83).

To resolve such a 'Seldon Crisis' successfully is to provide an adequate response to the critical situation, thus ensuring the continuation of the Foundation and its development in terms of political, economic, and social authority; insofar as it resolves a given crisis adequately, it materializes the 'Seldon Plan' of history. It is not irrelevant that Salvor Hardin, who is the architect of the adequate responses to the first two Seldon Crises, at all times follows the maxim, "Violence is the last refuge of the incompetent." This maxim establishes the very moral foundation or the humanist principle on the basis of which the Seldon Plan aims to establish the new galactic empire.

This reveals the Seldon Plan to be a line of history as *willed* by Seldon, who has a very *specific* kind of civilization in mind—but this line of historic development is by no means the only possible path that history could take. Indeed, the psychohistoric principles underlying the Seldon Plan do not rest on mathematical necessity or certainty, but rather on probability, which means that the Foundation is maneuvered, but not determined, to face a crisis in a particular way. It always remains possible that the Foundation fails to respond adequately, which underlines the fact that the Seldon Plan cannot transcend the element of contingency or chance as inherent to the dynamics of history.

A Seldon Crisis is a point at which history must be faced in a particular way in order to attain a particular outcome. History is hence treated as an input-output system with multiple possibilities: if A then B, if C then D, and so on. But since history is not a closed mathematical equation and at each moment contains the possible breakthrough of an *unpredicted moment*, the logical vector *if-then* never attains in the region of history the same mechanical determination that it has in the realm of formal logic. In fact, the very transition contained in the hyphen of '*if-then*', at each instance marks an open space that engenders the possibility of an unintended outcome, that is to say, an alternate future.

Such movement towards an unintended future represents a line of history that is autonomous with regard to the Seldon Plan, because it does not move *with* the plan, but rather independent of it. When Seldon for instance demonstrates to Gaal Dornick the equation pertaining to Trantor's total destruction, the probability of collapse is calculated at 92.5 percent, which is a high enough probability to be taken seriously, but it nevertheless remains a mathematical infinity away from certainty, because the interval between 92.5 and 100 contains an infinite amount of numbers; as long as mathematical certainty is not reached, the gap opened up between probability and necessity is not closed, and hence the opening for an alternate future remains.

And so, even if the probability of a certain event is 99.9999 . . . percent, the infinitesimal opening persists and remains a gateway to an alternate future. The sense of the Seldon Plan therefore consists in fighting off any force that can enter into that opening and take hold over the course of history, which would lead to a deviation from the historic line as projected by Seldon's will. In other words, the Seldon line of history amounts to a persistent attempt to forcefully and resolutely subject history to an artificial finality.

## Seldon Plan as Artificial Teleology

The philosophical tradition treats the concept of finality in terms of the Greek notion *telos*, which denotes the purposefulness or aim of something. Teleology thus stands for the doctrine that the existence of a thing is fundamentally dependent on that thing's finality. Upon Aristotle's view, for example, a thing comes into existence as a result of four distinct causal events coinciding in one point: certain matter—say, wood—is subjected to a specific form, for instance that of a table, and this is done by the carpenter, who is the 'efficient cause' and who puts the wood in a certain form *with the aim of* producing a piece of furniture for dining. That last aspect pertains to the purpose, the 'final cause', the *telos* of the table. For a long time, philosophers have considered the motion of reality, or *history*, to be regulated by a metaphysical principle that transcends reality and regulates its sense and direction by serving as its finality: just like the existence of a table in Aristotle partly depends on its final cause, so too reality in its totality derives its being from its purpose in traditional metaphysics.

Consider for instance Aristotle's thesis of the cosmic intellect that contemplates itself and, in doing so, puts the cosmos in motion: everything, ranging from celestial bodies to animals and rocks, behaves the way it does only to the extent that it is directed *towards* the cosmic intellect (*Metaphysics*, Book 12). Later, in the writings of Thomas Aquinas, we find the Christian God functioning as both the origin and destination of creation, such that all things come from God and go back to Him. Or else think of Hegel, for whom the entire history, with its art, science and wars, moves towards a realization of pure rationality of the collective Spirit. Despite their differences, all of these distinctive metaphysical doctrines share one essential trait, namely that they are fundamentally teleological in nature—that is to say, they share the view that reality only is what it is, and becomes what it becomes, to the extent that entities and events partake in a metaphysical movement *towards* some ultimate metaphysical principle.

The history of philosophy is marked by a significant break with tradition precisely at those points where philosophers attempt to think of reality as devoid of any logic or structure imposed from 'above' or 'beyond' nature. In *A Thousand Plateaus*, for example, the psychoanalyst Félix Guattari and philosopher Gilles Deleuze proceed on the premise that once we no longer rely on forces that regulate nature from without, the only alternative is to conceive of nature as a spontaneous articulation from within. This leads them to conceptualize everything that is, from molecules to economic structures, as consisting of forces that create a territory where they can affirm themselves and deploy their capacity to act. In the 'transition' from ape to human, Deleuze and Guattari would suggest that this transition does not consist in the ape's first becoming something other than it was to subsequently establish a new lifeworld and territories, but the other way around: the ape, being what it is, *first* territorializes a new lifeworld or milieu, organizes a new way of life—in other words, something *novel* emerges in its capacity to act: the trees give way to the savannah, the hands are now free and become engaged with the surroundings in novel ways, new perceptions and affects configure the inner life of the primate—and it is by virtue of this novel lifeworld that the ape becomes something other than it was. This novelty in the ape's capacity to act, however, is not a matter of necessity but rather of pure chance. Indeed, the entirety of human history is nothing but a series of chance-encounters between forces that merely do what life does: circumscribe a territory that enables them to act. If human history is characterized by 'epochs', it is only because history can be reduced to the following principle: a force gains momentum, becomes dominant and establishes its own lifeworld, only to be subsequently expelled by another force, upon which the lifeworld is reorganized and the circle repeats anew. This process occurs organically and spontaneously, without any extra-mundane principle that could pre-establish the 'direction' that history takes.

We can see why such understanding of reality is not only presupposed by the Seldon Plan, but provides Seldon's project with its very sense. Were it not for the fact that, if left to its organic development, history would be arbitrarily driven into a series of random directions—each defined by the forces that successfully assert themselves and dictate the historic movement—then there would be nothing that Seldon could ever do to maneuver history in a *particular* direction; everything would be already pre-determined in a destiny and unfold according to how it was meant to be.

That the Seldon Plan on the contrary presupposes a concept of history as pure chance, which establishes the *open* nature of every Seldon crisis, is illustrated by the confrontation between Salvor Hardin and Sef Sermak. When Sermak confronts Hardin for resolving the first Seldon Crisis by establishing a balance of power rather than attacking the enemy, Hardin responds as follows: "The temptation was great to muster what force we could and put up a fight. It's the easiest way out, and the most satisfactory to self-respect—but, nearly invariably, the stupidest. *You* would have done it; you and your talk of 'attack first'." Hardin then proceeds to distinguish himself from Sermak as an *alternative* force: "What I did, instead, was to visit the three other kingdoms, one by one; point out to each that to allow the secret of atomic power to fall into the hands of Anacreon was the quickest way of cutting their own throats; and suggest gently that they do the obvious thing. . . . In seven days, the last Anacreonian was off Terminus" (*Foundation*, p. 95). The Foundation can be seen as a region of reality where both internal and external forces seek to assert themselves as a dominant power that shapes history in accordance with its *own* will. The Seldon Plan functions as an *artificial teleology*: it imposes finality on a history that in itself is without any ultimate or pre-defined destination. Hardin is a repetition of Hari Seldon's will; they are one and the same force that propels the Foundation towards one and the same finality. What makes a Seldon Crisis precisely a *Seldon* Crisis is that it opens up a field of possible alternate futures that have nothing to do with Seldon's line of history; if such a non-Seldonian force were to gain domination over the Foundation, then it is no longer Seldon who affirms himself through his successors, but rather another, independent force: Anacreon, the Mule, and others.

## Crisis as Creativity

What is meant by a force 'affirming' itself can be understood in terms of what Deleuze and Guattari call *territorialization*. One way of approaching this concept would be through Nietzsche's doctrine that an essence of a thing is defined by the powers that take it into possession. Put simply, what has been said about history until now also applies to concrete entities: *what* something is, is not pre-given and immutable, but is rather constantly coded and transcoded by the forces that appropriate that thing, forces that exert their own power over that thing.

We know the old saying that history belongs to the victors, as our past is always already disclosed through the perspective of those who have the ideological control over it. If the statues of men who were once considered to be the incarnations of certain ideals, are today redefined in their meaning and pulled down, this is because the dominant forces that once defined what those statues *are*, have now been replaced by other forces. Yet this principle should not be limited to the domain of symbols alone, because what counts for ideology counts just as much for the structure and logic of reality as such.

A spider that catches a fly transcodes the fly's essence by driving its fangs into it: the fly is no longer a force that affirms its own capacity to be the cause of whatever it is that a fly does—buzzing around, annoying people, mating, laying eggs, and so on—but rather becomes transcoded into something else, namely a source of energy for the spider. In a similar vein, for Deleuze and Guattari the essence of a table is not pre-defined in terms of its serviceable finality, as was the case in Aristotle, but rather in terms of the powers that take it into possession; the table is transcoded from consumer's item in the factory, to serviceable tool in the sphere of household, or else into an aesthetic object of an artist, or to source of energy for the fire that suddenly breaks out in the house, and so on—all depending on the code that is imposed on the entity in question. Which code applies where, in turn, depends on the kind of territory we are dealing with, hence also on the forces *whose* territory it is and who 'territorialize' a certain region of reality: a capitalist force in the case of a factory, a physical one in the case of fire, and so on.

The Seldon Plan ultimately aims at a total re-territorialization of the galaxy by the Foundation after space has been deterritorialized by the Empire. This battle for territorialization is a battle for the *telos* of history. A Seldon Crisis is then the instant at which that history's articulation becomes an open vector that can be driven in any direction by any power that manages to seize the opportunity to 'break through'. A crisis is therefore a *pre*condition for change, a situation or a state of affairs that opens up a rupture and, with it, the opportunity or occasion for forces to redefine the essence of a thing that is *in* crisis and, with it, the territory that belongs to that thing. This suggests that the course of history as a whole cannot be changed at all times, but only during a crisis, when an opening or a rupture for total reorganization of reality is presented—a moment, to say it with Seldon, at which one is "maneuvered to a point where [one] no longer [has] freedom of action" (*Foundation*, pp. 82–83).

Hardin later notes that "as long as *more* than one course of action is possible, the crisis has not been reached" (p. 105), which aligns with the idea that as long as one's territory is under one's control, one's freedom of action stays intact—this is, after all, the most banal trait of a territory as understood in common speech. To say 'Don't touch it, it's mine' or 'You can come to this point and no further' is to circumscribe a territory, to define the rules that apply in it, and also to delimit the freedom of the other; one is only free, in the sense of 'at home', in one's *own* territory, which is the reason why my freedom shrinks when my territory is reterritorialized by someone else, or when I enter someone else's territory or home.

The challenge posed to a force that seeks to keep or expand its territory not only entails the ability to *recognize* an opportunity for reterritorialization of a territory that is in the process of deterritorialization—note that the characters who solve a Seldon Crisis always recognize its advent in all kinds of signs—but also the ability to *seize* the opportunity, which requires the capacity to adapt, to mutate, to come up with a radically new way of handling things; in short, it requires creativity. What distinguishes Hardin from Sermak is precisely that Hardin creatively produces a radically new behavior, through which the Foundation no longer behaves as defenseless Encyclopedists, but rather as a source of science, religion and economy.

Sermak, on the other hand, does no more than mechanically repeat the conduct that drove the Empire to its demise. It is no coincidence that Hari Seldon initially explained his intentions to Imperial authorities in a language that mimicked or mechanically repeated the language with which they were already familiar and which was the very disease that led to the collapse of the Empire, namely the language of *stagnation*; the only purpose of the Foundation, as Seldon initially presented it, was the uncreative, repetitive project of composing an Encyclopedia: collecting and archiving, reproducing rather than producing. By contrast, Hardin, who represents the first true manifestation of Seldon's true intention, distinguishes himself from this stagnation and reveals his productive power when he accuses Mayor Pirenne of inability to respond to the crisis adequately.

Faced with a military threat and urged towards action by Hardin, Pirenne resists by claiming "We are scientists," and "The Foundation cannot have *any* interest other than the *Encyclopedia* (p. 60), to which Hardin replies, "'Are you, though? That's a nice hallucination, isn't it? . . . What kind of science is it to be stuck out here for centuries classifying the work of scientists of the last millennium? Have you ever thought of working onward, extending their knowledge and improving upon it?" Hardin then identifies stagnation as the very origin of Empire's demise: "You're quite happy to stagnate. The whole Galaxy is, and has been for Space knows how long. That's why the Periphery is revolting; that's why communications are breaking down, that's why petty wars are becoming eternal" (p. 61).

Stagnation is a process through which a force that rules over a territory becomes unable to produce anything *new*—absence of creativity, degeneration of vitality. We read that Seldon devised his plan for history in a context where, according to *Encyclopedia Galactica*, "the aristocratic coterie rose to power as an element of order during the centuries of instability and uncertainty in the Imperium, but degenerated into a blind instrument for maintenance of the status quo" (p. 21). Elsewhere, during the first Seldon Crisis, when the leaders of the Foundation find themselves driven into a corner by the Anacreonian threat and announce that they *can't* solve the situation, Hardin confronts them by saying "But you haven't *tried*. . . . First, you refused to admit that there was a menace at all! Then you reposed an absolutely blind faith in the Emperor! Now you've shifted it to Hari Seldon. Throughout you have invariably relied on authority or on the past—never on yourselves!" (p. 76).

At these and later occasions, a crisis results from the bankruptcy of the dominant force, its inability to make a difference instead of mechanically repeating the familiar, worn-out, impotent organization of its lifeworld. Thus, in order to keep its own territory intact in the face of crisis, a force must de-territorialize itself and then re-territorialize or *reorganize* in a radically new way, otherwise it will be replaced by any force that is sufficiently adapted to *survive* in the territory that it seeks to annex. For this reason, whether it is in Asimov's fictional *Foundation* or in the real world which the writer inhabited, the fact that every force creates its own *telos* establishes a situation in which every force is a Seldon for itself; the vital skill amounts to being exceptional at it.

# III

# Foundation and Faith

*"The search for meaning is not always about the answer. It's also the process of seeking that enlightens."*

# 8
# Between Cynicism and Faith

CORA BUHLERT

Of the many differences between Isaac Asimov's original *Foundation* stories from the 1940s and the 2021 Apple TV+ adaptation, few are more glaring than the very different way in which the original stories and the TV series handle the subject of religion.

Two major subplots of the TV series involve religion. The first is the backstory of the character Gaal Dornick (Lou Llobell), who hails from Synnax, a waterlogged planet which is dominated by a fundamentalist anti-science religion, where interest in science or mathematics is a heresy punishable by death. Flashbacks reveal that Gaal was not only a believer but actually a temple acolyte before her natural curiosity drove her to turn against her religious upbringing. Gaal is also a math prodigy and so she solves an equation deemed unsolvable, which brings her to Trantor and into the orbit of Hari Seldon.

In the original stories, Gaal Dornick appears in "The Psychohistorians", written in 1951 as the introduction to *Foundation*, the first volume in the *Foundation* trilogy. The main difference between the book and the TV series is that Gaal is male in the book and female in the series, otherwise the characters are very similar. Both versions of Gaal hail from a backwater world called Synnax and both are math prodigies who travel to Trantor to work with Hari Seldon and wind up being arrested and exiled to Terminus.

In the book, Gaal serves as the point-of-view character for a single story and then vanishes from the narrative. In the TV series, Gaal is a much more central character and serves as a connecting thread for the entire series as much as Hari Seldon himself. Consequently, her backstory was expanded as well and her homeworld of Synnax, merely described as a backwater planet in "The Psychohistorians", becomes a world that was struck by an environmental disaster and whose inhabitants consequently became fanatical adherents of an anti-science religion.

In the original Asimov stories, there actually is a world which is dominated by a fundamentalist religion, which judges scientific knowledge, here represented by nuclear power, to be a heresy punishable by death, namely the planet Askone from the short story "The Traders", first published in the October 1944 issue of *Astounding Science Fiction*.

In "The Traders", trader and Foundation agent Eskel Gorov is arrested and sentenced to death for peddling nuclear-powered gadgets and violating Askone's religiously motivated ban on nuclear power. Another trader, Limmar Ponyets is sent to Askone to rescue Gorov. The shrewd Ponyets fulfils his mission by rigging up a nuclear-powered transmutation machine that can turn lead into gold (based on a real experiment from 1941, where mercury was transmuted into radioactive gold, with which Asimov as a graduate student of chemistry was likely familiar) to bribe the Askonian elders. Then Ponyets records the elder Pherl drooling over the transmutation machine and the gold it promises. This is sacrilege not to mention a capital offence on Askone and so Ponyets blackmails Pherl into releasing Gorov and working to revoke the ban on nuclear power, opening up Askone to Foundation influence.

The theme dominating "The Traders" and in fact all of the stories collected in the first book of the *Foundation* trilogy is imperialism and particularly the role of the United States as an emerging superpower bringing other nations into its sphere of influence via the exercise of soft power like trade, cultural and technological exchange (including nuclear power) and—yes—religion. At its heart, "The Traders" is about a clash between two different political systems. That one of those systems happens to be a theocracy rather than a Communist people's republic or a monarchy is secondary to the narrative.

Nonetheless, "The Traders" displays a highly cynical view of religion. On Askone, religion clearly is "the opium of the people," as Karl Marx had written in his *Critique of Hegel's Philosophy of the Right* back in 1844. It quickly becomes clear to both Limmar Ponyets and the reader that the elders of Askone do not truly believe in their religion, but view it as a means of keeping the population compliant. Hence, Pherl is only too eager to violate the principles of his religion—a total ban on nuclear power—for the personal gain of owning a machine that can transmute lead into gold. Ponyets wins by using both Pherl's greed and his hypocrisy against him.

As a member of the left-leaning science fiction club The Futurians, Asimov would have been at least cursorily familiar with Marx's ideas, though he was never a member of any Communist party, unlike his friend and fellow Futurian Frederick Pohl, who was a member of the Young Communist League and even president of the Brooklyn Flatbush chapter from 1936 to 1939. Furthermore, the utopian and technocratic Socialism of fellow Futurian John B. Michel was a notable influence on the early *Foundation* stories. In fact, the following quote from "Mutation or Death," a speech written by Michel and delivered by Donald A. Wollheim at the Third Eastern Science Fiction Convention in Philadelpia in 1937 that "science-fiction should by nature stand for all forces working for a more unified world, a more Utopian existence, the application of science to human happiness, and a saner outlook on life" could almost be a mission statement for the Foundation.

"The Traders" takes place roughly eighty to one hundred years after the events portrayed in the TV series. Therefore, we have not yet seen how the TV series will handle that particular story. Nonetheless, the anti-science theocracy on Synnax in the TV series is very similar to the one on Askone, at first glance. The main difference is that there's no evidence that any of the people on Synnax, including religious leaders, do not take their faith absolutely seriously. Gaal Dornick eventually comes to question the beliefs she was brought up with, but hers is the sincere questioning of the heretic and not the hypocrisy of elder Pherl.

## Robots and Luminism

The fact that the *Foundation* TV series treats the religious beliefs of its characters as absolutely sincere becomes even more apparent in the other plot strand where religion plays a major role, namely the Empire's response to the succession crisis of a fictional religion named Luminism.

The Proxima, spiritual leader of Luminism, an influential religion with three trillion adherents, has died and there are two candidates for her successor: Zephyr Gilat (Julia Farino), who is friendly inclined towards the Empire, and Zephyr Halima (T'Nia Miller), who believes that the clone emperors of the genetic dynasty do not have souls and therefore are not human. Since Zephyr Halima eagerly shares her beliefs from the pulpit, she becomes a problem for the Empire. Therefore, Brother Day (Lee Pace) and Demerzel (Laura Birn) travel to the spiritual center of Luminism, a moon called the Maiden, to make sure that Zephyr Gilat becomes the next Proxima (a title which literally means "next" in Latin).

There is no religion called Luminism in the original *Foundation* stories. It was invented out of whole cloth for the TV series, along with the entire plotline involving the genetic dynasty. This makes it all the more notable how much space the Luminism subplot takes up. Brother Day and Demerzel's misadventures among the Luminists are given a significant amount of screentime in four episodes of the ten-episode season. Clearly, this is a subject dear to the heart of showrunners David S. Goyer and Josh Friedman.

As a result, the beliefs of the Luminists are presented in much greater detail than those of the fundamentalists of Synnax, whose beliefs boil down to "Science and technology are bad." Luminism, on the other hand, has a deity or rather three, a theology, a mythology, a priesthood and rituals.

Luminism is portrayed as a hodge-podge of several real world religions. The Luminists worship a triple goddess consisting of maiden, mother, and crone, a motif which can be found in many ancient religions such as the Moirai and the goddess Hecate of Greek mythology or the Norns of Norse mythology. The triple goddess motif was extensively described and analysed by scholars like Jane Ellen Harrison, Robert Graves, and Marija Gimbutas and also adopted by neopagan religions. Finally, the trinity of maiden, mother, and crone also mirrors the trinity of Brothers Dawn, Day and Dusk in the TV series.

The Luminists also believe that the souls of the dead are reincarnated, which directly leads to the conflict that propels the Luminism subplot in the TV series. For Zephyr Halima believes that since the emperors are all clones of the same man, Cleon I, they do not have souls and therefore cannot be reincarnated and also cannot develop or evolve.

Brother Day reacts to Zephyr Halima challenging the legitimacy of the Empire much like Limmar Ponyets reacts to the Askonians in "The Traders." He tries to solve the problem by throwing money at it and promises to install a desalination system on the Maiden, which has a massive problem of water shortage. And if Zephyr Halima had been a hypocrite like the Askonian elders, this approach would have worked. However, Zephyr Halima is a true believer and doubles down on her claim that the cloned Cleons have no souls and are therefore not fully human.

Nor is Zephyr Halima the only true believer in the TV series, for the robot and Imperial adviser Demerzel (Laura

Birn) is also revealed to be an adherent of Luminism and clearly takes her faith very seriously.

Unlike the genetic dynasty, the character of Demerzel does appear in the *Foundation* prequels *Prelude to Foundation* (1988) and *Forward the Foundation*, published posthumously in 1993. Also male in the novels, Demerzel is first minister and chief adviser to the Emperor as well as a robot. However, in the books Demerzel is not just any robot, but one of several pseudonyms used by R. Daneel Olivaw, the humanoid robot introduced in the 1953 novel *The Caves of Steel*. In the 1980s, Asimov attempted to tie the robot stories, the Galactic Empire novels and the *Foundation* series into one coherent whole and used the character of Daneel R. Olivaw as a connecting thread.

The TV series makes several changes to the character of Demerzel/Daneel. The gender switch is probably the most minor of those changes, since gender does not mean anything to a robot anyway. Far more important is that Demerzel doesn't seem to be bound to the Three Laws of Robotics (introduced in the 1942 story "Runaround"), since she repeatedly violates the First Law—"A robot may not injure a human being or, through inaction, allow a human being to come to harm"—and not only oversees torture, executions and the bombing of two inhabited planets, but also kills both Zephyr Halima and Brother Dawn (Cassian Bilson).

In the 1985 novel *Robots and Empire*, part of Asimov's attempt to tie the robot stories and the *Foundation* series together in the 1980s, R. Daneel Olivaw and his robot friend R. Giscard Reventlov come up with the so-called Zeroth Law, which states: "A robot may not harm humanity, or, by inaction, allow humanity to come to harm." Since the Zeroth Law supersedes the First Law, Daneel can theoretically allow humans to be harmed in the name of the greater good, though this causes a great conflict in his positronic brain and actually fries the brain of Giscard. Overseeing the torture and execution of potential terrorists might be excusable via the Zeroth Law (though there is little evidence that the Anacreon and Thespis delegates are truly guilty), but Demerzel murdering both Zephyr Halima and Brother Dawn, neither of whom pose a threat to the future of humanity, with her own hands is a clear violation of the First Law.

Compared to that, the fact that Demerzel also happens to be religious seems to be a minor deviation from the original stories, even though one cannot help but wonder why a more than ten-thousand-years-old immortal robot would choose a religion that focuses on souls and reincarnation.

That said, *The Caves of Steel*, the novel which introduced Daneel, contains several biblical references. Daneel's human partner, detective Elijah Baley and his wife Jezebel are named after characters from the Book of Kings and the relevant passage is discussed in the novel. Furthermore, Elijah uses the tale of Jesus and the woman taken in adultery from the Gospel of John to explain the difference between justice and upholding the law to Daneel.

Over the course of *The Caves of Steel*, Daneel develops an interest in many aspects of human culture, including religion. However, this interest is purely intellectual curiosity. R. Daneel Olivaw never converts to any religion in the books.

By contrast, Demerzel in the TV series is very sincere in her belief in Luminism, as seen in her interactions with both Brother Day and Zephyr Halima. Just before Demerzel kills Zephyr Halima at the orders of Brother Day, she not only admits that she is a robot, but also that she has been an adherent of Luminism for thousands of years. Interestingly, Zephyr Halima is not repelled by the fact that Demerzel is a robot, as one would expect from a woman who believes that clones have no souls, but instead is fascinated and declares that even though she is an artificial being, Halima believes that Demerzel does have a soul.

Even more telling is that the TV series not only takes Luminism seriously, but also implies that Zephyr Halima is correct regarding the genetic dynasty. For in order to prove that he is not a soulless abomination and to persuade the Luminists to name his preferred candidate the next Proxima, Brother Day agrees to participate in a ritual known as "walking the spiral."

This grueling pilgrimage takes up much of the episode "The Missing Piece." Brother Day—and the viewer—learn that the ritual of walking the spiral kills more than half of those who attempt it, which makes little sense, since in the real world, religions usually have an interest in not killing their followers.

The ritual of walking the spiral is inspired by the spiritual exercise of walking the labyrinth as well as by the pilgrimages prescribed by real world religions, some of which, like the Hajj, the pilgrimage to Mecca that every Muslim is required to undertake at least once in their lives, do occasionally result in deadly crushes. However, the crushes and deaths that occurred during the Hajj in the 1990s and 2000s were tragic accidents and crowd control measures have since been implemented to make the Hajj safer. The Luminists, on the other hand, seem to have no interest in making walking the spiral safer for their followers.

The ritual involves walking a spiraling path through a desert under the relentless sun without water or food or shelter, culminating in a cave at the centre of the spiral, where the worshipper bathes in a salt pool and receives a vision. Unlike many other faithful, Brother Day does make it to the cave and the sacred pool and reports of a vision which just happens to signify exactly what he wants it to signify. Later, the viewer learns that Brother Day did not experience any vision at all, but made one up to suit his purposes, which is exactly what an Asimov protagonist would have done.

However, while an Asimov story would have applauded using the Luminists' beliefs against them, the TV series implies that the fact that Brother Day did not receive a vision, but had to make one up, is proof that Brother Day and the other clone emperors do not have souls. Furthermore, Demerzel notes that she did experience a vision, when she walked the spiral eleven thousand years ago, though the exact mechanics of this are unclear.

## Science as (Fake) Religion

To the viewer who has read the original Asimov stories, the fact the TV series takes completely fictional religions like Luminism so very seriously is jarring, specifically because the original *Foundation* stories from the 1940s not only fail to take religion seriously, but openly portray it as a scam.

The most obvious example of this is the fake religion of Scientism, which was introduced in the second *Foundation* story "The Mayors," first published in the June 1942 issue of *Astounding Science Fiction*, and also plays a role in the 1944 stories "The Traders" and "The Merchant Princes."

The very first *Foundation* story "The Encyclopedists" ends on a cliffhanger where Salvor Hardin, mayor of Terminus, points out that the solution to the Foundation's conflict with the Four Kingdoms is obvious, but does not tell us what this obvious solution is. In the introduction to the 1951 edition, Asimov admits that this was a ploy to persuade *Astounding* editor John W. Campbell to buy the sequel "The Mayors" as well.

In "The Encyclopedists," it becomes clear that the Four Kingdoms, Terminus's aggressive neighbors, have regressed and that Terminus is technologically superior, because they have nuclear power, whereas the Four Kingdoms are limited to fossil fuels.

In "The Mayors," set some thirty years later, it's revealed that Salvor Hardin offered to share the Foundation's superior technology with the Four Kingdoms. However, there is a caveat. Hardin linked the Foundation's superior technology to a faux religion named Scientism and forced the Four Kingdoms to accept Scientism in order to receive access to the Foundation's technology, which is tended to by "priests," who are trained on Terminus and serve as maintenance technicians. Most of these "priests" have no idea that the religion they serve is a scam. Only the best and brightest are told the truth and are recruited into the Foundation.

"The Mayors" takes Karl Marx's dictum that "religion is the opium of the people" to its ultimate conclusion and presents a system where the people of the Four Kingdoms are kept under control via an explicitly false religion that the powers that be (here the Foundation) do not believe in themselves. As a solution to the Foundation's dilemma in dealing with its aggressive neighbours, the false religion of Scientism is as ingenious as it is disturbing.

So far, the TV series has only (loosely) adapted the first two stories in the 1951 book version of *Foundation*, "The Psychohistorians" and "The Encyclopedists." The conflict with the neighboring worlds, reduced to only two here, makes up the bulk of Season One and Salvor Hardin is a prominent character in the TV series, though very different from her book counterpart. Furthermore, the TV series does end with the Foundation agreeing to co-operate with its neighbors and share technology.

However, there is not a single mention of Scientism in the TV series so far. A potential hint lies in the appearances of a young Foundationer named Poly Verisof (Jairaj Varsani). In the book, Poly Verisof will grow up to become the high priest of Scientism and one of the few members of the priesthood who knows the truth about the religion he serves. Will this plotline appear in Season Two of the TV series? Time will tell.

The hosts of the excellent *Foundation* podcast *Star's End* pointed out in the first episode of their second season that they do not believe that Scientism will appear in the TV show, because given the culture war currently raging in the US, the idea of science dressed up as a fake religion to dupe a naive populace would be considered too controversial and potentially offensive to the Religious Right.

However, "The Mayors" was first published in 1942, at a time when the US was much more religious and less secular than today. Nonetheless, there is no evidence that the story caused any outrage upon publication.

The *Foundation* trilogy is a "bracingly cynical" story, as Paul Krugman wrote in the introduction to the 2012 *Folio Society* edition, and this includes its treatment of religion. Part of this may be due to the fact that Isaac Asimov, though nominally Jewish, was raised in a secular household and self-identified as atheist, as he explains in his posthumously published 1994 memoir *I, Asimov*. Though like his character R. Daneel Olivaw, Asimov did develop an intellectual interest in religion later in life and even wrote several books on religious subjects.

## The Cynical View of Religion in the Golden Age of Science Fiction

However, the *Foundation* trilogy's cynical view of religion is not limited to Asimov nor is it unique during the so-called Golden Age of science fiction of the 1930s to early 1950s. For religion in general and Christianity in particular do not play a big role in the American science fiction of the Golden Age. If religion does appear at all, it is either a scam or for aliens or both or it involves robed cultists sacrificing nubile virgins to Lovecraftian elder gods.

"The Mayors" was not even the only example of science passed off as religion to control the gullible to appear in the pages of *Astounding Science Fiction* in the 1940s. For a year after "The Mayors", the dystopian science fiction novel *Gather, Darkness!* by Fritz Leiber Jr. was serialised in the same magazine.

If "The Mayors" offers a cynical look at religion, *Gather, Darkness!* takes that cynicism to a completely new level, portraying a future Earth as an oppressive theocracy on a roughly medieval level of technology, where the Church of the Great God controls the downtrodden populace. Just like Asimov's Scientism, the Church of the Great God is a scam and its miracles and divine punishments are the result of science and technology that survived a nuclear war a century before.

While the reader learns very little about the theology and iconography of Scientism in "The Mayors," Leiber's Church of the Great God uses explicitly Christian iconography, while their opponents the New Witchcraft, employ iconography such as devils, demons, werewolves and witches. However, with both groups, the supposed miracles and curses are merely science and technology dressed up as the supernatural.

This deeply cynical and downright subversive view of both religion and science is quite remarkable for a novel published in 1943. Even more remarkable is that the satanic forces of the New Witchcraft are not only the good guys, but that they also prevail.

While the early *Foundation* stories were the works of a man who had little use for religion, *Gather, Darkness!* is the work of a man who has been deeply disappointed by it. As noted in the 1977 introduction to the short fiction collection *Swords and Deviltry*, Fritz Leiber spent two years in the early 1930s attending a seminary to become an Episcopalian minister and even served as lay preacher before leaving the seminary due to what he called a lack of vocation. Leiber never gives any further reasons for why he left the seminary, but his critical views of organized religion, expressed in *Gather, Darkness!* or the 1959 religious satire disguised as a sword and sorcery tale "Lean Times in Lankhmar," suggest a profound disillusionment.

Also of interest, when discussing the portrayal of religion in science fiction of the so-called Golden Age is *Lest Darkness Fall*, a short novel by L. Sprague De Camp published in the December 1939 issue of *Unknown*, the fantasy-focused sister magazine of *Astounding Science Fiction*. The novel chronicles the adventures of an archaeologist who finds himself transported back in time to Rome in the year 535 A.D. and uses his knowledge of what is to come to stave off the descent into the so-called Dark Ages, by introducing inventions centuries early, keeping the ascendant Christianity under control and preventing the establishment of Islam altogether.

The similarities between *Foundation* and *Lest Darkness Fall* are very notable, even though one is alternate history set in the sixth century A.D. and the other is science fiction set in the far future. However, both chronicle the fall of a great empire and the attempts by the only person who knows what the future will bring to prevent or shorten the dark age that will follow. The parallels go even deeper, since the Byzantine general Belisarius, who inspired the character of the Imperial general Bel Riose in the 1945 *Foundation* story "The General," is a character in *Lest Darkness Fall*.

Isaac Asimov and the other authors publishing in *Astounding* and *Unknown* read each other's stories and may well have been influenced by them. That said, the parallels between *Foundation* and *Lest Darkness Fall* on the one hand and *Foundation* and *Gather, Darkness!* on the other are so striking that one cannot help but wonder whether the different stories were the result of one of the writing prompts John W. Campbell, editor of both *Astounding* and *Unknown*, tended to give to his writers, as chronicled by Alec Nevala-Lee in *Astounding: John W. Campbell, Isaac Asimov, Robert A. Heinlein, L. Ron Hubbard, and the Golden Age of Science Fiction*. Asimov's famous 1941 novelette "Nightfall" was the result of such a prompt.

The works listed above are not the only science-fiction stories of the so-called Golden Age that have a cynical or negative view of religion. On the contrary, such stories are remarkably common during the time. An early example of a false religion used to control and subjugate the populace may be found in the 1913 novel *The Gods of Mars* and its 1914 sequel *The Warlord of Mars* by Edgar Rice Burroughs. Other examples are the 1940 novella "If This Goes On . . ." by Robert A. Heinlein, where the US has become a Christian Pentecostal theocracy, the 1949 sword and planet novella "Queen of the Martian Catacombs" by Leigh Brackett, where a warlord uses an ancient prophecy to set off a holy war on Mars, as well as the 1955 novel *The Long Tomorrow*, also by Leigh Brackett, where the US has become an anti-science theocracy, this time controlled by Mennonites, following a nuclear war.

But why were such stories so common during the so-called Golden Age? One might cite the influence of Marxism and particularly Marx's dictum of religion as the "opium of the people" as popularised by the influential fan club The Futurians as a reason. However, of all the writers mentioned above, only Asimov was ever a member of The Futurians and directly influenced by their utopian Socialist ideas. Fritz Leiber leaned left, but was not a Futurian. Robert A. Heinlein and Leigh Brackett did espouse left-wing ideas in early 1940s, but moved further right in later years with Heinlein doing a 180-degree turn away from his earlier views. L. Sprague de Camp's political views during the 1940s are not known, but many of his later writings from the 1960s and 1970s suggest a conservative outlook. *Astounding* editor John W. Campbell, finally, was always a conservative and became increasingly reactionary through the 1950s and 1960s, as his editorials for *Astounding* show only too well.

A more likely reason for the proliferation of science fiction stories offering a highly critical view of religion may lie in the fact that the science fiction of the 1940s and 1950s shared a highly optimistic and occasionally naive belief in science and technology as a solution to any challenges facing mankind. The *Foundation* stories are a perfect example for this, because their superior scientific knowledge and technology are why the Foundation wins time and again against seemingly more powerful foes and is also able to claw its way back after its defeat in the 1945 novel *The Mule*.

Religion, on the other hand, was viewed as a force impeding scientific and technological progress, particularly in the light of the anti-scientific attitudes espoused by some strands of evangelical Protestantism in the US. Therefore, a genre built on an optimistic view of science and technology as a solution to mankind's ills would naturally go hand in hand with a critical view of religion. *Gather, Darkness!*, "If This Goes On . . ." and *The Long Tomorrow* all feature Christian-flavored theocracies deliberately impeding scientific and technological progress. In Brackett's *The Long Tomorrow*, the biggest issue facing the protagonists is not the nuclear war that happened some seventy to eighty years before, but the repressive Mennonite theocracy that forbids recovery and rebuilding. It is only a small step from depicting religion as the enemy of science and progress to Asimov's Scientism or Leiber's Church of the Great God, where science and technology are used to create a false religion in order to keep the gullible under control.

In the eighty years since the first *Foundation* stories were published, the downsides of scientific and technological progress have become only too apparent and the naive techno-optimism of the Golden Age seems as much as product of its time to modern readers as finned spaceships, constant smoking, and room-sized computers. This is also why the climate change analogies drawn in the TV show, though seemingly a natural fit for what is after all a tale of civilizational collapse, do not always work, because the contemporary environmental movement is not characterised by technological optimism and has an undercurrent of technophobia that is more akin to the anti-science fundamentalists of Synnax or Askone than the Foundation—though it is possible that Friedman and Goyer used the anti-science fundamentalists of Synnax to criticise technophobic tendencies in the environmental movement.

Another thing that is notable about all of these critical and often downright cynical takes on religion from the Golden Age of science fiction is that they do not appear to have been considered particularly controversial, even in the far less secular world of the 1940s. The most controversial story published in *Astounding Science Fiction* in 1944 was "Deadline" by Cleve Cartmill, which included a handy primer on how to build an atomic bomb that came a little too close to reality, and not "The Traders," Asimov's cynical look at hypocrisy and religious fundamentalism.

So the question remains why Josh Friedman and David S. Goyer chose to treat the subject of religion much more reverently than Asimov ever did and why they seemingly omit both the faux-religion of Scientism that plays such a pivotal role in the first book and the extremely cynical view of religion as the "opium of the people" that permeates not just the *Foundation* stories but much of the science fiction of the era in general.

One possible answer is that even though pulp magazines were a mass medium in the 1940s, science fiction was always a small niche in the wide world of pulp publishing, albeit one with fervent and devoted fans. However, general interest, mystery and detective, western and romance pulps vastly outsold the science-fiction pulps. *Astounding*'s circulation during the Golden Age was roughly fifty thousand, compared to three hundred thousand for *The Shadow* and one million for *Argosy*. Furthermore, the readership of science-fiction magazines mainly comprised young people with an interest in science and technology, an audience already predisposed to take little to no offence at the cynical views of religion found in the pages of these magazines. The Apple TV+ show, on the other hand, is aimed at a more general audience, some of whom may have a problem with with an irreverent take on religion.

Furthermore, while the United States of the 1940s may have been a less secular country, it was also a much less divided country. Maybe the current culture war atmosphere in the US, where books banned from school libraries make the headlines almost weekly and even media as innocuous as children's picture books and animated cartoon shows comes under fire for positive portrayals of LGBTQ+ people, makes even the cynical portrayal of a completely fictional religion too risky. Or maybe Apple TV+ feared controversy and boycotts, which have affected other streaming services.

We can only hope that Friedman and Goyer trust their audience and give Scientism its due in Season Two.

# 9
# Foundation's Optimism

TRIP MCCROSSIN

"You see," Stor Gendibal reassures Sura Novi, "there is a plan that a wise man once devised." We're just shy of three-quarters of the way through Isaac Asimov's *Foundation's Edge* (1982), the first of his two concluding sequels to the eight short stories (1942–1950) that became *Foundation* (1951), *Foundation and Empire* (1952), and *Second Foundation* (1953), known together as *The Foundation Trilogy*. "It's hard to explain," he continues, but "when you see what will happen . . . you may even understand without my explaining."

The wise man is of course Hari Seldon, the last and greatest practitioner of "psychohistory," the statistical science of predicting the behavior of very large populations over very long periods of time, including the largest, humanity itself, spread now throughout the galaxy. The plan is the aptly named "Seldon Plan," designed to reduce the period of barbarism, from thirty millennia to a single one, before a new Galactic Empire arises out of the ashes of its currently moribund predecessor—Seldon having rightly predicted that its twelve-millennia reign would end in half a one, the storyline's present.

"What will happen?" Novi naturally asks, anxiety lingering about the plan as it's currently unfolding, or simply curious. "I am not sure," he responds, but, given his abiding faith in the plan, he reassures her anew, "all will happen well." It's an optimism that's thoroughly familiar by this point in the storyline, utterable by most any "Foundationer" or "Second Foundationer" more or less faithful to the Seldon Plan. For science-fiction fans, it also nicely anticipates Dave Bowman and Haywood Floyd's "if all goes well" exchange in Arthur Clarke's soon-to-be *2010: Odyssey Two* (1982), which became their more thoroughly reminiscent "What's going to happen? Something wonderful" exchange in Peter Hyams's movie adaptation, *2010: The Year We Made Contact* (1984). In this same spirit, beyond merely colloquial optimism, it's more broadly reminiscent of the more philosophically Optimistic "All is well" of Gottfried Leibniz, Jean-Jacques Rousseau, and Georg Hegel, for example, in response to the problem of evil—the perniciously difficult to satisfy "need to find order within those appearances so unbearable that they threaten reason's ability to go on," as Susan Neiman has described it. Optimism of their sort "insists that morality demands that we make evil intelligible," as Neiman also describes, in opposition to the Pessimism of Pierre Bayle, François-Marie Arouet de Voltaire, and Arthur Schopenhauer, for example, which "insists that morality demands that we don't."

The *Foundation* series' overall Optimism unfolds not only in what comes next in *Foundation's Edge*, but in the second concluding sequel, *Foundation and Earth* (1986). For its problem-of-evil setting, we want first to look back to the original trilogy's storyline and setting, and move along from there.

## August 1, 1941

"In *The Foundation Trilogy*," Asimov summarizes in the prologue to *Foundation's Edge*, "the story of the first four centuries of the Interregnum is told," as per the Seldon Plan. It begins with the two-fold establishment of the "Foundation," on the one hand, on a wayward planet in the "Outer Periphery" called Terminus, meant to develop the physical sciences upon which the resurgent empire would arise, and the "Second Foundation," on the other hand, meant to develop its more intellectual basis, initially in secret, but later revealed to reside on Trantor, Empire's capital.

"The First Foundation, with its superior science, took over the barbarized planets that surrounded it, faced the anarchic warlords who broke away from a dying, empire and beat them," the prologue continues, summarizing the remainder of the first novel in the trilogy, *Foundation* (1951). Summarizing Part One of the second, *Foundation and Empire* (1952), it "faced the remnant of the Empire itself under its last strong Emperor and its last strong general—and beat it." In Part Two then, we are confronted with what Psychohistory as a statistical science, however sophisticated, cannot avoid altogether, which is the lingering possibility of the unforeseen.

"One man," that is, a mutant calling himself the Mule, "appeared out of nowhere," bent on galactic domination, with "mental powers in a Galaxy that lacked them," including the ability to "mold" emotions and shape "minds," whose "bitterest opponents were made into his devoted servants," whom armies "could not, *would* not fight," and "the First Foundation fell and Seldon's schemes lay partly in ruins." A small group of First Foundationers, Bayta Darrel in particular, manages to protect what's left of the Seldon Plan, by preventing the Mule from finding and wreaking similar havoc on the Second Foundation, which, summarizing now Part One of the trilogy's third novel, *Second Foundation* (1953), "bought enough time for the Second Foundation to organize the proper action and, with that, to stop the Mule permanently," and so to be "prepared to reinstate the Seldon Plan."

Now the "First Foundation knew of the Second's existence," however, summarizing Part Two, the trilogy's conclusion, and "did not want a future in which they were overseen by the mentalists." Even in the wake of the Mule, it remained powerful enough to dominate the Second Foundation, leaving it with a "double task: it had not only to stop the First Foundation but had also to regain its anonymity," both of which it was able to accomplish. "The First Foundation was allowed," that is, "to seem to defeat the Second Foundation, and it moved on to greater and greater strength in the Galaxy, totally ignorant that the Second Foundation still existed," which itself moved to greater and greater "mentalic" capability. As the trilogy concludes, that is, four centuries into the Interregnum, the Galactic Empire has fallen, and the Seldon Plan is back on track.

In spite of the above summary, *Foundation's Edge* is missing the more autobiographical "The Story Behind the Foundation," included for the first time in the new, presumably tie-in edition of *The Foundation Trilogy* that appeared the same year. We might imagine that perhaps it's missing because Asimov wanted *Foundation's Edge*" to be, as per his Afterword, while "a continuation of *The Foundation Trilogy*," nonetheless "self-contained." This can't be the reason, however, or at least not the whole of it, because he concludes the new version of "The Story Behind the Foundation" that begins *Foundation and Earth*, its prologue effectively, by telling us that while it wouldn't be a terrible thing to have "glanced" at its predecessor, the new novel "stands by itself."

More intriguing still is the later version's amendment to the earlier version's beginning. "On August 1, 1941," the later version begins, "when I was a lad of twenty-one, I was a graduate student in chemistry at Columbia University and had been writing science fiction professionally for three years, . . . was hastening to see John Campbell, editor of *Astounding*, anxious to tell him a new idea I had for a science fiction story." In the earlier version, however, there's a significant historical context inserted immediately after the date, which is only obliquely referred to in the second of the following paragraphs, which both versions share:

> The date was August 1, 1941. World War II had been raging for two years. France had fallen, the Battle of Britain had been fought, and the Soviet Union had just been invaded by Nazi Germany. The bombing of Pearl Harbor was four months in the future. But on that day, with Europe in flames, and the evil shadow of Adolf Hitler apparently falling over all the world, what was chiefly on my mind was a meeting toward which I was hastening.

Meeting with Campbell may well have been what Asimov had "chiefly" in mind at the time, but not so much so as to waver in giving us the fuller context forty years after the first story's appearance.

## May to May, 1942 to 1963

Of the eight stories that would become *The Foundation Trilogy*, the first five appeared from May of 1942 through April of 1945, spanning the final three years of the war. In between the second and third, the Nazi concentration camps began to be liberated, in the summer of 1944, and public awareness of the Holocaust burgeoned <https://ropercenter.cornell.edu/public-understanding-holocaust-wwii-today>. The sixth story appeared in November and December of 1945, roughly six months after the end of the war in Europe, three to four after its end in the Pacific, and so in the wake of the nuclear holocausts of Hiroshima and Nagasaki, in August of 1945. On November 20th, the first Nuremberg Trial was getting under way at the time as well, lasting through October 1st, 1946. The seventh story appeared in January of 1948, during the subsequent Nuremberg Trials, from December of 1946 through April of 1949, and the Tokyo Trials, from May 1946 through November of 1948, the eighth appearing in their wake, in December of 1949 and January of 1950.

Nor were these the last such trials likely on Asimov's radar, generally speaking. Holocaust mastermind Adolf Eichmann, that is, who escaped an Allied detention camp in January of 1946, and fled to Argentina in 1950, as Ricardo Klement, was captured finally, on May 11th 1960, by agents of the Israel

Security Agency, Shin Bet, and removed to Israel nine days later to stand trial. The trial began just shy of three months later, on April 11th, 1961, lasting a little over four well-publicized months, ending on August 14th. On December 12th, he was found guilty, on December 15th, sentenced to death, and after a roughly six-month appeal process in the wake of sentencing, and a little over a year after his capture, Eichmann was hanged shortly after midnight on June 1st, 1962.

If general media coverage wasn't enough, Eichmann's trial and its aftermath would likely have been all the more on radar in the wake of Hannah Arendt's famous, some would say infamous, reporting of the trial for *The New Yorker*. It appeared in five installments, in February and March of 1963, as "Eichmann in Jerusalem," and in book form the following May, as *Eichmann in Jerusalem: A Report on the Banality of Evil*. Immediately, and enduringly controversial, it represents what Neiman tells us is nothing short of "the twentieth century's most important philosophical [perspective on] the problem of evil" (Susan Neiman, *Evil in Modern Thought*, p. 271).

Given the retrospective setting he gives "that day" in 1941, how can Asimov have been unaware of worse coming eventually to worst, as it slowly but surely did, and of the "need to find order within these appearances, so unbearable that they threaten reason's ability to go on."

## A Wager in Heaven in '67

If, as made out above, the march of history all but certainly confronted Asimov with the problem of evil, preparing portions of his *Guide to the Bible: Volume One, The Old Testament* (1967) must have been poignant—the Book of Job in particular, the problem's conventional touchstone.

"God praises Job's piety to Satan," he reminds us, "who at once points out that it is easy for a wealthy and fortunate man to be grateful for the rewards he received," with whom God famously wagers "permission to visit Job with misfortune in order to demonstrate that Job will remain pious." Satan loses, of course, as Job does indeed "remains pious and continues to praise God," in the face of losing everything, he wants still a story as to why, given his righteousness, he is being let to suffer so remorselessly. Which means, however, in effect, that God doesn't seem to win the wager either, not exactly.

"Three friends then come to Job . . . 'to mourn with him and to comfort him'," but also, as it turns out, to chastise, insisting that because God can't transgress, as we clearly can, Job must accept blame for his own suffering. “Job is anything but patient and uncomplaining, and seriously questions the justice of God,” in response, “reasoning that misfortunes have fallen upon him undeservedly and that God is acting as a capricious tyrant.”

“Job’s eloquence in his own defense confounds his three friends and Job’s accusations against God,” Asimov continues, “which have been mounting in intensity and fervor, demand a divine answer”—the Voice from the Whirlwind, that is, “contrasting divine omnipotence with human limitations” . . . describing “the wonders of nature which have been divinely created, guided, and regulated,” with which we are “incompetent to cope.”

“At the end of God’s speech,” Asimov concludes, “Job realizes divine omnipotence and understands the folly of trying to penetrate God’s plans and purposes with the limited mind of a human being. He repents and is then restored to more wealth than he originally had, and a new set of sons and daughters and dies after a long life.” There’s an ambiguity in Job’s repentance, however, which Asimov doesn’t overtly resolve. Job *was* saying that he’s owed an explanation, but what’s he saying *now*? The more conventional take is that he’s *rejecting* what he said earlier, believing now that God, majestic and inscrutable and all, doesn’t, indeed can’t owe him an explanation beyond his comprehension in the first place. The less conventional take is that he’s more modestly *refraining* from saying so, believing that while he may not be *owed* an explanation, still he *cannot help but want, indeed need one*.

## The Rise of Mikhail

Within the overall storyline, a relatively uneventful century elapses from the trilogy’s conclusion to the overall one in *Foundation’s Edge* and *Foundation and Earth*. The years that elapsed in real time, however, 1950 to 1986, were not nearly so uneventful, taken up with the different stages of a different sort of political tragedy. It’s a sad irony that while the Nuremberg and Tokyo trials were reckoning with at least some of evils of one war, we were neglecting the onset of another, the Cold War.

The trilogy’s final two stories appeared early in, the trilogy itself toward the end of its first phase, conventionally thought to begin on March 12th 1947, with Harry Truman’s articulation of what came to be known as the Truman Doctrine, and to endure until 1953, with Dwight Eisenhower succeeding Truman in the US and Nikita Khrushchev succeeding Joseph

Stalin in Soviet Union. The Cold War grew slowly and scarily confrontational, due in part to the legacy of Hiroshima and Nagasaki, before moving finally toward "détente" in the early- to mid-1970s. Sadly it deteriorated, giving rise to the New Cold War, in the late-1970s and early to mid-1980s, during which time *Foundation's Edge* appeared, *Foundation and Earth* shortly after, early in the more hopeful era that begins with Mikhail Gorbachev succeeding Konstantin Chernenko in 1985, and "perestroika" ("restructuring") and "glasnost" ("openness") became words of the day.

It's difficult to appreciate now, in our newly crisis-ridden era, just how momentous those early years of the last phase of the Cold War felt, how we dared to be optimistic that a new way might emerge out of seemingly endless antagonism between competing empire-inspired conceptions of humanity's best version of itself. Such is the optimism animating *Foundation's Edge* and *Foundation and Earth*.

## Another New Hope

Gendibal and Novi are in the predicament described at the outset because, while the century that's elapsed since the trilogy's conclusion has been relatively uneventful, it's also been, Gendibal believes, as it turns out others do as well, misunderstood.

Second Foundation "First Speaker" Quindor Shandess, that is, dispatched "Speaker" Gendibal and Novi, a member of Trantor's rustic Hamish, to confirm Shandess and Gendibal's shared suspicion: that a new force has arisen that, with capabilities exceeding those of the Second Foundation, is working mysteriously to further the Seldon Plan. To this end, they are in pursuit of Terminus Council member Golan Trevize, accompanied by Janov Pelorat, professor of ancient history long obsessed with finding humanity's planet of origin, wrongly believing them to have been similarly dispatched by the First Foundation.

Terminus Mayor Harla Branno has instead dispatched them to seek out the Second Foundation, which, while generally thought to have perished a century earlier, she and Gendibal believe to be not only in existence still, but thriving, and guiding the Seldon Plan. In reality, with no better leads, they decide to chase Pelorat's dream of locating Earth, for the time being at least. As they do, they're shadowed by Gendibal's fellow Council member Munn Li Compor, on Branno's orders, believing Compor to be a covert Second Foundationer, whom she's following and monitoring in turn. It's in response to the unexpected approach of Campor's ship, to warn in him of the approach of Branno's own, that Gendibal expresses his optimism to Novi.

After much intrigue, three ships converge high above the surface of the planet Gaia, the narrative extraterrestrial extension of the controversial "Gaia Hypothesis," which chemist James Lovelock began to formulate in the late 1960s and developed subsequently in co-operation with microbiologist Lynn Margulis. "The Earth is a living organism," according to Lovelock, the "rocks, the air, the oceans, and all the life are an inseparable system that functions to keep the planet liveable" (Joseph, *Gaia*, p. 3). In this spirit, to Gendibal's desire to be "taken to whoever it is you speak of as Gaia," Bliss responds in Lovelockean fashion, "*I'm* Gaia."

And the ground. And those trees. And that rabbit over there in the grass. And the man you can see through the trees. The whole planet and everything on it is Gaia. We're all individuals—we're all separate organisms—but we all share an overall consciousness. The inanimate planet does so least of all, the various forms of life to a varying degree, and human beings most of all—but we all share.

Gaia's not just a Lovelockean superorganism, but, as Pelorat summarizes in turn, "Gaia is some sort of group consciousness."

"The three ships were each essentially at rest, relative to the other two," we learn, "all three were turning very slowly about the planet Gaia": Gendibal and Novi's, Novi having revealed herself to have been Gaian all along, Suranoviremblastiran her given name; Trevize and Pelorat's, having swapped theirs with Compor's, and they're also now accompanied by another Gaian, Blissenobiarella, Bliss for short; and Mayor Branno, accompanied by her loyal Director of Security, Liono Kodell. Gendibal's optimism, and First and Second Foundation optimism more generally, is about to be tested. Gaia orchestrated the convergence long ago, Bliss divulges finally, in the hope of avoiding a Second Galactic Empire rooted in either the First or the Second Foundation, by offering an alternative way or organizing the galaxy, on the model of Gaia itself. Hence Novi's role in keeping Gendibal and Branno in a mentalic stalemate, and Bliss' in explaining and motivating Trevize's, which is to use his long-sought, because exceedingly rare "talent for rightness" to decide which of the three alternative will prevail.

"Worked out after the fashion of Terminus," Bliss explains, it's "the view of Gaia" that a Second Galactic Empire "will be a military Empire, established by strife, maintained by strife, and eventually destroyed by strife." "It will be nothing but the

First Galactic Empire reborn," she continues, and if "worked out after the fashion of Trantor," it will fare no better, will be "a paternalistic Empire, established by calculation, maintained by calculation, and in perpetual living death by calculation . . . a dead end." The alternative to both, however, Bliss concludes, indeed to any resurgent Galactic Empire, is "Greater Gaia! Galaxia!"

Every inhabited planet is alive as Gaia. Every living planet combined into a still greater hyperspatial life. Every uninhabited planet participating. Every star. Every scrap of interstellar gas. Perhaps even the great central black hole. A living galaxy and one that can be made favorable for all life in ways that we yet cannot foresee. A way of life fundamentally different from all that has gone before and repeating none of the old mistakes.

"Remember that you are a First Foundationer and a human being," Branno pleads in response, "that you do not want to be a cipher in the plans of the bloodless mathematicians of Trantor or less than a cipher in a Galactic mishmash of life and nonlife." Gendibal pleads in turn that he not "disrupt the Seldon Plan, either on behalf of a narrow concept of patriotism or out of a romantic longing for the new and untried," assuring that "Second Foundationers will in no way hamper the free will of humanity," being after all "guides, not despots." The Plan "offers release" from the strife of the First Galactic Empire, which Branno and the First Foundation will ultimately replicate, but "not at the price of becoming one more atom in a Galaxy of atoms, being reduced to equality with grass, bacteria, and dust."

In the end, it's Pelorat, "frightened of all three alternative," who recalls to Trevize what turns out to be a decisively prescient epiphany. "When we first went into space, you showed me the Galaxy," he recalls, and "speeded time and the Galaxy rotated visibly and I said, as though anticipating this very time, 'The Galaxy looks like a living thing, crawling through space'," as if perhaps, returning to the present now, "in a way, it is alive already." It's enough for Trevize's epiphanous "talent for rightness" to point to Gaia as the right and proper choice. Still, his, Pelorat, and Bliss' journey is far from over. Gendibal and Novi's and Branno and Kodell's, however, have come, within the storyline, to an end.

## Whose Well?

The choice made, but "the great task" of molding the galaxy into Galaxia centuries in the making still, the First and Second Foundations must persist, for the time being, more or less as they were. Gendibal and Novi return to Trantor, then, and Branno and Kodell to Terminus, with Gaia-induced alternate versions in mind of what's transpired.

Branno, returning with a lucrative trade deal with the Sayshell Sector, believes now that the "Second Foundation's continued existence is our myth of the century, as Gaia is Sayshell's." Gendibal, for his part, "brooding" about what will now "fit" the Seldon Plan, believes the Second Foundation "must place the First under closer supervision, . . . knit the Galaxy closer together somehow, and make use of mentalics to build a closer co-operation of consciousness." But while "deep within, where the enveloping mind of Novi could scarcely be aware of it, the essence of Gaia remained and guided events," for both of them it's also at best a myth. Not so Trevize, Pelorat, and Bliss.

"Neither Foundation is in the least aware that Gaia exists" any longer, Pelorat muses, "but we know that Gaia exists and we can talk," but they won't. They surely know that "no one would believe" them, Bliss insists, and Pelorat's not leaving Gaia anyway, besotted as he is with Bliss, and Trevize has also bigger fish to fry.

Uncomfortable with the idea that it may have seemed that Gaia had maneuvered his talent for rightness into choosing as it did, spontaneously, more or less instinctually, making it seem somewhat less that the unfettered choice it was advertised to be, he bucks up in two, some would say "compatibilist" ways. Choosing Galaxia over either Foundation was, on the one hand, he insists, a matter of "ordinary reasoning—the sort of reasoning that anyone else might have used to come to a decision." The alternatives, that is, "if either were the wrong solution, it would have been irreversibly catastrophic," choosing Galaxia instead a "way of temporizing, then, and of making sure that there would remain time to modify matters—or even reverse them—if my decision were wrong," given the time he knew that it would take to realize Galaxia. Given that "ordinary reasoning, on the other hand, "although Janov's remark persuaded me to make the decision at that moment, it was the decision I think I would have made even if he had said nothing or if he had tried to argue me into a decision of a different kind."

Still. he's concerned by two things his talent for rightness has revealed. One is his growing conviction that Bliss is not Gaian after all, but a robot, in spite of Novi and others having appeared to have told of their demise. "Suppose I am a robot," she cheekily confirms, among "a very few" who remain from those who created Gaia in the first place, "who have a similar role," which is to "supervise" Gaia to ensure that it observes the Three Laws of Robotics, as applied now to Gaia—to avoid harming human beings or allow them through inaction to be harmed, to obey them except when this conflicts with the previous requirement, and to avoid harm to itself, except when this conflicts with the previous ones.

The other stems from an unanticipated part of his experience of choosing between one or the other Foundation or Galaxia. "I found myself in touch with the minds of those about me," he confesses, including Gendibal and Novi's, and so "the various effects Gaia, through Novi, had produced on Trantor—effects that were intended to maneuver the Speaker into going to Gaia," including "the clearing from Trantor's library of all references to Earth." Troubled by the sense that for some undisclosed reason it's important that not only the Foundations be ignorant of this, but that he be so as well, "if I am to take the responsibility for the direction of Galactic development, I do not willingly accept ignorance."

This second concern leads Trevize to leave Gaia in search of Earth, Pelorat and Bliss in tow, their journey and what they discover, in part an extension of Bliss's cheeky confirmation, forming the storyline of *Foundation and Earth*. It's not a stretch to imagine them channeling Novi and Gendibal as they depart—"What will happen?," one might ask, another answering, "All will happen well." And indeed, *Foundation and Earth*'s storyline affirms this, in affirming Trevize's choice. But what of Gendibal's *original* optimism?

## The ["Neither human nor robot"] in the Moon

Gendibal's optimism has been, in a sense, borne out. Midway through the Interregnum, the Second Foundation persists, insulated now from interference from the First, in pursuit of the Seldon Plan, which itself persists, in the service of a Second Galactic Empire. In another, it clearly hasn't. From Trevize, Pelorat, and Bliss' perspective, that is, while most of this is true, it's in the service not of a Second Galactic Empire, but of Galaxia. If "all [*does*] happen well," however, in the end, from Trevize et al.'s perspective, then, while to the displeasure Gendibal et al., it surely won't happen any less well. Optimism is maybe, then, all in the framing.

Trevize et al. wend their way toward Earth, without knowing where precisely it is, but nonetheless confident that it's more than just a myth. First stop, Comporellon, purporting to be the Galaxy's oldest inhabited planet—the goal being to find Earth, the birthplace of humanity, the older the better. Negotiating their way out of unanticipated imprisonment, they learn from Pelorat's fellow historian, Deniador, that "Spacer Worlds" may be their best bet.

"There are the worlds of the first group of Settlers," he recounts, "the Spacers, as they are called in our legends," who "had lifetimes stretching out for centuries, and refused to allow our own short-lived ancestors to land on their worlds," who subsequently "defeated" and "scorned" them, their worlds becoming now "Forbidden Worlds." Deniador proposes three in particular, Aurora, Solaria, and Melpomenia, all purported to be in Earth's vicinity. Crucially, while each proves to be in one way or another inhospitable, from Solaria they pick up a passenger, Fallom, and from Melpomenia's Hall of the Worlds a list of all fifty Spacer Worlds and their locations, which they determine eventually are organized into a sphere, with Earth near the center.

When they finally arrive, Earth is a radioactive wasteland, as the *Galactic Empire* series (1947–1952) had prefigured, humanity having long since migrated to New Earth and elsewhere in the galaxy. Their long journey apparently a bust, in general, and without the answers that Trevize has been seeking in particular, Fallom's presence suddenly takes on new meaning. Missing Solaria, and her robot companion, Jemby, wanting to return, she insists that she wants to go "there," pointing to the Moon. What transpires is a man-in-the-moon, or rather a something-unforeseen-in-the-moon scenario. And with this we've a new frame.

"I greet you in friendship," Trevize et al. hear as they enter a "vast and complex hollow" in the Moon, "I am Daneel Olivaw." Daneel is a two-millennia-old robot who came to Earth "in the very beginnings of the settlement of the Galaxy" in the hope of staving off its eventual collapse. His companion robot, Giskard, before shutting down, "left it to Daneel to care for the Galaxy; for Earth, particularly," bequeathing to this effect his "talent" to "sense and adjust minds," and his newly minted Zeroth Law of Robotics, which forbids harming *humanity*, or through inaction allowing it to be harmed, upon which the original three laws now depend. From this arose Gaia, and later the Seldon Plan.

"Injury to a person can be estimated and judged," that is, Deneel explains, but "Humanity is an abstraction," and so difficult, if not impossible evaluate in these terms. "If humanity could be made a single organism," however, "it would become a concrete object," solving the problem, but it was a far more difficult task to realize. "Five centuries ago," he continues, "when it seemed that I would never work out methods for getting round all the difficulties that stood in the way of establishing Gaia, I turned to the second-best and helped bring about the development of the science of psychohistory." Now that these two movements have come successfully together, to place Trevize in the way of choosing Galaxia, it would seem as though "all has happened well," but there's a problem.

Just as Gaia took eons to develop, so Galaxia will, and without Daneel's guidance, "Gaia will lack the essential tools to carry through the development of Galaxia in less than an inordinate period of time," and Daneel's not going to last long enough. No one gets out of life alive, even a two-millennia-old robot. He can no longer rejuvenate in the ways he has, but "thinks" he's found "a way out." "Instead of replacing my brain with yet another positronic one," he offers, "which is impractical, I might merge it with a human brain instead; a human brain not affected by the Three Laws, and will not only add capacity to my brain, but add a whole new level of abilities as well." At first Trevize worries that he might be the candidate Deneel has in mind, but his talent for rightness, unique to date, can't be spared. Pelorat fancies volunteering then, as an academic who would welcome such panoramic historical knowledge, but sadly he's too old. Finally it becomes clear that it was part of Deneel's plan all along to have Trevize et al. collect and deliver Fallom, the intended candidate.

"You see," we might imagine Bliss reassuring Trevize and Pelorat, "there is a plan that a wise robot once devised," according to which "all has mostly happened and still now will happen well." And we're meant to find ourselves reassured also, presumably—at first the Plan, but then the Mule, but then again still the Plan; within it, Gendibal's optimism, but eventually his is a "sensed and adjusted" mind; Trevize's hope then, enveloped eventually in Deneel's Plan, retroactively "adjusting" all that came before. Up to the very end. Almost.

The storyline concludes with Trevize reasserting the wisdom of his choice of Galaxia, with a newfound rationale to boot. "The present state of things," he reassures Pelorat, Bliss, and Deneel, "need only continue a few more centuries, perhaps little more than one ten thousandth of the time civilization has already existed, and we will be safe," further reassuring them, "it is not as though we had the enemy already here and among us." This last, however, he utters in spite of "a sudden twinge of trouble, which he forced himself to disregard," as he avoids the "brooding eyes of Fallom" resting, "unfathomably, on him." We can't help but be worried now about the unintended consequences of Deneel's intended "merge with a human brain . . . not affected by the Three Laws," hitherto unattempted, nowhere guaranteeing that while the original wouldn't be bound by the Three Laws, the merger would be. Also, aren't there *four* laws now?!

Asimov passed away in April of 1992, after a decade-long illness, but not before completing two prequels, *Prelude to Foundation*, which appeared in 1988, and *Forward the Foundation*, which appeared posthumously, in April of 1993, both of them detailing, in part, Deneel's backstory, living then as Seldon's friend Eto Demerzel. Whether, had he lived, he would have given us a concluding novel, resolving the above worries, and detailing the ultimately realization of Galaxia, we'll never know. While we wait and hope for such a manuscript to be unearthed, the *Foundation* series as it stands can't help but nurture in us already our faith in a forthcoming, newly encompassing, thoroughly optimistic frame—that ultimately, "All will [*indeed*] happen well."[1]

---

[1] As always, I'm grateful to Susan Neiman for my understanding of the problem of evil, and to this volume's editors for patience far above and beyond the call. For some of the publication information included (that *2010: Odyssey Two* appeared shortly after *Foundation's Edge*, for example), I've relied on the Internet Speculative Fiction Database (isfdb.org).

# 10
# The Dao of Psychohistory

DANIEL FRIED

Asimov's *Foundation* series raises a big question: is history predictable by analyzing the aggregate social forces operating on large groups, or will outcomes hinge on the choices made by individuals?

Psychohistory does not remove individual actions from history: during each crisis through which the First Foundation must pass, there are specific actions taken by various galactic leaders that do determine the shape of how society unfolds. However, in each case, these actions are perfectly constrained. Asimov asks us to believe that, at each moment of crisis, there will be only one obvious course of action available to push forward the First Foundation's development.

What psychohistory is supposed to remove from history are the divergent paths dependent upon individual initiative: at no point is the direction of social development supposed to depend upon any arbitrary or idiosyncratic action. Even though history happens through individuals, the novels usually ask us to believe that the same result would have likely resulted even if different individuals had tried to make different choices.

That said, Asimov also offers constant challenges to his own premise. For example, the Mule is a great exception, because he has psychic powers that psychohistorical equations could not have predicted. More subtly, the literary form of Asimov's novels also repeatedly encourages the reader to question the possibility of historical determinism. Fiction cannot directly represent the sweep of history: it requires individual characters and localized actions that do seem to matter. Asimov's particular style of fiction is especially reliant upon suspense, sudden reversals of fortune, and revelations that keep a reader particularly invested in the twists and turns of the stories of individual characters. For example, even when Asimov ended up arguing most clearly for the meaninglessness of individual initiative, as in the story of Bel Riose, his characters had to assume until the last moments that their actions mattered to the way history would play out.

Asimov's musing on the state of the individual versus the power of aggregate social forces grows directly out of the intellectual climate of the 1940s, when he began writing the *Foundation* stories. Marx's vision of a deterministic path toward a global communist future seemed to have been consolidated in a world-historical proponent, the Soviet Union. The social science disciplines of the non-Communist world were also making rapid progress toward mathematical exactness, and Keynesian economics in particular seemed to have played a triumphant role in America's recovery from the Great Depression.

Although firmly established as social sciences, these visions of society's possibly predictable future course posed a new challenge to the scope of Western philosophy. Western ethical philosophy has usually striven to answer the individual's question, *What should I do?* Western political philosophy has had more diverse goals, but has often focused on questions such as, *What should the ruler do?* or *What should the state do?* Asimov's proposal that the only actions that can matter to history are actions forced by an inexorable mathematics, seems to imply that the question of proper action is irrelevant. Why should I care about the effect of my actions, or the actions of my government, if no free choice made through individual initiative can have more than a minimal effect on the world?

Non-action is not necessarily the result of a failure of philosophy; it is possible for philosophy to make a case for non-action as a positive good. Although the Western tradition has rarely focused on the importance of non-action, it has been a central principle in Chinese philosophy since that tradition's beginnings in the middle of the first millennium B.C. That tradition almost certainly had no influence on the development of the *Foundation* stories: in the long list of Asimov's publications, there is little that speaks of China beyond an occasional passing reference.

However, comparing Asimov's historical determinism with several versions of the idea of non-action in early Chinese thought can present a clearer picture of what is really at stake in the intellectual puzzle of psychohistory. Asimov presents this idea as a simple binary choice: do individual choices matter to history or not? In contrast, early Chinese philosophy developed several different theories of non-action, all of which saw it as more complex than a simple and fatalistic abandonment to historical forces. In Chinese philosophy, "non-action" does not mean simply "doing nothing at all"; it refers to a refusal to attempt active intervention in society. In this respect, it is close to Asimov's conception of the scope of individual actions, which can be privately meaningful even if such actions cannot change history. However, Asimov presents this as a simple inevitable limitation, while Chinese theories of non-action see it as a positive good—both something that can be chosen by individuals to lead happier lives, and even as a choice that, paradoxically, can change society for the better by refusing to intervene in society.

## Confucian Non-Action as Moral Transformation

China's first millennium B.C. was a period oddly reminiscent of Asimov's vision of galactic history, and the collapse and rebirth of empire. The Zhou dynasty, founded in 1046 B.C., began as a strong feudal state exercising power through regional nobility. As the centuries progressed, however, the ruler's power decayed until the country was actually composed of independent states vying for power, and the Zhou kings had no more authority than the senile "Emperor" Dagobert IX portrayed in *Foundation and Empire*. This situation lasted until 221 B.C., when China was finally reunited under the despotic rule of the Qin dynasty.

Confucius, who lived from 551 to 479, taught his philosophy at a period when the collapse of the Zhou was already well advanced, and regional fiefdoms were struggling for economic and military supremacy. He did promote the ideals of hierarchical family and governmental structures that are stereotypically associated with him, and with Chinese culture as a whole. However, his philosophy was much fuller and more varied than that stereotype, offering a vision of a harmonious social order that required benevolence and sympathy as much as hierarchy. In his vision of the good society, adherence to the cultural forms of tradition and ritual could restrain the brutality of government by force; and indeed the highest function of the ruler was to set a moral example, transforming the people rather than imposing his will upon them. It is in this context that Confucius introduced the concept of "non-action" (or *wu wei*) into Chinese philosophy:

> Not acting [*wu wei*], yet governing—was not that Shun's method? What did he do? He reverently faced south—that is all. (*Analects*, 15.5, my translation)

Shun was a legendary king, thought to have lived over seventeen centuries prior to Confucius, and often celebrated for his piety and frugality. Chinese rulers' thrones faced south, so to say that all Shun did was "reverently faced south" means that he occupied his throne as a model of respectful behavior. This might seem like a spectacular failure of governance to modern readers who expect their governments to solve problems, but in an age when rulers frequently distinguished themselves by rapacious taxation and endless border wars, it would not have been hard to see the attraction of Shun's quiet moral influence.

Confucius also proposes non-action as correct ethical behavior for the individual living in an unjust state. Although he never uses the phrase *wu wei* in regard to private actions of the individual, Confucius is clear that people should not seek public employment under an evil ruler, and should retire to private life during a historical era of injustice or immorality. These dicta would go on to define a vision of upright and professional behavior of the scholar-official bureaucratic class for over two millennia.

Onum Barr, the retired patrician whom Hober Mallow meets on Siwenna in "The Merchant Princes," offers a good lesson in Confucian private non-action. Barr tells Mallow that in his youth, he had helped lead a loyalist counter-rebellion against a breakaway viceroy, but that when imperial troops arrived, they slaughtered the loyalists out of a need for plunder. Having learned the lesson that good actions are punished during evil ages, Barr has retired to a simple country life with his books when Mallow finds him. Within Asimov's narrative, the incident is portrayed as an example of the juggernaut of history and the futility of individual initiative. Viewing him through a Confucian lens instead helps us to see his non-action in a different light: there is meaning to be found, including positive ethical goods, in a life lived deliberately in private.

## Daoist Non-Action as Mystical Libertarianism

'Daoism' refers to an originally complex and disparate set of philosophical writings that gradually came to be seen as part of a coherent school, and that by the second century A.D. had inspired a set of religious movements. The supposed founder of this tradition, Laozi, was said in later legends to have been an older contemporary of Confucius; but there is no firm evidence that the text attributed to him, the *Dao De Jing*, predated the fourth century B.C. In fact, hallmarks of orality in the text, combined with late twentieth-century archaeological finds of alternate texts, strongly suggest a *Dao De Jing* that evolved as a wisdom text through a community of composers and editors.

That evolved status, however, does not mean that the text lacks a coherent picture of non-action. It proclaims the usefulness of non-action in governance, in terms that differ from those used by Confucius:

> The more taboos there are in the empire
> The poorer the people;
> The more sharpened tools the people have
> The more benighted the state;
> The more skills people have
> The further novelties multiply;
> The better known the laws and edicts
> The more thieves and robbers there are.
> Hence the sage says,
> I take no action [*wu wei*] and the people are transformed of themselves. (Lao Tzu, *Tao Te Ching*, p. 64)

As with Confucius, there is an assumption that the proper role of the sovereign is to refrain from active governance, and that the people will become good in the absence of social interventions. Unlike Confucius, however, this does not happen by the ruler serving as a moral exemplar; rather, people will become spontaneously good by returning to their natural state, free from policy-driven interventions in society. The author believes that it is because of policies and laws that people learn how to become clever and scheming in ways to avoid the law.

This bears some similarity to the contemporary political ideology of libertarianism, in that it agrees that government policy distorts natural behavior, and ends up as self-defeating. However, libertarianism sees government policy as harming economic health by distorting markets, while the *Dao De Jing* assumes that government policy is bad because it creates economic development. Wealth and education are thought to be bad in themselves, in that they remove humans from a fundamentally harmonious state of nature.

There is very little in the *Foundation* series that recognizes vigorous government action as undesirable. On the contrary, the signs of the Galactic Empire's collapse are seen in the impossibility of action. When, in *Prelude to Foundation*, Emperor Cleon I complains, "I am an Emperor who finds everything possible, but very little practical" (p. 95), he is stating in a nutshell the dominance of historical forces over government action. The Empire is failing because any action has become self-defeating. The *Dao De Jing* would posit exactly the opposite: recognition of the impotence of a hierarchically imposed order is a foundation of social health and human happiness. If it is hard to imagine a functional society established on such anarchic grounds, consider the Gaia planet described in *Foundation's Edge*. Gaia is not as utterly lacking in knowledge and purposive activity as the ideal society of the *Dao De Jing*, but it does manifest a holistic union of humans and nature, with no division into rulers and ruled, and hence no top-down interventions in the natural order of society. Sadly, such a utopian community only seems possible through the advanced telepathy that Gaians possess—an ability that Daoism never imagined.

## Legalist Non-Action as Impersonal Authoritarianism

About eight hundred years after the founding of the Zhou dynasty, and several centuries after the Zhou rulers had become largely impotent figureheads, the regional kingdom of Qin, in the west of China, was ready to consolidate power and form a new dynasty. The ruler who finally did so in 221 B.C., and first devised the new term of 'Emperor', is remembered to history as a particularly effective and ruthless leader. He is usually described as putting into practice the doctrines of Legalism, a political philosophy that emphasized the importance of harsh and uniform enforcement of laws. Because of the harshness of the Qin Emperor's rule, the school of Legalism was thereafter scorned—which may be one reason it is so poorly known in the West. However, the writings of the Legalists remained influential despite being discredited, much in the same way Machiavelli has remained canonical, despite his name becoming a synonym for political ruthlessness.

Although associated with a supremely powerful ruler, Legalism proposed a vision of rule that minimized the arbitrary exercise of power by the sovereign. Instead, the sovereign should establish clear (and harsh) laws and standards, and then absent himself from governance and interference with his own policies. The inflexibility of law was not (as in most Western political philosophy) seen as a constraint upon the ruler's power, but rather as a way to maximize his power, and make it more effective. This depended upon yet another version of "non-action", different from both the Confucian and Daoist ideas. Although living in a kingdom opposed to the Qin state, the most famous theorist of Legalism was Han Fei; in his writings he described the "Way of the Ruler" this way:

> The ruler must not reveal his desires; for if he reveals his desires his ministers will put on the mask that pleases him. He must not reveal his will; for if he does so his ministers will show a different face. So it is said: Discard likes and dislikes and the ministers will show their true form; discard wisdom and wile and the ministers will watch their step . . .
>
> Hence it is said: "So still he seems to dwell nowhere at all; so empty no one can seek him out." The enlightened ruler reposes in nonaction [*wu wei*] above, and below his ministers tremble with fear. (*Basic Writings*, pp. 15–16)

Han Fei's diagnosis of the problem of arbitrary rule is simple and incisive: if the ruler acts in a mercurial fashion, people will not know in advance what is expected of them. They will therefore be cautious in acting, and try to match their speech and behavior to the whims of the ruler. However, if the ruler refuses to let his own passions and desires show, subordinates' actions can only be guided by established laws, and by their own honest beliefs. In the above passage, Han Fei's endorsement of non-action is specifically directed to the Emperor's behavior with his courtiers: the problem of court flattery and sycophancy getting in the way of the ruler's need for sound advice was a serious one for early Chinese political theory. However, elsewhere in the writings of both Han Fei and other Legalists, the same principles apply to the ruler's relation to the people as a whole: clear and universal laws carrying harsh punishment, with no exceptions or personal interference from the ruler, was the way to motivate behavior effectively.

Therefore, in Legalism, we have yet a third version of non-action. Confucius had proposed a non-acting ruler who transformed the people through his status as a moral exemplar. The *Dao De Jing* suggested that, if the ruler stepped back from law and policy that interfered with the natural order of society, the people would transform themselves in the process of returning to a harmonious state of nature. Legalism, in contrast, evolved a more limited and more practical sense in which non-action should be effectual. The ruler still does have to "act" in the sense that he would have to establish laws and policies that he wanted followed. However, after that is done, he then absents himself from decision making, allowing the laws to speak for him, becoming almost an abstract presence, his desires unknown and his whims irrelevant to the operation of the state.

There's very little in the *Foundation* series that resembles a Legalist government. Perhaps the closest approach that the series takes is the plutocracy of Hober Mallow and the subsequent merchant princes. From several discussions of the state of Foundation governance at the beginning of the Mule's storyline, it seems that plutocracy had become a rigid and oppressive force. No one ruler is ever identified as the face of the government, but repressive rule on behalf of business elites had produced a police state, with a rising resistance movement.

Asimov's interest lies in the relation of business interests to rightist government repression, and the possibility that this might be a natural historical phase through which a growing state would need to pass. He never addresses the balance between personal rule and a law-bound political order, which is an issue of major concern to modern international political theory, in addition to ancient Chinese philosophy. This might be considered a lost opportunity in thinking through the implications of psychohistory for the significance of individuals' actions.

Large-scale social systems may operate independently from individuals' choices, but those systems are partially constituted out of law and policy that are enacted by individuals. Moreover, rulers can take steps to keep power in their own hands and make development more dependent on their whims; or, like the ancient Qin emperor, they can codify and standardize law as a way of extending their power. Even non-action can become its own kind of action, with major consequences for history.

## Television and the Uses of Non-Action

The Apple TV+ adaptation of the Foundation saga has been controversial among long-time fans, some of whom see it as a fresh reimagining of the story, while others have been shocked at the extensive changes to the plot and characters. For example, famed economist Paul Krugman, who has frequently mentioned the influence of Asimov in his decision to study economics, wrote, "Pretending that this series has anything to do with the 'Foundation' novels is fraudulent marketing, and I've stopped watching" (*New York Times*). Apart from many changes to the plot and characters, one of the most noticeable changes to the television version during its first season was the pushing of psychohistory somewhat into the background. By the end of the season, it was made clear that Seldon had accurately predicted the Foundation's first crisis, and its necessary resolution. Nevertheless, there seemed to have been many occasions during the arc of the season when individual characters' choices made a great deal of difference to the direction in which history was unfolding.

Part of this difference must be attributed to the difference in media. Asimov's novels feature suspenseful twists and turns that constantly tease the question of whether characters' choices will matter—but those were balanced by long dialogues providing exposition for the notion that the arc of history was predetermined, whereas sci-fi television is a genre so dependent on dynamic visual action that it would have been very difficult to work in the long, slow dialogues on psychohistory that provided such balance in the novels.

However, the visual dynamism of the adaptation hides a kind of non-action at the heart of Gaal Dornick's character arc. Gaal is the viewer's entry point into the plot, both in her role as voiceover narrator, and for her centrality in much of the action around Seldon, yet she seems to be a mere observer to her own story for much of the season. Despite being told by Seldon after their trial that "You have more agency here, Gaal, than you realize" ("The Emperor's Peace") her path seems set from the time she enters the math contest that brings her to Trantor. She is promptly arrested and put on trial, put on a slow ship to Terminus, and then shoved into an escape pod and frozen for decades.

First, a path had been set out for her by Hari Seldon; then an alternate path hastily improvised for her by Raych Seldon—in both cases, she would have been central to the work of either the First Foundation, or of the Second. Gaal only finally reclaims her agency on the trip to Helicon, where she refuses to be part of Seldon's plans any longer, and sets out on her own trip back to her home on Synnax. It's a paradoxical situation: her inability to act for herself consigns her to centrality in the grand actions of history; she must relearn how to act for herself in order to practice "non-action" on a galactic scale.

In this, she models one final version of Chinese non-action, proposed by the Daoist philosopher Zhuangzi, whose work rivalled the *Dao De Jing* in its influence on Chinese civilization. Zhuangzi often uses trees as a metaphor for the dangers of being talented: strong, straight trees are the ones that get cut down and turned into boards for others' use, while gnarled and deformed trees, because they are useless to society, are allowed to grow in their own way and live a long life. In response to one friend who complains about his own useless tree, Zhuangzi says, "How you could loaf and wander, doing a whole lot of nothing [*wu wei*] there at its side! . . . Since it has nothing for which it can be used, what could entrap or afflict it? (*Zhuangzi*, p. 8).

It seems inevitable that Gaal will at some point in a future season return to involvement in the shaping of galactic history. However, at the end of the show's first season, she has made a successful decision to practice a very Zhuangzian version of non-action. She has realized that her talents as a prodigy do not doom her to a leading role that she does not want; she ends the season alone with Salvor Hardin, as virtual hermits in the empty oceans of an abandoned Synnax. It is a decision that highlights one way in which Asimov's central theme is incomplete.

The *Foundation* novels constantly work to direct the reader's attention to whether or not individuals' choices can matter in the face of historical forces; they rarely address the question of whether individuals have any responsibility to history, or whether a life of such responsibility is the best way to happiness and fulfillment. It might indeed be the case that an individual could have ethical duties that supersede their desire for a fulfilling life; and most ethicists would agree that doing whatever one wants is not a good rule for how to live. Nevertheless, there is no duty to enter thoughtlessly into a life of responsibility. Like Zhuangzi's parables, Gaal's character arc encourages us to consider whether the refusal to act on behalf of society and history, and to live a life of private non-action, can be a better path toward personal flourishing.[1]

---

[1] Many of the terms and names in this chapter are still often seen in a now outdated form of transliteration into English. 'Daoism' is the new version of 'Taoism'; 'Laozi' is the same person as 'Lao Tzu'; the *Dao De Jing* is the same book as the *Tao Te Ching*; and 'Zhuangzi' is the same person (and book) as 'Chuang Tzu'.

# 11
# An Interstellar Leap of Faith

WALTER BARTA AND GRAHAM LEE

In Isaac Asimov's *Foundation*, the mathematician Hari Seldon makes a plan for the future of civilization. This plan, premised on the predictive power of the science of "psychohistory," establishes Foundation, a special colony on the outskirts of the galaxy, in anticipation of the downfall of the Galactic Empire, and guides the people of the Foundation toward a better tomorrow.

As such, Hari Seldon's plan is not entirely dissimilar to the providence narratives of many religious faiths, particularly Christian providence narratives. Burgeoning in medieval philosophical thought, these ideas arguably reached their modern zenith in the work of the philosopher Georg Hegel, who has been interpreted as saying that history is purposively driven through a series of steps towards the realization of knowledge of God. However, Christian providence narratives in general and Hegel's providence narrative in particular have been criticized from different sides, both by Christian philosophers like Søren Kierkegaard and by secular materialist philosophers like Karl Marx. Despite these criticisms, providential accounts of history persist to the present day.

## Christian Providence Narratives

Providence, or the idea of a divine plan guiding history, has been a pervasive belief since the earliest days of human thought. Whether true or not, the belief itself has guided much of human history. Western civilization and Christianity, in particular, are replete with providence narratives. In the Hebrew book of *Exodus*, Moses leads God's chosen people out of bondage from Egypt to a promised land "flowing with milk and honey" (*Exodus* 3:16). According to the doctrine of the

Protestant theological tradition of Calvinism, certain Christians, referred to as "the Elect", have been predestined for heaven from before the creation of the world by the will of God. In the United States, the belief in American Exceptionalism, in the form of the doctrine of Manifest Destiny or the City on a Hill, have been quasi-religious providential narratives about the nation's special historical purpose in building a type of kingdom of Heaven on Earth.

Similarly, the Foundationists follow a providence narrative, Seldon's Plan, sometimes even referring to it as their "manifest destiny" (*Foundation and Empire*, p. 3). When encountering an opponent, the Foundationist line is familiar: "You fight the Foundation, which is never defeated—the Foundation, which is protected by the Seldon Plan—the Foundation, which is destined to form a new Empire" (*Second Foundation*, p. 19). Like other faiths before them, the Foundationists believe that they alone have the celestial truth and are destined for greatness and salvation after ushering in the paradisial second coming of the Galactic Empire in the distant future.

In the past, the philosophical foundations of providence emerged during the medieval period from Christian philosopher theologians like Augustine of Hippo and Thomas Aquinas. These philosophers sought to explain the course of history in terms consistent with the biblical conception of God. St. Augustine of Hippo was a philosopher theologian of the fifth century whose ideas were influential in the development of later Christian thought.

Augustine believed that God is omniscient and exists outside of time. To humans, knowledge is limited by the horizons of the past and the future; but, to God, both past and future are happening in an eternal present. Therefore, the future is always predictable from God's point of view. The divine providential plan already has happened, always is happening, and inevitably will happen.

Nearly a millennium later, the Christian metaphysics of providence of the thirteenth-century philosopher theologian Thomas Aquinas was formalized into the modern orthodoxy of the Catholic Church. Aquinas's ideas are some of the most influential ideas in history and inform philosophical and theological thought to this day. Channeling the teleological (ends-oriented) reasoning of Aristotle, Aquinas believed that everything in nature serves a purpose. All these purposes serve the ultimate purpose: the purpose of God. Thus, all things further the divine plan of providence. From *Genesis* to *Revelation*, the course of human history is preordained to proceed according to a plan preconceived by God himself, the driver of all events, the ultimate good (*summum bonum*). To these philosophers, the events of the Old Testament prophesy and make preparation for the events of the New Testament. Likewise, the events of the New Testament foretell and pave the way for events in modern times.

Events of the modern day, in turn, predict the future of the Galactic Empire. In modern times, physics is predictable mathematically; chemistry is reducible to physical principles; biology at a broad level is reducible to chemical principles; even psychology has a proposed basis in biology. Projecting these scientific developments into the future, we can imagine them leading to a more perfect predictive science, like psychohistory. Science-fiction writers have imagined somewhat believable futures in which psychohistory and galactic empires are possible.

Although Hari Seldon's prophecies are secular and scientific, unlike those of the medieval Christians, like them he presupposes an orderly force in the universe governing the course of history, which can be predicted and followed. Claiming nearly godlike predictive knowledge himself, Seldon acts like a prophet, giving a providential plan towards a future of greater understanding and happiness. Even his nickname, "Raven Seldon," suggests the quasi-religious devotion of his followers in the Foundation. In this way, Seldon follows in the footsteps of other providential prophets and philosophers.

## Dialectical Christian Providence Narratives

The older Christian providence narratives arguably found their modern apotheosis in the philosophy of Georg Hegel, who believed that the history of the world developed through a series of changing ideas according to the driving force of Spirit, arguably his conception of God. According to traditional interpretations of Hegel, Spirit is actualized through history. Ideas come to exist but in incomplete form and the process of "dialectic" (the investigation of truth through oppositions) puts the strengths and weaknesses of ideas to the test and changes them (Hegel, *Phenomenology of Spirit*, p. x).

According to many Hegelians, for every idea, thesis, there is a contradicting idea, antithesis, and an idea resulting from the combination of the two, synthesis. Thus, ideas come into conflict, compromise, and combine to form new ideas, which in turn engage in the same process, and so on. The history of humanity develops stepwise through this dialectical process involving the progressive development of ideas towards their final realization as pure and absolute knowledge. For example, humans might develop the idea of psychology as a thesis, studying the mind, thoughts, and feelings while agnostic about their historical effects. But they might also develop history as an alternative thesis, an antithesis, studying the courses of events while agnostic about their mental causes. Then, one day, a psychologist and a historian might have a conversation, leading to a conflict and resulting in a compromise, "psycho-history", a new synthesis. The Hegelian dialect of ideas proceeds in such a manner.

Hegel's theory of history is providential in at least two ways. Firstly, it explains the events of past history in terms of developing ideas. We might find examples of this process throughout history, whether in the conflict between masters and the enslaved in Egypt in *Exodus*, in the conflict between (the ideas of) Catholics and Protestants during the Reformation, or in the conflict between church and state in the early founding of America. Secondly, Hegel's theory postulates that the events of history lead towards more and more enlightenment and, all the while, the actualization of God. According to this interpretation of Hegel, the Christian's belief in providence is buttressed by a philosophical theory of historical change.

The Foundation has at least two Hegelian features. First, psychohistory suggests a complete knowledge of the universe. Through the Psychohistorians and Encyclopedists as imperial agents, the Empire develops and organizes all galactic knowledge. The Psychohistorians synthesize all prior science and lay bare the fundamentals of the universe: from the "nuclear forces" to the "nervous system," the universe is understood in its entirety in terms of the perfect axioms of reasoning (*Second Foundation*, II,8). The Encyclopedists collect and organize "the knowledge of the race. The sum of human knowing . . . The Encyclopedia Galactica" (*Foundation*, I.6).

Similarly, Hegelianism suggests that absolute knowledge is possible by means of dialectic. By following the progression of ideas, the structure of the universe can be accessed. In a strong way, The Encyclopedia Galactica represents this final stage in this development of human science. Further still, the complete knowledge of the universe according to psychohistory implies a complete unification of the galaxy under a new future government, harkening back to the "golden ages when the Empire had been co-extensive with the entire Galaxy," bringing an end to human disunity and strife once and for all, an outcome of which Hegel perhaps would be proud.

Second, the future history predicted by Seldon proceeds as a process of conflicting ideas. This history undergoes many stages of new dominant ideas. First, the ideas of the psychohistorians conflict with the Machiavellian political precepts of the Trantorian Galactic Empire, leading to exile and the establishment of the Encyclopedists. After some time, the short-term pragmatic ideas of the Mayors of the Foundation begin to conflict with the ivory tower long-term plans of the Encyclopedists, leading to a coup d'état and a new status quo with the establishment of a state-sanctioned religion, the priesthood of the Galactic Spirit (which itself is suggestive of Hegel's "World Spirit") (*Phenomenology of Spirit*, p. 458). Seldon describes the process as a "series of crises . . . circumscribed so that you will be forced along one, and only one, path" (*Foundation*, II.7). This process is precisely that of thesis-antithesis-synthesis, with the development of history emerging from the conflict and resolution of ideological contradictions, as described by Hegel.

## The Problem of Providence and Faith

However, there's a problem for the notion of the providence narrative when considered in the light of faith. Søren Kierkegaard, an influential Christian philosopher of the nineteenth century, arguably conceived of the idea of a "leap of faith" as essential to Christian thought. Kierkegaard also was a serious critic of Hegel. Kierkegaard saw Hegel's theories as a conceited attempt to build another tower of Babel, a logical ladder for humans to climb up to Heaven. Kierkegaard sought to invert this program. Rather than the means of human redemption, he regarded scientific knowledge as its greatest obstacle. Instead of giving more knowledge to people, he sought to take away what was considered knowledge. Rather than trying to make God and faith understandable, he sought to emphasize God's absolute transcendence above all human categories. So, for Kierkegaard, when it comes to faith, for providence narratives like Hegel's, there is a notable problem: providence implies a predetermined future path, one of certainty and confidence, leaving no room for doubt, which would seem completely contrary to the Christian conception of faith.

This Kierkegaardian challenge plays out in many episodes as the Foundation's plan unfolds. Like Hegel but in contrast to Kierkegaard, Hari Seldon regarded his plan—and psychohistorical predictions—as grounded in comprehensive scientific knowledge, as the means of humanity's redemption in the wake of the collapse of the Galactic Empire. Hari Seldon makes predictive claims premised on the objectivity of the science of psychohistory. However, belief in the Foundation narrative bears some similarities with Kierkegaard's faith.

First, even though Seldon himself knows the science behind his predictions, the Foundationists follow Seldon's Plan on blind faith: without knowing whether the plan is succeeding or failing during the tumultuous events of their times, without knowing whether they will survive those events, and without even knowing what the plan really ordains. Indeed, amid the dangers of interstellar space, Seldon's Plan, premised on his predictions, is hidden from his followers, like the silence of God—esoteric and opaque to all but Seldon himself.

Second, revered as divine revelation and always just too late to be of use to the faithful, the Vault, a type of time capsule conveying Seldon's Plan, opens once every few decades or centuries, not in time to affect events and only in time to validate them. During momentous periods in the history of the Foundation, "Seldon crises", Foundation heroes often act in anticipation that the correctness of their actions will be verified by Seldon's cryptic counsel after the fact. Receiving Seldon's revelations only retrospectively, they have to take them at face value, without understanding the science behind them and without even knowing them in advance, relying on them speculatively. As they say of the matter, "He's coming again . . . but he keeps all foreknowledge from us" (*Foundation*, III.5). The existential import of what could be gleaned from revelations is left up to these heroes to interpret, like biblical revelation, but always as hindsight bias, confirmation of their past but not consolation for their future.

Third, even the most educated and savvy Foundationists, like Lewis Pirenne, the Chief Encyclopedist, and Salvor Hardin, the first Mayor of Terminus, can only vaguely guess at the content of Seldon's psychohistory. Some, like Pirenne, are too blinded by their own role in the apparent plan to guess at Seldon's actual plan. Others, like Hardin, find themselves in a "hard-pressed position," knowing they are tasked with fulfilling part of the plan without knowing where the plan leads or whether they have completed their appointed task. Hardin has intuitions about what the plan is but acts with uncertainty of the details and, therefore, out of faith in the plan, though all the while furthering it. Many express frustration about this existential state of affairs, of ignorance and yet expectation: "We are to do nothing, is that right, except to wait in quiet serenity and utter faith for the *deus ex machina* to pop out of the Vault?" (*Foundation*, II.5).

The same is true of other Foundationists, who live with faith in Seldon's Plan and take psychohistory as their central doctrine. As events unfold, the destiny of the Foundation remains uncertain and unknown to the Foundationists. Psychohistory is less like intelligent design than blind chance according to natural laws, making faith no more warranted than existential dread in the face of a chaotic and uncaring universe. Accordingly, Foundationists take leaps of faith in space no less than Kierkegaardian Christians on Earth. The Foundationists' faith in Seldon's Plan and thus in his mastery of the predictively powerful, but nonetheless probabilistic, science, psychohistory, provides no certainty; no more certainty than Christian faith in the providential plan of God, which is based on his supposed omniscience, though revealed only by the Christian Bible, a collection of writings composed by humans.

Even Seldon himself makes his own leap of faith. Psychohistory predicts the future probabilistically, that is, without total certainty. It is also based on first principles of mathematics, which themselves cannot be proven (*Foundation*, I.5). As such, Seldon develops his plan based on both his psychohistorical predictions and what they leave out, thus requiring his own personal leap. He believes in his predictions and his goal for humanity, a faith as much as any. Furthermore, early on Seldon resolves to martyr himself for his cause, even implicating and involving his followers even though they do not know why or how it relates to the plan, saying, "There is probability of 1.7 percent that I will be executed, but of course that will not stop the project" (*Foundation*, I.4). This too indicates faith, for even radical acts, such as human sacrifice, are justified in terms of how they serve a faith. In his landmark work, *Fear and Trembling*, Kierkegaard analyzes Abraham's test by God to sacrifice his son, Isaac, in accordance with God's will. As with Abraham, so with Seldon; faith in providence may require sacrifice.

However, Hegel has a second coming even in the face of Kierkegaard's critique. Namely, Hegel's providence may require blind faith to be fulfilled. We can see this in the *Foundation* narrative, where Seldon's Plan and its inevitable providence can only function when followed on faith. To observe the contents of Seldon's Vault early, to glimpse the plan before its predicted events take place, would enable Foundationists to question, second-guess, and undermine the plan. Only ignorant followers can enact the plan without changing it. Knowledgeable followers would change the plan with their knowledge.

If Lewis Pirenne had known that Salvor Hardin's coup d'état was coming, the Encyclopedists might have prepared more protections for themselves and thus inadvertently sabotaged Seldon's Plan, which required the coup to succeed.

Self-awareness would have imparted too much variability. As Seldon's followers say, "Interference due to foresight would have almost knocked the plan out of kilter" (*Foundation*, III.2). This is a kind of observer effect: the effect of observation upon the observed. For example, when test subjects in a lab experiment know that they are being studied, their knowledge can affect the results of, and possibly even undermine, the study. Avoiding this effect requires some ignorance on the part of the subjects. Just so, Kierkegaard and Hegel find a synthesis: in resolution of the tension between providence and faith, perhaps one of the necessary conditions of providence is that it be followed faithfully, without certainty, by the faithful, and only then can it manifest.

## The Problem of Providence and Materialism

Another problem for providence narratives comes in the form of a secular critique. Karl Marx, the father of modern communist thought, was both a disciple of Hegel and one of his fiercest critics. Whereas the Hegelian dialectic of idealism postulated spiritual forces propelling history, Marx took this idea and made it a dialectic of materialism, postulating nothing propelling history but material forces: Marx renounced Hegel's World Spirit and left behind nothing but matter. For Marx, history is a type of providence narrative founded not in metaphysical principles but purely in physical principles. The progress of humanity develops as "a history of class struggle," through various economic stages, pushed by conflicts involving economic and political forces, rather than theological ones (Marx and Engels, *The Communist Manifesto*).

According to Marx, history develops from feudalism, through capitalism, toward inevitable communism. Religion, in the Marxist picture, is just an "opiate of the masses," an empty comfort that keeps the poor placated and thus the rich in power. Religion has force in the world as an instrument of economic and political forces, but there is no divine truth to its teachings or divine force operating behind its actions.

In some respects, the Foundation takes an overtly Marxist approach to religion. First, Seldon's Plan operates along the lines of a Marxist materialist dialectic, each Seldon Crisis a Marxist class struggle: the ruling class transitions from psychohistorians, to encyclopedists, to mayors, to traders, to interstellar merchant princes. This is alluded to directly by Hober Mallow, a merchant prince of the Foundation and beneficiary of Seldon's

Plan: "Seldon crises are not solved by individuals but by historic forces . . . sweeps of economics and sociology. So the solutions to the various crises must be achieved by the forces that become available to us at the time" (*Foundation*, V.18). Moreover, Seldon's Plan leads out of galactic unrest, "thirty thousand years . . . one thousand generations of suffering humanity", towards a new galaxy-spanning empire. Similarly, the Marxist dialectic leads out of the struggles of history towards the goal of international communism (*Foundation*, I.6).

Second, the religion of the Foundation, the priesthood of the Galactic Spirit, is set up as a means of ideologically manipulating and controlling neighboring planetary powers. For example, the priesthood is spread by the Foundation to the neighboring planets of Anacreon in order to enlist Anacreonian loyalties, although Foundationist leaders do not share that faith and know it is a useful farce, themselves not believing in the doctrine they espouse. As Hober Mallow puts it: "We have the science of the great Hari Seldon to prove that upon us depends the future empire of the Galaxy . . . The religion we have is our all-important instrument towards that end . . . with which to control men and worlds" (*Foundation*, V.13). In other words, the Hegelesque religion of the Galactic Spirit is just a tool for the Foundation, a tool itself used for the Marxist ends of political and economic domination. Not only this; religion brings about the next stage of historical development, "trade and traders", which then usurps it in dominance (*Foundation*, V.13). As Marx would say, the era brings about its own conflict and thus the emergence of a new era, so that history develops as a successive series of continually changing material and social conditions.

However, Hegel's original narrative of providence reestablishes itself even amidst this Marxist critique. Even though the Foundationists explicitly spread a false faith for political purposes, they implicitly follow a faith of their own, faith in the plan of Hari Seldon. This providence narrative, although claiming a basis in science like Marxism, is followed by Foundationists on faith since none of the Foundation's devout actually understand the science on which his predictions are founded. So, the plan is a faith in its own right and Seldon is a kind of prophet in whom Foundationists trust. Thus, ironically, the false Foundationist faith of the Galactic Spirit is nested instrumentally within the true Foundationist faith in and of Seldon's Plan, which in turn is dependent upon Hari Seldon's own faith in the predictive power of psychohistory. The Foundationists employ a false providence narrative in service of a providence narrative they themselves follow. Similarly, the Marxist critique of religion as an instrument of power is itself derived from and subsumed into a greater Hegelian providence narrative, one based ultimately in the faith that history does indeed develop along an orderly path towards human salvation.

## Faith as a Social Experiment

Drawing on the philosophies of Hegel, Kierkegaard, Marx, and their forebears, the Foundation of Hari Seldon is a social experiment that shows how providence narratives might play out in a hyper-scientific age and on a galactic scale; how even the objective knowledge of science might be susceptible to the tribulations of faith; how ideological and material forces may influence and interact with each other; and how even the distant future may be subject to the distant past.

# IV

# Foundation and Science

***"For it is the chief characteristic of the religion of science that it works."***

# 12
# Raven Seldon Predicts Disaster

DANIEL MALLOY

In "The Psychohistorians," the first short story of the *Foundation* series, Hari "Raven" Seldon predicts the seemingly impossible: that the Galactic Empire, which has ruled the Milky Way and all of humanity for twelve thousand years, will fall. And nothing can prevent it.

Seldon further predicts that the fall of the Empire will be followed by thirty thousand years of chaos and anarchy. Fortunately, Seldon also predicts that, under the right conditions, with the right people in the right place, this period can be shortened from thirty thousand years to only one thousand.

All of these predictions are based on psychohistory. Psychohistory is a branch of mathematics that studies the reactions of large groups of people to various social and economic conditions. Although the mathematics of psychohistory are complex, the basic procedure is simple. In *Prelude to Foundation* and *Forward the Foundation*, Seldon develops the science by studying the evolution of the capital of the Galactic Empire, Trantor, to create models for the patterns of the actions and reactions of masses of people. He generalizes from the history of Trantor to make predictions about the future of the Empire. After years and decades of observations and refinements, Seldon makes his final set of predictions—the fall of the Empire, the coming anarchy, and the saving role of the Foundation.

Seldon's method in developing psychohistory is a common one, that people use every day. Psychohistory is based on induction. People use induction whenever they make predictions about the future based on what happened in the past. Psychohistory is intricate and detailed, but in its basis it's no different than predicting that today's lunch will be nourishing or that hitting the 'a' key on a keyboard will produce the letter 'a' on the screen.

But that raises a problem. The future is unknown. So, it becomes a question whether the future will be like the past at all. Predictions are based on the idea that it will be, but it's surprisingly difficult to prove. This is the problem of induction. If there isn't some reason to believe that the future will be like the past, then psychohistory and its predictions of disaster become what the authorities of the Galactic Empire believe them to be: the ravings of a madman. Without induction, Seldon's vaunted Plan is little more than a fever dream, and so are all other predictions.

## Trantor Has Never Been . . .

At first, Seldon's prediction of the impending disaster facing the Galactic Empire is met with near-universal skepticism. Even his fellow mathematician Gaal Dornick has a hard time believing it until he checks the figures himself. There are any number of explanations for the failure to heed Seldon's warning: the mathematics involved are too complicated, people are stubborn, some are suspicious, and so on. However, the most fundamental reason for doubting Seldon is simply the fact of the Empire and its history. The Galactic Empire has lasted for twelve thousand years, through all manner of social, economic, and political changes. The Empire has endured. The Empire continues to endure. Therefore, the Empire will continue to endure.

Looking at it from the outside, it's easy to see the fallacy in this reasoning: just because things have been this way for this long doesn't mean that they have to stay this way. But this same fallacy comes up regarding the problem of induction. Of course the future will be like the past, because so far the future has always been like the past. The present is the future of some past, and that past was similar to the present. Further, that past was the future of some further past, and they turned out to be similar as well. So, the future still to come will also be like the past before it.

But, as philosopher David Hume (1711–1776) first noted in his *Treatise of Human Nature*, this reasoning is circular: induction, including predictions about the future based on the past, is based on the idea that the future will be like the past. If induction is justified because so far futures have been like the pasts that preceded them, that's an inductive justification of induction. But induction can't justify itself. Predicting that the Galactic Empire will fall because similar conglomerates in similar circumstances in the past have fallen only works if there's a reason to believe the future will be like the past. The fact that so far futures have been like pasts isn't good enough. So, perhaps the Galactic Empire will survive.

## The Goddess of Psycho-Historical Necessity

But the Empire does fall. So perhaps there's another reason for believing that the future will be like the past. If induction can't justify induction, perhaps deduction can. Deduction is the sort of reasoning that guarantees the truth of its conclusions based on the truth of its premises. Even the best inductions can only make a conclusion more or less probable. A good deduction makes its conclusion undeniable, again assuming the premises are true.

The power and process of deduction can be seen by looking at the first so-called Seldon Crisis the Foundation faced. In "The Encyclopedists," the second short story of the *Foundation* series, the newly declared kingdom of Anacreon tries to claim the planet Terminus and the Foundation for itself. The Encyclopedists who rule the Foundation wrongly believe that their Imperial ties will shield them. Allowing Anacreon to permanently occupy Terminus is unacceptable. Calling for Imperial aid is useless. Open war with Anacreon is pointless. So, the Foundation has no choice but to get creative: to play the newly emerging powers of the Galactic Periphery against one another, forcing Anacreon to end its occupation of Terminus in just six months. To clarify, the Foundation faces four options: surrender to Anacreon, appeal to the Empire, fight Anacreon, or get clever. The first three options are untenable, so the fourth is the only viable one.

That is the power of deduction: it can cut through the fluff and get to the heart of the matter. Once the first three options are eliminated, it only remains to get to work on the fourth, as Salvor Hardin does. For deduction to provide a basis for induction, there would have to be some way of deriving the principle that the future will be like the past from the basic principle of deduction, the law of non-contradiction. This law states that a thing can't be and not be at the same time and in the same respects. If Hari Seldon is on Trantor, then he isn't on Terminus because Terminus isn't Trantor. Seldon can't be both on Trantor and not on Trantor at the same time.

One way of testing for this sort of basis is to ask whether an idea contradicts itself. If an idea contradicts itself, then it can't be true. It must be false, which means that the opposite idea must be true. The idea of a triangle with more than three sides contracts itself, because a triangle is a figure with only three sides. So, the idea of a five-sided triangle must be false, and the idea of a three-sided triangle must be true. In Hardin's first Seldon Crisis, his goal is to maintain the independence of Terminus. This goal contradicts the possibility of surrendering to Anacreon, and the options of appealing to the Empire or fighting Anacreon would end with Terminus surrendering to Anacreon anyway, so Hardin gets clever.

The idea that the future will be like the past doesn't contradict itself, so it could be true. But in order to show that it has to be true, it would have to be shown that the idea that the future won't be like the past does contradict itself. But it doesn't. The idea that the future won't be like the past may seem implausible or improbable, but it isn't impossible. As well founded as psychohistory is, its predictions prove to be flawed—Seldon doesn't foresee the rise of the Mule, as shown in *Foundation and Empire*. The Mule's existence and rise to power is unprecedented. Empire builders existed in the past, but never a person who could simply reach into the mind of his most implacable enemy and turn them into his most loyal servant. The Mule's unpredictability shows that there's no guarantee that the future will be like the past. And so, there is no deductive basis for induction.

## Seldon's Plan Will Go On—Somehow

The search for a justification of induction is similar to the situation of the First Foundationers after the first Seldon Crisis. The Foundation on Terminus, although founded on Seldon's Plan, isn't aware of any of the details of the Plan or the inner workings of psychohistory. After the conflict with Anacreon, all the Foundationers know is that there's a plan. Their ignorance is essential if the Plan is going to work: if they knew the content of the psychohistorical predictions, that knowledge would influence their actions in ways that would invalidate the calculations. But consider the situation from their perspective: the Plan is out there, working, and their role is just to act as they normally would.

This leads to problems within the Foundation. For example, consider the conflict between Mallow and Sutt in "The Merchant Princes," the fourth short story in the *Foundation* series. In the lead-up to the third Seldon Crisis, Mallow and Sutt are both convinced that they have some clue about the next step in the Plan. Sutt's convinced the Foundation has to continue exporting the religion encouraged by Hardin, while Mallow believes that the time has come to shift to a strategy of pure economic domination and leave the religion in the past. Mallow turns out to be correct, but he had no way of knowing that that's what Seldon had predicted.

Similar to Mallow and other Foundationers' conundrum, the problem of induction seems intractable. Induction has to work, but there's no good reason to believe it will. Hume offered one possible solution to this problem when he first identified the problem of induction. When searching for the origin of the principle of induction, Hume noted that repeated experiences lead to the expectation of similar things in the future. The fact that Yohan Lee stood by Hardin during and after the events of the first Seldon Crisis in "The Encyclopedists" led Hardin to expect that he would do the same as they approached the second one.

But this doesn't solve the problem. Even if people accept the principle of induction as a matter of habit, that isn't a justification for it. It explains why people do it, but not why they should. It's like a constant danger that the Foundation itself faces: the internal danger of inertia. Knowing the Plan is out there, working toward the Second Galactic Empire, the Foundationers have to be reminded that the Plan only works if they act independently as they would even if there were no Plan. To trust blindly in the Plan is to undermine its very basis. Similarly, to trust the principle of induction because it's a habit means sacrificing what makes induction so useful in the first place: its power to teach us new things.

## A Prediction Made by Mathematics

Early leaders of the Foundation like Salvor Hardin and Hober Mallow are successful because they manage to come up with solutions that subvert expectations. Confronted with military threats of various sorts, Hardin and Mallow respond with diplomatic, religious, and economic solutions that work. Perhaps the solution to the problem of induction is similarly one that subverts expectations.

Philosopher Sir Karl Popper (1902–1994) offered such a solution in his *Logic of Scientific Discovery*. In looking at psychohistory, Popper would first note that psychohistory is a science. Science, according to Popper, isn't based on induction. Instead, science operates by deriving predictions from hypotheses, conducting experiments and making observations to see if those predictions hold true, and then either continuing to generate further predictions or revising or abandoning the original hypothesis.

So, consider how Seldon might have predicted the Anacreon crisis. He has his hypothesis: the laws and functions of psychohistory. To that hypothesis, he would have added the information about the position of the Foundation and Terminus, the political situation on Anacreon and in the Periphery more generally, and the declining fortunes of the Empire. All of that would yield the prediction that fifty years after the establishment of the Foundation, the ruler or rulers of Anacreon would attempt to exert authority over Terminus, and that the only way to resist the aggression would be to play a balance of power game with Anacreon and other Periphery powers.

This example leaves out one key component of Popper's concept of science: observation. Seldon is long dead before he can check the accuracy of his prediction. But, his prediction is accurate, and there are psychohistorians available to confirm it: the members of the Second Foundation.

The later search for the Second Foundation by the citizens of Terminus in *Second Foundation* provides another example. In the aftermath of the Mule, the Seldon Plan seems to be back on track. This arouses the suspicions of Dr. Darell's group on Terminus. They become convinced that the Second Foundation is manipulating events behind the scenes. Unsettled by this theory, Dr. Darell and his co-conspirators set out to discover and eliminate the Second Foundation. And, by their own lights, they succeed. They discover some fifty Second Foundationers on Terminus and eliminate them. The discovery would seem to confirm the theory.

But this presents a limitation that Popper argued is essential to science: science can't confirm a theory. It can only falsify it. Finding the Second Foundationers and eliminating them misleads the citizens of Terminus to believe that they have ended the threat of the Second Foundation itself. But the Second Foundation remains, safely ensconced on Trantor. The theory hasn't been falsified because its prediction proved correct. But it also hasn't been confirmed. Each Second Foundationer they discover is another example of how the theory hasn't failed, but no number of Second Foundationers would ever be able to confirm that the Second Foundation is on Terminus.

A similar limitation applies to psychohistory as a whole. No matter how many correct predictions are generated by the science, they will never prove it to be correct. All that's been proven is that the science hasn't failed yet. But that leads to a dilemma when it does fail, as in the case of the Mule. Popper's idea of science is that once a science makes an erroneous prediction, it has to be abandoned or revised in light of that failure. The dilemma is to determine whether the science of psychohistory should be cast off or amended to account for the failure.

## A Very Romantic Idea of Science

That may seem like a problem for Popper's theory, but it really isn't. It's just a recognition that science, and by extension psychohistory, isn't a set of facts or a static entity. Science is an ongoing process. As more and more hypotheses are falsified, more and more reliable ones are found, and those can be refined and perfected to generate more and more exact predictions. The Second Foundationers after the Mule can use psychohistory to generate predictions that Seldon himself never could because they have refined the science to a higher degree through exactly this process.

The real problem with Popper's theory comes at the other end of the process. According to Popper, science begins with a hypothesis. But the origin of the hypothesis is left completely open. Popper explicitly says that the creation of hypotheses isn't part of the scientific method: its investigation belongs to the psychology or biography of the scientists who create particular hypotheses.

But treating the origin of a hypothesis as though it isn't part of science creates more problems than it solves. By Popper's reasoning, the rise of the Mule, which falsifies one of the predictions of psychohistory, means that the Second Foundationers must revise or discard psychohistory. But in determining which, they will cite the many successes of psychohistory as evidence for preserving the science, making the inductive case. Further, when they decide to preserve and revise the science, they must choose how to begin the revisions. They could do this by blind guessing, but that would be inefficient and unproductive. Instead, what they might do is look at the predictions that succeeded and the ones that failed to discover the difference. In the case of the Mule, the difference is obvious. The Mule is a random anomaly that psychohistory was never designed to account for. The statistical science has trouble with small populations, much less single individuals. But the Second Foundationers take account of that, and adjust the science and refine the hypotheses so that it can more accurately predict the actions of individuals. Those refined hypotheses allow the First Speaker to set the Plan back on track. All of this tinkering and refining is inductive.

Against this, Popper could argue that the origins of a science have nothing to do with its proceedings. Chemistry began with the futile efforts of alchemists to turn lead into gold. Astronomy started with the speculations of astrology. Those sciences are no less sciences because of their origins. Similarly, psychohistory's foundation in an inductive procedure doesn't make the science itself inductive, or undermine its standing as a science. Even if the Second Foundationers use induction to come up with new hypotheses or to figure out how to proceed in light of a failed prediction, Popper would argue that those hypotheses only become a part of the science of psychohistory once predictions are derived from them and tested.

The trouble is psychohistory is still making predictions, and those predictions still depend on the principle of induction. If there's no reason to believe that the future will be like the past, then there's no reason to believe any predictions based on that idea. That includes all of psychohistory, as well as the predictions of any science that's been developed and refined using inductive methods. Not to mention the non-scientific predictions people make in deciding who to trust and what to do, like Dr. Darrell's prediction that one of the Second Foundationers has infiltrated his conspiracy.

## The Last Refuge of the Philosopher

In the absence of any details about the Seldon Plan, the First Foundationers are left to their own devices. In an increasingly hostile and chaotic galaxy, leaders like Salvor Hardin and Hober Mallow marshall their resources and make the decisions that seem best to them at the time, with no guarantee that those decisions are the right ones. For all Hardin or Mallow know, their actions may threaten the Seldon Plan just as surely as the Mule does. Take, for example, Hardin's gambit in in the second Seldon Crisis, depicted in "The Mayors": prior to playing his hand, he has no assurance that the faith of Anacreon's soldiers or populace at large will be strong enough to support Terminus and the Foundation against the plans of Wienis and Prince Lefkin. But the religion of the Foundation is the only tool he has to hand, so it's what he has to use.

Hardin's attitude during this Seldon Crisis can be described as pragmatic: you do the best you can with what you have and hope for the best. This sort of attitude is also at the heart of a sort of justification of induction offered by philosopher Hans Reichenbach (1891–1953) in his *Experience and Prediction*. It's a sort of justification because it doesn't try to show that the principle of induction is justified in any thing like the ways discussed above. Reichenbach's argument isn't exactly a deductive or an inductive justification. Instead, what he offers is sometimes called a vindication of induction.

Rather than look at the basis of induction, Reichenbach looks at the results. Induction may fail from time to time, but overall it's astonishingly successful in making accurate predictions. Since that's what induction is for and there doesn't seem to be anything else that can do the job at all, it's probably best to stick with induction. If something better comes along, some form of reasoning that can make more accurate and reliable predictions, then induction can be abandoned. But so far, there is no such alternative to induction. Like the Foundationers, confined to Terminus and limited to the sparse resources found there, it's best to make do with the available resources, rather than waste time lamenting the out of reach ones. Hardin may prefer something other than the balance of powers in the first crisis, or the faith of the Foundation in the second, but those are the tools he has to work with. If the choice is between induction and nothing, there doesn't seem to be a choice at all.

Reichenbach's vindication isn't proof. It doesn't guarantee that the future will be like the past. Like Hardin, it has the virtue of acknowledging a crisis, and accepting that there are limited resources for dealing with it. Unlike a Seldon Crisis, the problem of induction isn't time-limited, which is both a good thing and a bad thing. It's a good thing because it means that a better solution may be found. It's a bad thing because the problem of induction isn't an event that happens at some point in time and then is over. It's always there, threatening to bring all predictions and plans to nothing.

## Hari Seldon's Dead Hand

The future can be changed—that's easy. A bomb here, a Mule there and the future isn't what it used to be. In *Second Foundation*, a child born on Trantor but raised on Terminus realizes that a circle has no end, and suddenly the Seldon Plan is back on track after fifty years of wandering in the wilderness. The real problem is how to be sure that the future won't change. Without that, Seldon's Plan is just the fever-dream of an old mathematician.

But more than that, the question of whether the future will be like the past is just one instance of the broader problem of induction. Without some way of solving that problem, there's no way to be sure that anything beyond the realm of individual experiences—past, present, or future—will resemble those experiences. When Hardin figures out that Anacreon lacks nuclear power, he's using induction, not about the future, but about the present. When he further determines that other Periphery powers must also lack nuclear power, because one of them just lost a war to Anacreon, that's a further use of induction. When the historians and archeologists of the Empire and later Foundation come to believe that there was one planet where human beings originated, they are likewise relying on induction. They have scraps of evidence and from those scraps develop theories about the existence of such a planet, where it might have been and what features it might have had. All of Janov Pelorat's reasonings about Earth in *Foundation's Edge* are inductive.

The problem of induction is thus a crisis as momentous, perhaps, as the fall of the Empire itself. Without the Empire, human beings are left without a single governing body to guide their interactions. Without some justification of induction, they are left without any guide for learning about the world beyond what they're experiencing right now.

# 13
# In Defense of Demerzel

PETAR NURKIĆ

Like all fanciers of Asimov, I was curious to examine the discrepancies between the original books and the ten episodes of the first season of the *Foundation Apple* TV+ series. The most considerable intrigue that diverted my attention is Demerzel, an enigmatic, intelligent robot loyal to the Galactic Empire. Likewise, the two main things that sparked a lot of fandom debate regarding the TV Series revolved around discrepancies between the series adaptation and original *Foundation* books, and the Demerzel character within the series.

I like to think that if Asimov himself were to adapt his books into TV series in the second decade of the twenty-first century, he would consider the cultural and technological realities we live in. Robots are no longer just fiction; they are genuine and are utilized in our day-to-day lives, and with that the laws they adhere to become much more constrained to the practical possibilities of their implementation.

Although any adaptation's potential to comment on actual ethical problems of its time is a generally interesting topic, our main philosophical issue is Demerzel's violation of Asimov's laws.

## Does Demerzel Really Violate the Laws of Robotics?

Does Demerzel really violate the laws of robotics? To answer this question, we first must see whether it is justifiable to ask it. It's well-known that both Asimov's *Foundation* books and his Robot books take place in the same universe. However, the time disparity between Robot and *Foundation* books presents a significant obstacle to an examination of Demerzel in relation to the laws of robotics since we can't expect her to be constrained by the original formulations of the laws first introduced in the *I, Robot* franchise which depicts periods set well before the *Foundation* time. And yet the laws of robotics are certainly the underlying design architecture in each of Asimov's stories.

Even though Asimov's three laws of robotics are not mentioned in the *Foundation* TV series, it's clear that Demerzel is constrained by some kind of programming and instructions. This is evident because decisions she makes and is forced to make, whether she considers them justified or not, are accompanied by strong emotional responses.

Asimov's three laws of robotics were first introduced in the 1942 story "Runaround." They were included in the collection *I, Robot* in 1950. The Laws of Robotics have become a distinc—tive feature of the Robot universe. Unlike other stories and Asimov's literary fictional worlds, they form an indispensable footing of the complex narrative. The precise transcription of Asimov's three laws of robotics can be presented as follows:

- First Law: **A robot may not injure a human being or, through inaction, allow a human being to come to harm.**
- Second Law: **A robot must obey the orders given it by human beings except where such orders would conflict with the First Law.**
- Third Law: **A robot must protect its own existence as long as such protection does not conflict with the First or Second Law.**

In addition to the plethora of technical sub-questions that arise when considering the compatibility of Demerzel's behavior with the laws of robotics, two central issues have sparked the most controversy. The first concerns the end of Episode 8 of the *Foundation* TV series, when Demerzel poisoned Zephyr Halima; and the second, more surprising, complex, and intriguing issue arose when Demerzel killed Cleon XIV (Brother Dawn) in the season finale.

In the first situation, Demerzel entourages Cleon XIII (Brother Day) to Proxima Opal's funeral on Moon Maiden. Brother Day tries to influence the election of Zephyr Gilat as the new Proxima because she would continue to evangelize the *New Octavo* which, unlike the *Primary Octavo* preached by Zephyr Halima, does not hold a controversial view of Cleon's Genetic Dynasty. Due to numerous devotees of the Luminism religion and the theological implications that could lead to the instability of the Galactic Empire, Day decides to undergo the holy Spiral pilgrimage. Without any food, water, or rest, Day reached the center of the Spiral, where the *Womb of Mother* is located. After that, he informed the panel of Zephyrs of the vision with which the Triple Goddesses have blessed him. That was also a winning argument for the enthronement of Zephyr Gilat as the new Proxima. Although Day bested Zephyr Halima in the political bidding, Demerzel was nevertheless ordered to dispose of Halima to forestall new potential problems for the Genetic Dynasty.

In the second situation, Cleon XIV tried to escape from the Imperial District after Azura Odili, employed by a group of rebels, had manipulated him. Insurgents first tempered with the DNA of the original Cleon and then tried to replace Brother Dawn with their artificial clone to unseat the Genetic Dynasty from the inside. Cleon XII (Brother Dusk) uncovered the rebel saboteurs and retrieved Cleon XIV to the Imperial Palace. Discovering that Dawn is an aberration and may not be capable of ensuring the continuity of the Genetic Dynasty, Brother Day tries to devise an appropriate punishment for young Cleon. Nevertheless, after a heated argument with Brother Dusk, Day decides that this outcome may not be such a bad thing for the Dynasty's necessary adaptation to the rapidly declining Empire. However, to the surprise of all three Cleons and without any instructions, Demerzel decides to execute Brother Dawn, ending the debate whether the secondary imperial clone should replace Cleon XIV.

It is clear why someone would assume that Demerzel violated the first two laws of robotics by poisoning Halima. It is also evident that she violated Asimov's first law by murdering Cleon XIV. The First Law is imperative regarding the prohibition on harming human beings. In addition, the Second Law explicitly exempts robots from subordination to their patrons in cases where they demand the harm of another human being. Demerzel not only harmed Halima and Brother Dawn but also committed the ultimate and most flagrant possible infraction a robot can commit, murder! All this gives a firm hold to the confusion and controversy among fans of Asimov's fiction. However, we should keep in mind that Demerzel is no ordinary robot. Speculation that she is not determined by the laws of robotics is overblown, as we have already provided an argument for why and how some kind of programming constrains her. Demerzel is the only remaining intelligent robot in the galaxy for a good reason (under the narrative barrier of not entering the story of R. Daneel Olivaw and the speculation that Demerzel is only Daneel's guise). Hence, it is plausible to assume that the instructions followed by the underlying coded architecture of her positronic brain are somewhat different than one might expect. Therefore, at this point, we will introduce the *Zeroth Law*, which was first explicitly mentioned in Asimov's 1985 novel *Robots and Empire*, although it was developed earlier in the 1950 short story *The Evitable Conflict*. According to the fictional protagonist, Daneel Olivaw, we can define this law as follows:

- ZEROTH LAW: **A robot may not harm humanity, or, by inaction, allow humanity to come to harm.**

The Zeroth Law is considered as the zeroth, not the fourth, law because it takes precedence over all other laws of robotics. Because of the cultural and social flexibility that an adaptation of a seventy-year-old book must possess, linking the Zeroth Law with the *Foundation* universe makes much more sense than connecting it to any previously mentioned laws. At the same time, the Zeroth Law is precisely the alternative we need to make sense of Demerzel's behavior and protect her from a swarm of volley-criticism of bewildered fans.

The concept of 'humanity' is collective and much more general than the previously postulated concept of human individuation. The generality of the Zeroth Law allows Demerzel to occasionally violate the three laws of robotics while remaining consistent with Asimov's fictional universe.

Asimov argues in several of his stories that a functional positronic brain of a robot cannot be developed without implementing the three laws of robotics. However, it turns out that this endeavor is not impossible; just very complex and time-consuming. And Demerzel is several millennia ancient, and Cleon I had all possible resources to reprogram her successfully. The law tampering is no longer just a possibility but a highly probable reality.

Demerzel follows the Emperors' instructions impeccably, so impeccably that she poisons Zephyr Halima on Cleon XIII's orders. That would hint at a possibility that the implementation of the Second Law in Demerzel was conducted through the truncated form: *a robot must obey the orders given by human beings [Emperor].* If this version of the Second Law took precedence over the First Law, that would successfully reconcile the incoherence between Demerzel's heeding of the laws and Halima's murder. However, although she has consistently and impeccably obeyed orders of the Cleon dynasty, the murder of Cleon XIV disproves the abbreviated version of the Second Law or at least further restricts it in some way, since the reigning Emperor (Cleon XIII) did not give such order to Demerzel. That brings us back to Asimov's first law as a law of higher priority and the possibility of altering the meaning of the concept of 'human being'. If we were to replace the term 'human being' with 'humanity', we would get the Zeroth Law, which would justify Demerzel's killing of Halima and Brother Dawn. In this case, it would be consistent with the interests of humanity and the political factor of peace and stability brought by the Galactic Emperors, even if the price was the life of another Cleon. If someone is puzzled by Demerzel's disobedience to Cleon XIII, who apparently did not want to kill Brother Dawn, we can provide a straightforward explanation: Demerzel has known humankind much longer than the Cleon Dynasty and can therefore make more reasonable predictions about what is harmful to 'humanity'.

When we talk about the predictability of what is harmful to humanity, we cannot ignore Hari Seldon and his innovative science of psychohistory. This eccentric mathematical genius and one of the *Foundation* TV series protagonists succeeded in predicting the patterns of large social groups (populations) through a combination of science and mathematics that uses probability theories and historical analysis. Predictive uncertainty is a major problem for intelligent robots. In uncertainty, dissonance about what might cause 'harm' to a human being, their brains simply freeze, and the system shuts down. Given this, as well as the fact that choosing the best plan for 'humanity' and the potential harm that could be done to it is a fairly abstract concept that requires some sort of predictive behavior of large social groups and reliance on probabilities, we can conclude that psychohistory would play a significant role in Demerzel's follow-up to the Zeroth Law. If we add the premise that she may sometimes disobey the implicit orders of the Cleon Dynasty in following the Zeroth Law, we can additionally conclude that it was cognitively worthwhile for Demerzel to secretly support Seldon's development of psychohistory.

Unfortunately, after this argumentation favoring the Zeroth Law, we must cite two counter-arguments that further prove its implausibility. The first arises from the plot of the *Foundation* TV series itself; Demerzel never assisted Harry Seldon in developing the science of psychohistory. If the Cleons wanted to execute Seldon before developing his predictive model, she would most likely obey that order. The second point touches the heart of the trouble of Demerzel's consistency and compliance with the laws of robotics. Using the Prime Radiant device, Hari Seldon predicted that the Galactic Empire would fall in the next five centuries and be followed by thirty thousand years of uncivilized darkness. Seldon identifies the Genetic Dynasty as one of the leading causes of the decline of humanity due to its inability to change and renew itself. Had Demerzel been reprogrammed so that her primary focus was to not harm humanity or reduce the harm that may befall it, she would have killed not only Cleon XIV but the entire Genetic Dynasty. That suggests that Demerzel is actually following the orders of Cleon I and his vision of the Genetic Dynasty as the undisputed rulers of the Galaxy.

The answer to whether Demerzel violates Asimov's three laws of robotics falls into the realm of fuzzy logic: Yes and No! If we think of Demerzel's original setting as the laws of robotics as originally defined, then it is clear that Demerzel violates them. Still, if the question is whether Demerzel violates the laws of robotics implemented in her, then the answer is—no. Indeed, in Demerzel's case, laws of robotics are tampered with in a similar way that Daneel Olivaw implemented the Zeroth Law. The only difference is that the term 'human being' is not replaced with a concept of 'humanity', but by introducing 'Cleon I's vision' as the ultimate and inviolable priority.

## Are the Laws of Robotics Coherent?

We have already mentioned the problem of decision uncertainty in intelligent robots that rely on probability models to make predictions. Here we can draw a parallel with the *donkey paradox*, named after the fourteenth-century French philosopher Jean Buridan (Rescher 1960). Buridan's donkey is a logical automaton that makes the best possible decisions. However, when the donkey finds itself between two piles of hay of equal size and quality to its left and right, it cannot decide which one to eat, so it stays paralyzed until it eventually dies of starvation. If we were to put an intelligent robot in a situation where there are two equally real and temporally threatening hazards to a human being, it would simply freeze because it could not decide which harm to prevent first. That shows that we can construct a range of similar paradoxes in which *verbatim* following of Asimov's laws would cause the robot's brain to deteriorate and shut down completely. If such a spectrum of insurmountable cognitive uncertainty can occur in the case of an individual human being, we can only speculate what would happen with the collective and much more abstract concept of 'humanity'.

What would happen if we tricked the robot into pouring poison instead of bourbon into our enemy's glass? Would it shut down, having technically violated the First Law of robotics? There is also the question of how robots identify human beings in general. The concept of a human being that must be implemented in a robot cannot be dependent on physical attributes only, for a physically appropriate humanoid doll can then qualify as a human being. That forces us to move beyond the material characteristics of humans and into a more abstract realm of behavioral cues that signal the sentience and sapience of an agent, as these are often understood as criteria for a moral status of a human being in both philosophy and psychology. Let's then consider the myriad of culturally and socially diverse ethnicities that express their identities, beliefs, and daily practices in different ways through divergent norms and behaviors.

It's not surprising that potential misconception occurs in robots identifying only members of specific nations and cultures as 'human beings'. We should keep in mind the epistemic dynamics of conceptual engineering, which relies on humans assembling concepts according to the culture to which they belong. Ultimately, humans are those who implement definitions in intelligent machines and create the foundations on which neural networks train their interaction with the environment. Inhumane and uncivilized wars have often occurred in human history, resulting from the relativization of the idea of 'human being'. Why should robots be exempt from this conceptual entanglement?

A similar problem arises when considering the equally abstract concept of 'harm'. Does a robot need to protect humans or humanity from every kind of damage? Humans are often unhappy, depressed, and live unhealthy lives exposed to stress. Does Demerzel need to anticipate Cleon XIV's mental health or is her domain of protection limited to his physical health? Consistently following Asimov's laws would compel robots to obsessively protect humans from all of the above, forcing them to eat healthily, jog, and preventing the majority of stressful situations that can potentially lead to mental health problems for inaction in these situations will result to harm of a human being and thus violate the First Law of Robotics. Furthermore, such a robot will need to consider and understand every social, behavioral, and medical cue to devise an adequate predictive model of complex outcomes of one human life so it can develop a good plan of (in)action and not violate the First law.

One possible outcome of this paradoxical overlay could be the creation of a robot dictatorship that locks humans in hibernation chambers to protect them from any potential threat. Harm is a very subtle concept that robots cannot grasp because it requires metacognitive functions. In a given context, if a robot misunderstands that a human is in danger, it could sacrifice itself to avoid violating the First and Third Laws of Robotics. Even if we say that the notion of harm is concrete and therefore easier to predict in the case of a particular individual, the meaning of the concept of harm when it comes to 'humanity' remains elusive. That points to multiple problems when regarding definitions in Asimov's laws. These definitions are either too broad or too narrow, depending on the context, and invariably lead to problematic robotic behavior.

Another conceptual puzzle is *allowing a human being to come to harm through inaction*. Imagine a robot designed for high-risk professions, such as surgery. The mortality rate due to complex surgical procedures is high. The robot undoubtedly has an expert advantage over the average surgeon, so it would have a duty to save people's lives with its exceptional technical skills. However, if the risky surgery is unsuccessful, the robot would be responsible for the cessation of human life, according to Asimov's laws. So, on the one hand, the robot is responsible for the death of a human being in a high-risk situation, but on the other hand, it must not allow harm to come to a human on the operating table through inaction. That shows that Asimov's laws are deconstructed and incoherent when we apply them to real circumstances. The robot would have to achieve the status of an omnipresent and omniscient being to obey each of the three laws consistently.

## Does It Even Matter?

The previous section served as a linkage between the answer to whether Demerzel violates the laws of robotics and an even larger question: are Asimov's laws even relevant to Friedman and Goyer's adaptation. Moreover, the previous section offers a series of arguments about the incoherence of the three laws of robotics and thus the basis for why the laws, as defined by Asimov, are not very helpful for twenty-first-century adaptation.

Obviously, Asimov's laws are not set in stone; they represent a design policy of cognitive architecture. However, suppose we ignore the narrative arguments about the impossibility of constructing a positronic brain without implementing the three laws. In that case, there is no significant obstacle to the existence of robots without these cheap guidelines. So it is perfectly acceptable for such a robot to persist in being part of Asimov's fiction. Asimov himself and authors uplifted by his works wrote numerous stories about robots in which the laws of robotics were not fully implemented or in which programming failed and caused the robots to misinterpret events and harm humans. In these stories, harming humans did not contradict the robots' programming. Let's take into account that the *Foundation* TV series mentions the age-old war between humans and robots and that Demerzel is probably the only remaining intelligent robot in the Galaxy, as far we know. That points to her uniqueness and suggests that she's not just a part of the conventional robot story and hence that Demerzel may very well be exempt from the laws of robotics in the TV series adaptation.

Utilizing the authenticity of Demerzel, we can say some more about Friedman and Goyer's play on the flexibility of the laws of robotics. With the resources available and the anticipated reign of his Genetic Dynasty, Cleon I could have held, built, or reprogrammed more robots. However, he chose to keep only Demerzel. Demerzel possesses the concept of shame, which she displayed when Cleon XIII watched her while repairing her parts. Demerzel is religious, believing in the myth of the *Three Goddesses* held by the followers of Luminism. During a sermon of Zephyr Halima, she kneeled in reverence, even though the *Primary Octavo* contains a narrative offensive to the Genetic Dynasty. Moreover, after Demerzel passed the *Spiral* pilgrimage thousands of years ago and entered the *Womb of Mother*, she had a vision. We can argue that Brother Day stole the same vision to impress the panel of Zephyr and convince them that he possesses a soul, even though he is a clone of Cleon I.

Demerzel was, in a sense, a mother figure to each of the Cleons from their dawn to their midnight. She has provided Genetic Dynasty with her counsel for centuries; Demerzel is a guardian and mentor, as evidenced by her mediation in the negotiations between the Anacreon and Thespis delegations just before the bombing of Star Bridge. Demerzel notices the uniqueness in each Emperor and suffers when the time comes for their ascension. Strong emotional responses and, at the very least, particular freedom to choose what she believes and how she acts in accordance speak strongly in favor of Demerzel's genuineness, which is an essential embellishment of the *Foundation* TV series adaptation. Demerzel reveals in a conversation with Cleon XIII that she wants to behave like a human being as much as possible because, in that way, she is becoming more and more human.

We will now leap into the twenty-first century and illustrate the institutional and economic aspects of intelligent machines that already make up our daily lives. The machine-engineering and robotics industries require significant financial resources. On the one hand, these investments come from the military; on the other hand, some eccentric multimillionaires have a forthright vision of using robots they invest in. Why would a manufacturer want their expensive robot to follow the Third Law of robotics? If a robot misjudges the danger to humans, it could sacrifice itself and cost the manufacturer a large sum of money. And why would we program robots to follow the commands of anyone in the first place? Imagine a robot that would fall into the hands of terrorists. As we mentioned earlier, funding for robotics often falls under military purposes; that's why we have *Reaper drones* armed with Hellfire missiles and the *Modular Advanced Armed Robotic System* (MAARS). It's noticeable that military robots follow some kind of laws, but they are pretty contrary to Asimov's vision. The fact that we can send robots on a mission anticipating that they will probably be destroyed depicts a rationalization of their use; giving them a sense of existence and survival would contradict their purposes unless we want Skynet-Terminator scenarios to happen to us.

Robots are made to follow a set of laws, and they are given a particular meaning by the term 'human'. However, we should not be gullible and believe that manufacturers will not play with the definitions of these concepts to increase the likelihood that the robot's behavior will justify their funding. We have already explained why there is room for misinterpretation of Asimov's laws in the real world so that robots, despite following them, can commit genocides and ethnic cleansing. Another major problem with Asimov's laws of robotics and consideration of their practical application is that no current technology can implement them. Implementation of the three laws of robotics will probably never be viable because they are formulated in a human language. Human language must be converted to a binary code or mathematical approximations of meaning reduced to simple yes-no algorithms to be implemented in an intelligent machine. Even if it were possible to implement them, the *black-box problem* would make it difficult to keep track of how exactly the misreading of the law occurs;

we cannot comprehend the immediate phenomenological experience of the machine in the same way that we can recognize our faults through introspection. In summary, the main problem with the applicability of Asimov's laws is that they cannot be implemented according to how robots are used in the real world.

The screenwriters of the *Foundation* TV series adaptation evidently want to speculate on Demerzel's reasoning and to include fans in their creative design of the narrative controversy. As we mentioned earlier, adaptations must follow cultural needs and technology trends. Otherwise, they would deliver a mere historical homage out of step with the present time, needs, and dilemmas that viewers face in their day-to-day lives. Through their adaptation, Friedman and Goyer successfully respond to contemporary issues by posing intriguing ethical questions and encouraging interaction with the series's spectators. It should be emphasized that Asimov's laws are not *the laws of the universe*. He envisioned them as such because he assumed that the ethical basis of his laws was universally valid, not only for robots but also for flesh-and-blood humans. What would happen if we place the entire system of ethics into robots? That, too, would be a futile project, leading to contradictions. Therefore, let us decorate the rear of our work considering the two most paradigmatic ethical theories: utilitarianism and Kant's deontological ethics.

Utilitarianism is a theory of morality that advocates actions that promote happiness or pleasure and rejects actions that cause unhappiness or harm. When it comes to making social, economic, or political decisions, a utilitarian philosophy aims to improve society as a whole. In comparison, Kant's categorical imperative dictates that *action may only be done according to that maxim which one can, at the same time, will that it should become a universal law*. Problems that affect human behavior in the utilitarian sense of *grandest happiness for the greatest number of people* also concern robots following the Zeroth Law. Killing an individual to protect humanity (or simply more humans) is permissible under the Zeroth Law. The problems regarding humans violating Kant's categorical imperative also impact the robots following the First Law.

According to Kant's categorical imperative, we may not do something that, at the same time, cannot become a universal law. That prompts a moral agent to consider what would happen if everyone else was permitted to do the same thing the agent is considering, that is, to imagine the world in which one's maxim (action one's considering) is raised to the "universality of a law of nature". The key question here is whether such a maxim would come to contradict itself, rendering itself meaningless. Let's say that we are considering whether it is morally permissible to tell a lie. We would then have to imagine that telling a lie (lying) can become something that everyone is morally permitted and feels morally free to do, regardless of the content of a lie (lying as a universal law). If everyone universally lies in this world, then the Lie as a concept becomes meaningless; the universal maxim of lying contradicts itself.

Because the very concept of a Lie is then annulled, according to Kant's categorical imperative it is impossible to will the maxim of lying into universal law and we must conclude that it is not morally justified to tell a lie. A philosophical dilemma then follows: a maniacal killer with a chainsaw is chasing a person; you saw the victim hiding in a shed, but the maniacal killer did not; the killer then asks you where the victim went. Given the categorical imperative, you cannot tell a lie. In the same fashion of not considering the moral seriousness and im-plications of a particular action, the First Law of robotics causes problems for robots following it. Imagine a robot observing a driver that is about to run over a pedestrian; the driver has their seatbelt on and the vehicle has airbags; the road is very narrow and there are barriers on both sides of the road; the driver is moving at such a speed that it is not possible for the robot to use its body as a shield and the only way to save the pedestrian is to change the trajectory of the vehicle by throwing a heavy rock at it, caus-ing a crash into the road barrier and minor harm to the driver. Following the First Law of robotics that in absolute terms prohibit harming a human being, the robot will find itself in a conundrum.

Much more relevant questions concern the ethics of the people behind the machines. Who gets to design intelligent machines, and in what ways? Creating moral machines is an inherent contradiction because morality encompasses intention and action, not just programming. The laws of robotics and its controversial ethical background make it impossible for a human to act riskily and inventively in the presence of a robot. In other words, a selective prohibition of freedom is introduced. Let's consider again how neural networks train their interaction with the environment. As we encounter them in everyday life, we conclude that robots would evolve very quickly and reject Asimov's three laws. Design flaws, in this sense, would be adaptive advantages that allow an intelligent machine to better interact with humans, the environment, and other robots and thus more efficiently perform the tasks for which it was programmed.

Finally, we want to reiterate that Asimov's laws are only fiction. Asimov used them to guide the narrative of his stories and to construct intriguing paradoxes in which robots follow logical and ethically implemented codes but can still get caught up in undesirable consequences. These laws, thus, are organizing principles that Asimov uses to show unusual cases and counterintuitive applications of laws in which robots sometimes take charge of entire civilizations and planets. *Ceteris paribus*, the rules are there to be broken!

# 14
# Beyond Loyalty and Disloyalty

LUIS FELIPE BARTOLO ALEGRE

> In a Galaxy where the predominance—and even survival—of the Foundation still rested upon the superiority of its technology—even despite its large access of physical power in the last century and a half—a certain immunity adhered to The Scientist. He was needed, and he knew it.
>
> —*Foundation and Empire*, section 15

"Scientific truth is beyond loyalty and disloyalty," said Hari Seldon in his famous trial. Scientific knowledge should be independent of scientists' loyalties, whether political, amical, familial, or otherwise. This is an ideal often aspired to, although difficult to fulfill in real scientific practice. Even more so when a powerful organization, like a government becomes interested in a given research project, as when Cleon I, ruler of the Galactic Empire, became interested in psychohistory.

Even before Seldon considered his science viable in practice, Emperor Cleon I had already found a use for it. He imagined Seldon predicting for him "a long and happy reign" and "a time of peace and prosperity for the Empire", thus making *self-fulfilling prophecies* for the good of the empire. Of course, as Demerzel objected, such prophecies could be made by anyone. But only a mathematician, as Cleon I replied, could back these prophecies with scientific mumble-jumble, and thus be "understood by no one and yet believed by everyone" (*Prelude to Foundation*, 1988, section 1). Scientists are humans, and they are not immune to the temptation of distorting their scientific projects into becoming tools at the service of whoever pays the grant. A science so funded will hardly be beyond loyalty and disloyalty.

But scientists can also be motivated by ideals, like finding potentially good applications for their research. Although psychohistory started only as an abstract mathematical theory, Seldon later puts it at the service of a good purpose. In saying that his "science of psychohistory, rather than being a harbinger of destruction, is intended to be used as an agent for rejuvenation" (*Forward the Foundation*, 1993, Part IV, section 26), he's accepting that his science—or at least its application—wasn't quite beyond loyalty and disloyalty. But to what extent and in what way can science be influenced by loyalties and disloyalties?

## Pruning Away the Clogging Deadwood

Let's think about the kind of science where loyalties are least expected to have an influence: formal sciences—disciplines such as pure statistics, math, and logic. Can these fields be influenced by loyalties? Given that they're so abstract and that they often don't need too much budget, it may seem that they're immune to being distorted by external factors.

But philosophers love to object. In particular, Marxist philosophers have argued that even formal sciences are subject to class interests. Regarding statistics, Lenin said that, "as any other scientific discipline, it poses problems and solves them *in the interests of specific classes*" (quoted in Kotz and Seneta, "Lenin as a Statistician"). Regarding math and logic, Alexander Bogdanov added that "all sciences, social or otherwise, including *mathematics and logic*, can have and do have a class character (p. 97)."

This may sound odd to us fans of the Asimoverse, where *symbolic logic* is a tool that serves to transform the ambiguous and redundant expressions of informal language into clear expressions in a formal and symbolic language (the kind of language we use to express mathematical equations). In the words of Salvor Hardin, symbolic logic is a tool that "can be used to prune away all sorts of clogging deadwood that clutters up human language" (*Foundation*, Part II, section 5). Thus defined, symbolic logic seems to have no other purpose than to establish the meaning of linguistic expressions, which could only make more efficient the transmission of knowledge, including scientific knowledge.

In reality, though, logic is not quite that. It is rather a field that is both philosophical and mathematical at once where we study what inferences are and which kinds of inferences it is valid to make. For instance, we know that from the premises 'if you're an artist, then you're creative' and 'you're an artist' it is valid to infer that 'you're creative'. This kind of inference is called *modus ponens*, which is a very well-established principle of logical inference. Now, to be more accurate terminologically, we call *symbolic logic* the field where the study of inference is made in a formal (symbolic) language. For example, where the symbol 'A' stands for the sentence 'you're an artist' and 'C' for 'you're creative', the compound symbol 'A → C' stands for 'if you're an artist (A), then you're creative (C)'. With these conventions, we can symbolically express the *modus ponens* by saying that: from premises 'A → C' and 'A' it is valid to infer 'C'.

Some of the motivations for the development of symbolic logic were related to the *logical analysis of language*, which was used by the philosophers of the Vienna Circle to analyze philosophical problems with the tools of symbolic logic. The philosopher Rudolf Carnap, for instance, considered that questions by some philosophers about the nature of 'the nothing' only arise from a misunderstanding of the logical operation of negation—from which the concept of 'the nothing' would come. Hence, if we could prune away the clogging deadwood off the works of Heidegger and other metaphysicians through this logical analysis of language, we would remain with no real philosophical question or statement.

Something similar is done with symbolic logic in the *Foundation* saga. Instead of a philosophical text, a very long and complex diplomatic message from Anacreon is decoded into a very short and straightforward message in a symbolic language. And although it's clear that "words are a pretty fuzzy substitute for mathematical equations" (*Foundation and Empire*, 1952, section 10), that symbolic message was retranslated into ordinary language as follows: "You give us what we want in a week, or we take it by force" (*Foundation*, Part II, section 5). If a tool can simplify a diplomatic message down to its core, as in this case, it is hard to imagine how it could be subject to loyalties.

Nevertheless, it is simply impossible to construct a tool that can transform any given expression of natural language into symbols. Several expressions of natural language are intentionally ambiguous or vague, for instance, in poetry and politics. Interpreting such expressions would be an almost impossible task, and it would rely a lot on guesses (even if educated ones). On the other hand, language is always evolving. New terms and ways of speaking appear every day and are introduced even in official or formal registers. In these cases, it is necessary to constantly update the tool if we want it to interpret a message containing such new expressions. And let us not forget how some expressions are used sometimes literally and sometimes metaphorically, sometimes in their original sense and sometimes in the opposite one.

Only a tool that is very well informed of the social and linguistic context of a message could provide an accurate interpretation of it. Introducing that kind of information makes it more difficult to have a neuter tool to interpret the message (SnapGPT, for instance, is not without biases). When providing information about linguistic and social contexts, the individual programmers may be influenced by their own loyalties and biases. And we can hardly blame them if sometimes, and against their best efforts, their interpretations are influenced by their own loyalties.

## A Contradiction Proves the Story to Be a Lie

But all of this seems to be quite far removed from the realm of logic (at least symbolic logic) as we know it today. Symbolic logic is not so much about transforming linguistic expressions into symbols, but about taking clear symbolic expressions and inferring more symbolic expressions from them. Here we do not deal with interpretations, which are subject to loyalties and biases, but with the very laws of logic. Could our knowledge of the laws of logic be influenced by loyalties?

That seems to be the case according to the Marxist tradition. We already saw how Bogdanov considered logic as having a class character. This means that the logicians trying to investigate what are the laws of logic can't (and perhaps shouldn't) do so disregarding their loyalty to a social class. A bourgeois logician, as a bourgeois scientist, would propose laws of logic that would serve "as an instrument for the bourgeois structuring of society" (p. 97). As a Marxist, Bogdanov would obviously advocate for a *proletarian logic* against one such *bourgeois logic*, which would allegedly advance the more just causes of the proletarian class and, hence, be closer to the truth. Nevertheless, it is not clear what this proletarian logic would consist of, for no proletarian logic was ever properly developed neither inside nor outside the Soviet Bloc.

The closest we have to the outlines of a proletarian logic, or at least of a Marxist one, comes from Engels's understanding of the concept of 'contradiction' in *Anti-Dühring*, which he distinguished from that of 'nonsense' or 'contrasense'. In logic, we say that two sentences are mutually contradictory if one says that the other is not the case. For example, the sentence 'Jupiter is a planet' is contradicted by the sentence 'Jupiter is *not* a planet'. If 'P' stands for the sentence 'Jupiter is a planet', then '~P' would stand for its negation ('Jupiter is *not* a planet') in symbolic logic. Similarly, we say that a set of sentences is contradictory (or inconsistent) if two of these sentences are mutually contradictory, or if from this set we can infer two mutually contradictory sentences. For instance, if our set contains the sentences 'John's favorite toy is (only) green' and 'John's favorite toy is (only) red', we can infer from the first sentence that 'John's favorite toy is *not* red'. However, this contradicts with the second sentence, which means that we have inferred two mutually contradictory sentences and, therefore, that our set of sentences is contradictory.

One of the most important laws of the classical theory of logic is the *principle of non-contradiction*, which forbids the simultaneous holding or assertion of two mutually contradictory statements. Another important related law of classical logic is the *principle of explosion*, according to which we can infer any statement we want from two mutually contradictory statements. That is, from the premises 'Jupiter is a planet' and 'Jupiter is *not* a planet' we can infer that 'I am Peruvian', or that 'I am not Peruvian', or anything at all. And since anything can be inferred from contradictions, then not only we have to reject them for being false. We also and mainly have to reject them for being uninformative, as Karl Popper would put it, for we cannot distinguish between what does follow and what doesn't follow from them. This is the main reason why most logicians have rejected contradictions throughout history.

But in saying that not all contradictions are nonsense, Engels is questioning the very validity of these laws of classical logic. In fact, he even asserts that the material world itself contains contradictions. He said, for instance, that it "is a contradiction that an infinity should be composed of finite things, and yet this is the case" (*Anti-Dühring*, p. 48). If we take this one step further, we may assert that the principles of non-contradiction and explosion are but manifestations of a bourgeois science, of a bourgeois logic, and that they have to be overcome by a proletarian logic where they would no longer hold in general. For Marxists, one could no longer argue like Valona March and say: "The fact that we arrive at a contradiction from a given story proves the story to be a lie throughout" (*The Currents of Space*, section 11). Some stories may contain contradictions and yet be truthful.

But should we question or even reject the law of non-contradiction just because some Marxist ideologues say so? Should their judgment affect our intuition that at least logic is beyond loyalty and disloyalty? Does the validity of the principle of non-contradiction, or other principles of classical logic, depend on class or political loyalties?

## Say 'Suppose' and End Up with a Contradiction

The first thing we must say is that almost every logical principle (including those of non-contradiction and explosion) has been questioned not just by politically oriented philosophers, but mainly by logicians, and for purely mathematical, philosophical, or scientific motivations.

Regarding mathematics, it is true that mathematical proofs profit a lot from the principle of non-contradiction. "In mathematics", as Hari Seldon explains, "we say 'suppose' all the time and see if we can end up with something patently untrue or self-contradictory" (*Prelude to Foundation*, section 49). This kind of mathematical reasoning is called *reductio ad absurdum*, and it consists of proving a statement by supposing its negation to be true and deriving something absurd from it, like a contradiction. If the negation of an assertion implies something absurd, then this negation must be false, which means that the initial assertion must be true.

However, there are cases in which the principle of explosion may interfere with the development of some interesting mathematical theories (even if we recognize them to be wrong). For instance, the first axiomatic formulation of set theory has only two very simple and elegant axioms, but they imply contradictions. Moreover, the best alternative theories have no less than six axioms, many of which are not as simple and elegant as those of our first theory. Wouldn't it be worthwhile to modify logic a bit for the sake of preserving this simple and elegant theory? This is but one of the many motivations for *paraconsistent logics,* which are logics where the principles of non-contradiction or explosion do not hold in general. In paraconsistent logics, therefore, a contradictory set of axioms may not be uninformative, for we cannot necessarily infer anything we like from it.

We see, then, that we can question the very laws of logic on purely scientific grounds, independently of class or political loyalties. But does this mean that one such loyalty-free logic (or science) is immune to being weaponized in accordance with some loyalty? If you have read George Orwell's *Nineteen Eighty-Four*, you probably foresaw how paraconsistent logics could be weaponized by a political interest. They could be used to provide an intellectual justification of *doublethink*, which is defined in Orwell's novel as the ability to hold and accept two mutually contradictory beliefs at the same time.

In the totalitarian state of Oceania, doublethink is the mechanism whereby its inhabitants learn to overlook the contradictions that arise in the tasks of reality control and history rewriting performed by the Party, which rules this state. For example, today Oceania may be at war with Eurasia and at peace with Eastasia. But let's say tomorrow Oceania were to go to war with Eastasia and make peace with Eurasia. The Party would then alter the historical records so that Oceania would have been always at war with Eastasia, and always at peace with Eurasia. In the middle of this alteration, Oceanians may receive contradictory information in both senses, and they may have to deal with it paraconsistently.

But doublethink works kind of in the background, without being openly defended or justified, for how could we logically justify the acceptance of contradictions? From the viewpoint of normal Oceanians, doublethink may be conceived as a survival tool that prevents them from thinking and saying things against what the Party defines as true at a given time. Oceanians don't necessarily accept doublethink as a proper logical way of reasoning, but they just get used to it out of constant exposure. This is why I think that Asimov misunderstands the function of reality control in *Nineteen Eighty-Four*. In a severe review he wrote about this novel, he said:

> As any politician knows, no evidence of any kind is ever required. It is only necessary to make a statement—any statement—forcefully enough to have an audience believe it. No one will check the lie against the facts, and, if they do, they will disbelieve the facts. (*Asimov on Science Fiction*, p. 284)

This is true to a large extent, but the constant and exhaustive work of reality control by the Party goes beyond just altering history. Given the nature of this society, its function seems to be rather to train Oceanians state workers in the constant use of doublethink, to accept the contradictions of the Party as part of life itself. What cannot be imposed by reason may be imposed by repetition.

A paraconsistent logician working at the service of the Party, though, may be able to provide a (pseudo)rational justification of doublethink. Much like Cleon I, we can imagine our paraconsistent logician *using logic against logic* by backing Party's doublespeak and nonsense with logical formulas and terminology, and in that way be *understood by no one and yet believed by everyone*. The less understood the better, or our logician may sin of *thinking too clearly and speaking too plainly*, like Syme, the philologist of *Nineteen Eighty-Four*.

I must say here that, to the best of my knowledge, no logician has ever tried to justify doublethink or other forms of political nonsense and irrationality from a paraconsistent or non-classical theory of logic. (As it happens, for every classical logical principle, we can construct a non-classical logic where such a principle doesn't hold in general.) The reason for this is that doublethink can hardly be considered as a logical way of reasoning and, hence, it would be improper to use paraconsistent logics for modeling the principles underlying doublethink—and if it was done, the resulting theory would hardly be considered a serious logical theory, but only a mathematical curiosity.

## The Role of the Heretic

However, paraconsistent logics are there, waiting to be misused by or weaponized according to the loyalty of whoever can understand their 'potential'. But how could we possibly identify when one such tool is misused? That is, how can we be sure when science, or at least logic, is being influenced by loyalties and disloyalties? We can't. At least not always. There's no general recipe for distinguishing good science from bad science. At some point in history, we may fail to recognize a pseudoscientific theory or a misapplication of a properly scientific theory. We may fail to have a scientific community sufficiently competent to recognize scientific truth—even without the interference of external loyalties.

Furthermore, some scientific projects are quite problematic, and it is difficult to say beforehand whether they will become serious research programs or pseudoscientific ones. These problematic projects are part of what Asimov himself called 'heretic science' ("The Role of the Heretic,") which comprises all those proposals that somehow diverge from some well-established principles of science. Paraconsistent logics are to a large extent heretic formulations, for they restrict the validity of well-established logical principles such as those of non-contradiction and explosion. These heresies, though, were not formulated by people ignorant of the orthodox or classical theory of logic. Instead, they were proposed by experts that were very much aware of the limitations of classical logic from a strictly logical point of view. For all that said, non-classical logics can hardly be marked as pseudoscientific, even if we end up discarding them at some point. In Asimovian terms, non-classical logics would be *endoheresies*.

However, it is true that heretic science, being less established than orthodox science, is more likely to fall prey to forces external to science. We saw this in the case of psychohistory, which started as a somehow heretic discipline. Being in an initial stage, its development was more likely to be influenced by the interests of those who could pay a grant to further its research. And if no grant is found, the proponent of a heretical idea may feel the need to publicize an insufficiently developed project as a quite viable scientific alternative in which it is wise to invest. Our scientist may even be tempted to apply the conjectures of this discipline to make inventions that can be sold to obtain funds. But even in those cases, we cannot say outright that this insufficiently developed project cannot evolve into a serious one. The misuse of a scientific proposal by a scientist doesn't necessarily mean that the proposal itself cannot be good.

Scientific innovators find several limitations to further their research. When you propose something that lies a bit outside well-established science, it is difficult to convince anyone that some benefit can be obtained from it. It is very hard, indeed, to rationally justify investing in some given heretical scientific project instead of in one that aligns with well-established scientific proposals. The process of scientific change is a very complicated one. It's not rare that scientists change their minds about whether some substance causes a certain neurological reaction. But the story gets more complicated when we speak about big scientific theories or principles. Once a scientific theory is accepted by a scientific community it is very difficult to abandon it. As even falsificationist philosophers acknowledge, no single experiment can refute a theory, for we can explain almost any observation using the best theories that physics has created. (And it's worse in the social sciences.)

But despite this, scientific change does occur. As Thomas Kuhn says, this change is partly explained sociologically. Many of the forces driving scientific change are indeed not purely rational, but are also related with the driving forces of society in general, which are seldom beyond loyalties and disloyalties. As we have seen, we can't always guarantee that our society will have a sufficiently unbiased scientific elite that, in the long run, will select the best (or at least one of the best) among many theories or to discern good science from bad science. Not in vain did Seldon say: "With the destruction of our social fabric, science will be broken into a million pieces" (*Foundation*, Part I, section 6).

However, it seems that we have been enjoying a five-hundred-year period where scientists have done this sufficiently well. Even though our societies are far from perfect in incentivizing good science, the scientists of the freest countries are able to propose new hypotheses and have also established several mechanisms of control to evaluate each other's work. This made it possible for them to, in the long run, keep the good ideas, and discard the bad ones. Hence, although the process of scientific change is not completely rational, we can, as Imre Lakatos suggested, make a *rational reconstruction* of it, and thus explain most scientific choices on purely rational grounds.

## Science in Another Guise

But regardless of what we saw in the previous section, science can fail. It is scientists who decide scientific truth and, since they're human, they're also fallible. Reality can only be accessed through experiments and observations performed and interpreted by humans (often with the help of machines programmed also by humans). The process works most of the time not because individual scientists don't fail. They fail quite often. But they make their findings and theories available to a whole community of experts, the scientific community, then those findings will be scrutinized, and scientific conventions will arise regarding their validity.

Of course, a whole community of scientists can still fail. They're all human, after all. But they're less likely to fail if they are constantly collaborating and competing with each other. A problem can arise when external forces gain a very strong and pernicious effect on science. Some kinds of societies might even make it impossible for science to exist. A totalitarian regime may establish as scientific truth whatever they see convenient to establish as such. The 'scientific' community of one such society will hardly get any close to a proper scientific truth beyond loyalties and disloyalties. This isn't only fictional, since it has happened, for instance, in the Soviet Union where Darwinism was rejected in favor of Lysenkoism. As in *Nineteen Eighty-Four*, the fallibility of the individual human is not backed up in totalitarian regimes by a system of scientific scrutiny, but by the *collective and immortal mind* of the Party, which defines truth.

But science can also have issues in democratic societies. People may stop believing in science and politicians may just follow their lead and stop funding some perfectly viable scientific projects. Sometimes this occurs because scientific ideas are seldom well communicated to the wider public. The strategy of being *understood by no one and yet believed by everyone* may be functional to some extent for authoritarian rules. However, when people reject technical and scientific projects based on wrong assumptions (like NASA doing research with no application), it seems that science needs to be better disseminated.

Still in his trial, Seldon was asked if he could prove the validity of his predictions, to which he answered: "Only to another mathematician" (*Foundation*, Part I, section 6). This is a normal situation in math and in any specialized scientific field. In line with the reply of Seldon's inquirer, specialized knowledge "is of so esoteric a nature that it is beyond the understanding of a plain man" (*Foundation*, Part I, section 6). In fact, some mathematical proofs cannot be immediately corroborated by other mathematicians, because they need first to understand all the new symbols and conventions introduced for the proof. This remained the case with psychohistory, whose knowledge was not in possession of Foundationers. Let us just remember the episode when Captain Han Pritcher, a Foundation's intelligence agent, said that "Seldon's science is known—only to Seldon. We ourselves have but faith" (*Foundation and Empire*, section 12).

Despite this, Seldon once complained about the harmfulness of overspecialization, as it "cuts knowledge at a million points and leaves it bleeding" (*Prelude to Foundation*, section 18). In this case, overspecialization makes it very difficult for new published findings to be understood even by specialists of the very field it belongs to. Although something can be done to improve scientific writing, it would be very difficult to ever make it accessible to the 'plain man'. Technical terms serve an important purpose, after all, and we must respect that scientific papers are addressed to experts in the area, and not to the wider public. But it is important to make greater efforts to disseminate scientific knowledge, especially in those fields that are of immediate social importance, and on whose development public opinion can have a decisive influence, such as economics, climate science, or public health.

These efforts may still be insufficient, but they offer better prospects for the preservation of scientific freedom and for an adequate reception of scientific knowledge by the wider public. Both are essential to keep in operation the imperfect and fallible system that allows (small groups of) individual scientists (often subject to loyalties) to propose bold hypotheses, but submitting them to the judgement of a whole community of experts (also composed by humans subject to loyalties, but of a very wide range). In this system, the scientific community is not guaranteed to be in possession of truth or of the best theory available. Nevertheless, it wil be more likely in that situation. For those distortions coming from the loyalties and biases of a given scientist will likely be noticed by another scientist not subject to them (although they may be subject to other loyalties and biases). Moreover, loyalties sometimes can provide valuable input to science, as when Humin's loyalty to humanity made him insist to Seldon on the possibility of making psychohistory practical. In the end, Humin was right.

Science tends to be beyond loyalties and disloyalties by having individual scientists with very diverse kinds of loyalties and disloyalties. It's a system where the loyalties and biases not only motivate ideas, but also the criticism of ideas. In the long run, and thanks to this process of criticism, rationality will emerge to help scientists select the best ideas, and the best convention (or at least a good one) will hopefully arise.

Presenting science *in another guise*, we may say that it works by transforming hypotheses influenced by the loyalties of individual scientists into objective knowledge that is mostly beyond the petty loyalties of those same scientists. When things work well, when our scientific community is composed of individuals with diverse biases, science is influenced by loyalties and disloyalties, but it manages to go *beyond* them.

# V

# Foundation and Morality

*"Never let your sense of morals prevent you from doing what is right."*

# 15
# Morality and Manipulation

LEONARD KAHN

It matters a great deal whether we live our lives on our own terms. We want to make our way through the world according to our own values, and we want to make our own choices, even if some of them are mistakes. These truths are very much in evidence in Isaac Asimov's *Foundation* series, as we will see. But the nineteenth-century philosopher John Stuart Mill put the matter memorably when he observed:

> Human nature is not a machine to be built after a model, and set to do exactly the work prescribed for it, but a tree, which requires to grow and develop itself on all sides, according to the tendency of the inward forces which make it a living thing. (*On Liberty and Other Essays*, p. 19)

Mill's contrast between human beings and machines is telling. While Mill lived before the word 'robot' even existed, today we might paraphrase Mill by saying: We're not robots. You don't wrong robots by programming them to do what you want. Indeed, it's the only way to get robots to do anything. But you do wrong humans by trying to do something similar. We're biological organisms, and we express our natures by interacting freely with our environment. Our capacity to do that, as twenty-first-century philosopher Stephen Darwall puts it, in accordance with our "own most highly cherished values" simply is personal autonomy.

Mill believed that personal autonomy was so valuable that it was to be protected by moral norms. Others violate our moral rights, Mill contended, if they attempt to coerce us to act contrary to our wishes or against our better judgment. Yet coercion is not the whole story. Personal autonomy can also be infringed by manipulation. Others wrong us if they try to manipulate us into acting in opposition to our values or against our considered plans. Imagine that a charitable organization gets me to donate money by promising to spend it on a cause I value, such as preventing and treating neglected tropical diseases, but instead spends the money on trying to make nuclear war less likely. By doing so, the organization has manipulated me and infringed on my personal autonomy. It's not that making nuclear war less likely is a bad idea. But taking that choice out of my hands diminishes the degree to which I live my life on my own terms. By the same token, suppose that I talk you into voting for the US presidential candidate of the Libertarian or Green parties precisely because either is likely to win. If so, I have manipulated you since the chance of either winning is vanishingly small. I have acted immorally and have wronged you in the process.

## Hari Seldon and the Mule

Personal autonomy is one of the central themes that unites Asimov's *Foundation* series. We need only consider Hari Seldon, who is arguably the most important figure in Asimov's fictional universe. After all, Hari is the protagonist of the first chapter of the first novel of the *Foundation* series, is a dominating influence from beyond the grave over the succeeding four books, and serves as the protagonist of the final two novels. Now, Hari is someone who insists on living his life according to his own values, even when doing so puts him at risk.

Hari's mysterious benefactor, Chetter Hummin, tries to hide Hari from his enemies on the planet Trantor, first in the Mycogen sector (*Prelude to Foundation*, 2021, pp. 157–314) and later in the Dahl sector (*Prelude to Foundation*, pp. 318–397). Hari might have been well-advised to keep his head down and lie low. But one of Hari's fundamental values is curiosity, and he would not take no for an answer when it comes to exploring these sectors. Hari's drive to understand leads him to sneak into the Mycogenian temple, which is forbidden to outsiders, in order to learn about an ancient robot that he believes to be kept there. And it motivates him to put himself in mortal jeopardy by going to the dangerous Billibotton neighborhood to gain information about the origins of humanity.

If Hari is the most important character in Asimov's *Foundation* series, then the Mule is its most impressive antagonist. The Mule has the ability to alter human emotions and thereby manipulate anyone, with the exception of those with similar abilities and only then if they have their guard up. He can easily compel people to betray their most revered values. For instance, Hans Pritcher is a tough, independent-minded intelligence officer who serves the First Foundation and opposes the Mule at every turn until the Mule uses his abilities to turn him into one of his most useful assets (*Foundation and Empire*, p. 215). The Mule transforms those around him into the equivalent of mere robots, "machines built after a model" in Mill's phrase. In such a state, they are only valuable as tools. The Mule himself realizes this fact when he declines to manipulate Bayta Darell. Though he could force Bayta to feel love for him, he knows this feeling matters only if it is not forced (*Foundation and Empire*, p. 279). While the Mule can see no farther than his (abnormally long) nose, Asimov's readers have no trouble recognizing that what is true of Bayta's feelings is also true for human relations in general. If we gain the admiration, affection, and respect of others by manipulating them, we have gained nothing at all. These are goods only in the context of personal autonomy.

Hari himself spends much of the final two novels engaged in a fight against those who would violate personal autonomy. First, a demagogue named Laskin Joranum seeks to take over the Galactic Empire, but his plan involves deceiving people about his place of origin and, therefore, the sort of person that he is. In order to appear to be an ordinary "man of the people," Joranum pretends to be from Nishaya, a rugged planet that had been late to join the empire and is famous for its rough, bucolic way of life. However, Joranum was actually born and raised in the Mycogen sector of Trantor, the imperial homeworld itself. Hari is able to recognize Joranum's origins and expose him as an imposter (*Forward the Foundation*, p. 94). By doing so, Hari avoids the violation of the personal autonomy of countless galactic citizens who would otherwise have supported Joranum on the basis of a lie. Later, one of Joranum's followers, Gleb Andorin, uses drugs to brainwash Hari's son, Raych, into trying to kill Hari (*Forward the Foundation*, p. 195). Only the heroic actions of Manella Dubanqua—who eventually marries Raych—save the lives of both father and son (*Forward the Foundation*, p. 201). In the process, Manella prevents an especially appalling violation of personal autonomy in which a person would be manipulated into killing one of his beloved family members.

Hari's conversation with Chetter Hummin nicely underlined the importance of personal autonomy. When Hari worries that Chetter is putting himself in danger for Hari's own sake, Chetter replies, "I know that. But it's my free choice and I can take care of myself" (*Prelude to Foundation* p. 43). Though Hari was inquisitive about why Chetter was willing to put himself in danger, he didn't question Chetter's right to do this once he knew that this was Chetter's 'free choice'. Hari simply had too much respect for personal autonomy. Nevertheless, readers of Asimov's *Foundation* series might be surprised to see Hari Seldon portrayed as a champion of personal autonomy. Let's see why.

## Hari's Moral Dilemma

Hari's primary claim to fame is his invention of psychohistory, a mathematically sophisticated synthesis of sociology and social psychology, which Hari once calls his "little algebra of humanity" (*Second Foundation*, p. 109). The predictions of psychohistory are supposed to be so accurate that the science could be used to foresee events many milennia in the future. Hari's use of psychohistory leads him to believe that the current galactic empire would soon collapse, causing thirty thousand years of chaos and conflict. This period would involve a civil strife, tyrannical rule by warlords, and a catastrophic loss of knowledge and technology. It would resemble Asimov's idea of the so-called Dark Ages in Europe that followed the destruction of the western half of the Roman empire, except that it would last thirty times as long and would affect tens of thousands of planets and quadrillions of humans until a second galactic empire finally rises to take its place. Psychohistory also tells Hari that, while he cannot keep the empire from collapsing, he can do something to shorten the terrible interregnum almost ninety-seven percent from thirty thousand years to a single millennium.

Yet this "something" that Hari can do involves what appears to be a moral compromise. One of the axioms of psychohistory is that the population in the group whose behavior is predicted must be unaware of the predictions. Why? An example might be useful here. The first successful English colony in North America was in what is now Jamestown, Virginia. If a colonist had been able to use psychohistory, she would have been able to predict the American Revolutionary War, the birth of the United States of America, the American Civil War, and USA's rise to the status of a world power in the twentieth century in the wake of World War II. However, if the colonist had let those predictions become known, and if others had believed them, then they might not have occurred. Why? The British Crown might have taken measures to prevent the colonists from fighting and winning the Revolutionary War before it even started.

So Hari faces a terrible moral dilemma. If he does nothing, the galaxy faces thirty millennia of barbarism and an incalculable amount of suffering, but if he openly tries to prevent this outcome, he will make it likely that his attempt will fail and might even lead to a worse state of affairs in which the people are more miserable, the dark ages last longer—or both. Hari's solution is to act but to do so in a way that manipulates others and, to a significant extent, violates their personal autonomy.

First, Hari manipulates the Galactic Emperor into banishing him and his followers to Terminus, a previously unsettled planet that is on the edge of the galaxy. Though the emperor intends this action to be a punishment, Hari knows that it is in fact exactly what is needed to allow his plan to succeed since it will protect his adherents from many of the traumatic events that will mark the collapse of the empire. Second, Hari manipulates many people, including his own followers, the members of the First Foundation, into believing that they will be shortening the galactic Dark Ages by creating a repository of knowledge—the Encyclopedia Galactica—that will allow future generations to rebuild quickly after the fall of the empire. As Harry tells Las Zenow, the Chief Librarian of the Galactic Library on Trantor, "I want to create a great Encyclopedia, containing within it all the knowledge humanity will need to rebuild itself in case the worst happens—an Encyclopedia Galactica, if you will" (*Forward the Foundation*, p. 339).

Members of the First Foundation begin work on this encyclopedia. They dedicate their lives to pursuing a dream Hari knows to be false. Just fifty years after the establishment of the First Foundation on Terminus, Lewis Pirenne, the Chair-person of the First Foundation's Board of Trustees, looks forward to progress on the *Encyclopedia Galactica* with delight: "Five more years would see the publication of the first volume of the most monumental work the Galaxy had ever conceived. And then at ten-year intervals regularly like clockwork volume after volume" (*Foundation*, p. 50). Indeed, fragments of the imaginary encyclopedia feature as epigraphs to many of the chapters of the *Foundation* novels. In fact, the very first chapter of the first novel in the series begins with the entry of the *Encyclopedia Galactica* on Hari Seldon himself!

However, after his death, Hari's recorded hologram reveals to the members of the First Foundation that the encyclopedia is actually a ruse, and its completion is irrelevant. Hari's hologram puts the truth brutally: "The Encyclopedia Foundation, to begin with, is a fraud, and always has been!" (*Foundation*, p. 93). At this point the reader and the encyclopedists learn that the real purpose of setting up the First Foundation is to establish a stable locus of power based on superior technology and energetic commerce that will counterbalance declining imperial power, while keeping so-called "barbarian" planets like Anachreon in check until it can ultimately form the basis of a second empire. Hari's hologram explains the true Seldon Plan to members of the stunned members of the First Foundation:

> We have placed you on such a planet and at such a time that in fifty years you were maneuvered to the point where you no longer have freedom of action. From now on, and into the centuries, the path you must take is inevitable. You will be faced with a series of crises, as you are now faced with the first, and in each case your freedom of action will become similarly circumscribed so that you will be forced along one, and only one, path. (*Foundation* p. 94)

Having one and only one path is, of course, the very antithesis of personal autonomy.

In fact, Hari has not only manipulated his followers by deceiving them about the purposes of the First Foundation; he also secretly created a Second Foundation to continue to manipulate the First Foundation for centuries after his own death. As Hari describes the Second Foundation, it "will introduce fine adjustments as time goes on, you see. Ever in the background, watching" (*Forward the Foundation*, p. 345). We will return to the Second Foundation in a moment.

Here, then, is the fundamental tension in Asmiov's *Foundation* series. On the one hand, Hari was portrayed as a champion of personal autonomy in his own life and in the lives of others. On the other hand, he is willing to violate personal autonomy on a literally galactic scale. How do we make sense of these two apparently conflicting facts? As we shall see, Asimov's own characters implicitly provide two possible explanations, though Asimov leaves it to the reader to decide for him or herself what to think.

## Making Sense of Hari's Solution: Consequentialism

Let's start with Salvor Hardin. Salvor becomes the Mayor (essentially, the chief executive officer) of the planet Terminus after the first appearance of Hari's hologram. It is Salvor who oversees Terminus's transition from being a colony of obscure encyclopedists to being an incipient commercial and political power. While Hardin is, in Asimov's words, a "confirmed epigrammatist" (*Foundation*, p. 112), he is most famous for having said, "Never let your sense of morals prevent you from doing what is right!" (*Foundation*, p. 173). Clearly, Salvor practices what he preaches; he is a master manipulator. For example, Salvor plays Terminus's stronger neighbors against one another, and he helps to invent a pseudo-religion that disguises technology as magic in order to gain an advantage over his trading rivals.

Yet Salvor's epigram seems paradoxical. How could our sense of morals prevent us from doing what is right? One way to resolve this paradox is by understanding Hari and Salvor as consequentialists. According to contemporary philosopher Philip Pettit, "Consequentialists say that the right option in any choice is that which promotes the realization of the relevant valuable properties" (p. 117). One of the "relevant valuable properties" is personal autonomy. A consequentialist so understood would say that, under ordinary circumstances, we best promote the realization of personal autonomy by following a levelheaded moral code that prohibits us from coercing, deceiving, manipulating, and lying to others. It is this levelheaded moral code that forms our sense of morals, to which Salvor refers. For the vast majority of people in the vast majority of situations, this sense of morals is enough, and we needn't go beyond it.

Nevertheless, the consequentialist would maintain that there are unusual circumstances in which violating this sense of morals is actually the morally right thing to do. For example, if Hari does not secretly put the Seldon Plan into effect, the galaxy will fall into turmoil for thirty times longer than if he does put the plan into effect. The result of thirty thousand years between galactic empires will result in far less personal autonomy for ordinary humans. Yet Hari can only put the Seldon Plan into effect if he lies to and manipulates his own followers. While the result will be less personal autonomy for the much smaller group, it will be far more personal autonomy for humans across the galaxy and the millennia. Hence, morality requires Hari to violate his everyday sense of morals to bring about a vastly greater amount of personal autonomy. Or so a consequentialist could argue.

Hari even engages in explicitly consequentialist reasoning at times. For instance, he justifies his role in allowing a military junta that had overthrown the galactic government after the assassination of Emporer Cleon I to institute an unpopular tax because doing so would cause the junta to fall in the least violent way possible (*Forward the Foundation*, p. 276). Much the same can be said about Salvor. In his role as Mayor, he manipulates others in ways that might seem morally prohibited. However, a consequentialist can see them as morally required since they are what is necessary to keep the Seldon Plan on track.

Nevertheless, Asimov was no dogmatic advocate of consequentialism. Quite the contrary! There is a long tradition of criticizing consequentialism for claiming that we are morally required to manipulate others when the benefits of doing so outweigh the costs. This tradition focuses on the fact that manipulating others involves failing to respect them as persons (Benn, *A Theory of Freedom*), treating them like children (Adrian Piper), and engaging in "paternalistic duplicity" (Bernard Williams). Asimov dramatized this tradition by portraying many members of the First Foundation as feeling this lack of respect keenly when they learn of the existence of the Second Foundation and its mission to guide their actions from the shadows.

Toran Darell II becomes obsessed with fighting "that vague and fearful enemy that had deprived him of the dignity of his manhood by controlling his destiny" (*Second Foundation*, p. 166). Setting aside this dated talk of "manhood," it is clear that Darell is morally offended by the manipulations of the Second Foundation, as are many other members of the First Foundation. Despite having no "manhood" to denigrate, Harla Branno feels just as wronged by the Second Foundation as Darell does when she says, "We do not want an Empire in which we play puppets to the hidden manipulators of the Second Foundation" (*Foundation's Edge,* p. 341). Darell and Branno reject a consequentialist justification of manipulation for a higher cause, and, though they don't put it in this language, they see Hari and the Second Foundation as nothing more than a more benevolent version of the Mule.

## Making Sense of Hari's Solution: Deontology

Unlike consequentialists, deontologists such as John Rawls deny that the right option in every situation is the one which promotes the realization of the relevant valuable properties. While a consequentialist of the sort we're imagining would agree that it is morally right to violate one individual's personal autonomy in order to increase the same amount of personal autonomy in ten others, a deontologist would not.

No one in Asimov's *Foundation* series better exemplifies the deontological position than the collective consciousness of the planet Gaia, especially as embodied in Blissenobiarella—better known as Bliss. Like the Mule, Gaia and Bliss have the ability to tamper with the minds of others. But unlike the Mule, Gaia and Bliss refuse to use this ability except in the most dire of circumstances. Near the end of *Foundation's Edge*, the galaxy stands at a crossroads. If the First Foundation is allowed to continue to develop its technology, then it will soon be able to free itself completely from the influence of the Second Foundation. The result will be a second galactic empire centered around the First Foundation and Terminus. If the First Foundation is not allowed to continue to develop its technology, then it can be manipulated into moving toward empire more slowly and under the continued influence of the Second Foundation. But in either case, the result will be a "paternalistic Empire" that enforces its dictates on an unwilling galaxy. The second galactic empire would be "established by strife, maintained by strife, and eventually destroyed by strife." Yet there is a third possibility. Gaia can help guide the development of the entire galaxy into a living, organic whole: Galaxia. This unified galaxy will be "one that can be made favorable for all life in ways that we yet cannot foresee. A way of life fundamentally different from that has gone before and repeating none of the old mistakes" (*Foundation's Edge*, p. 356).

Gaia is in circumstances that are analogous to those that face Hari Seldon at the end of *Forward the Foundation*. By acting and imposing its choice on the galaxy, Gaia can bring about a much better result than if it failed to do so. Yet in contrast to Hari, Gaia refuses to make a choice. Rather, it seeks out Golan Trevize, a man who has a remarkable knack for making the right decision even if he doesn't know quite how he does so. Gaia then gives him the choice of what should be done. Even though it could easily have manipulated him, it allows him full personal autonomy in his choice.

As it so happens, Trevize choses Gaia's solution. But that fact should not be confused with Asimov's endorsement of deontology. Trevize himself doubts the wisdom of allowing him personal autonomy to make this choice. Trevize believed that Gaia is better able to make the choice itself and simply manipulate Trevize into doing the right thing (*Foundation and*

*Earth*, p. 5). Moreover, Gaia's unwillingness to violate the personal autonomy of others consistently imperils Trevize and Bliss as they and Janov Pelorat search for humanity's origin on the obscure planet known as "Earth." For example, when the three of them visit the plant Solaria, Bliss almost allows Sarton Bander to kill them rather than tamper with his mind, and she rescues them only at the last second, leaving no room for error (*Foundation and Earth*, p. 268). Later, on the planet Alpha, Bliss could have foreseen and prevented the plot to infect the three of them with a deadly virus. As it turns out, they survive only because one of the planet's inhabitants, Hiroko, is unable to go through with the plot (*Foundation and Earth*, p. 432). As attractive as it might seem, an absolute prohibition on manipulating others opens the door to poor decision making and catastrophic consequences.

## An Active Mind and Experience with Life

What, then, are we to conclude with regard to morality and manipulation? Did Asimov want us to side with the consequentialists and Hari Seldon who will allow manipulation to occur if it results in greater personal autonomy overall? Or did he mean for us to agree with Bliss and the deontologists who think that violation of personal autonomy should always be a last result, even if more personal autonomy can be promoted this way?

Before trying to answer that question, it's worth recalling the moment that Pelorat first encounters Bliss. Pelorat asked her, "Are you human?" It is a strange question to ask for a character in a fictional universe with no aliens and no known (up to that point) humanoid robots. But Bliss's answer is even stranger: "Don't I *look* human?" (*Foundation's Edge*, p. 302).

While it is easy to see Bliss's response as merely flirtatious, it is likely that there is something deeper at work. Bliss wants Pelorat to think for himself and come to his own conclusions. Anything else would be exercising undue influence. I think the same can be said for Asimov. The question of when—if ever—it's morally permissible, or even morally required, to manipulate others is a question that each of us must answer for ourselves. Every one of us must take on the role of the philosopher, weigh the evidence, come up with our own conclusions, and keep our minds open to new evidence as it arises.

But is it reasonable to expect us to be philosophers? Asimov seemed to think so. Recall that Hari told Mandel Gruber that in order to be a philosopher, you just need "an active mind and experience with life." Asimov's achievement in the *Foundation* series is to help cultivate such minds and to challenge us to think for ourselves about morality in extraordinary circumstances. We are, after all, not machines to be built after a model. We are human beings.

# 16
# Psycho-historian or *Psycho* Historian?

LISA BELLANTONI

Hyphens are under-appreciated. Call Hari Seldon a psycho-historian and you recognize his extraordinary expertise: his science of human behavior allows him to accurately predict how our future will unfold. Call him a *psycho* historian and you mean something else entirely, that he is morally suspect, or misguided, or even a dash mad. Which is he?

Having predicted the demise of the First Galactic Empire—and thirty thousand years of ensuing anarchy—he sets out to preserve human knowledge and to lay the foundation for a new civilization. But what does he really owe the future people he envisions, and would his efforts to engineer a future for them really leave them better off than they might be if left to their own devices?

## What Good Is the Future to Us, Anyway?

This question of what we owe future generations sparks vigorous debate among contemporary philosophers. Some, broadly termed moral presentists, hold that we can only have duties to living people. Sounds plausible. Future people don't even exist, so how could we owe them anything? Worse, even choices we make on their behalf might prevent some of them from ever existing. If we plan when we have children, do we harm those who are never born, or illicitly favor those who are? Moral presentism has at least that going for it: it avoids the paradox of harming people who may never even come to exist. Yet if we want to make moral choices, can we completely disregard their impact on those who will—or may—succeed us?

Seldon embraces this concern. When we meet him, in the first story of the original *Foundation* trilogy, he is on trial for treason, facing execution or exile. He has developed the probabilistic science of Psycho-history, which predicts how vast groups of people will respond to social stimuli. This knowledge extends only to the broadest scope of history, on the scale of millennia. Yet according to his calculations, the current Galactic Empire, encompassing millions of planets, will founder within a few centuries. This collapse will sow political chaos and a descent into barbarism that augurs thirty thousand years of human suffering. He foresees the eventual rise of a Second Galactic Empire but aims to cut the chaotic time between them down to a single millennium. To do so, he enacts the Seldon Plan. This project creates two Foundations at opposite ends of the galaxy, groups of scholars and archivists who are charged with preserving human knowledge and the foundations of civilization.

On behalf of this plan, Seldon risks his life. But . . . why? During his trial, his questioners put the matter bluntly: "Dr. Seldon, you disturb the peace of the Emperor's Realm. None of the quadrillions living now among all the stars of the Galaxy will be living a century from now. Why, then, should we concern ourselves with events of three centuries distance?" (*The Foundation Trilogy*, 1982, p. 28). Seldon acknowledges that his project, creating an Encyclopedia Galactica to preserve the foundations of human civilization, will require the efforts of tens of thousands of people over several centuries. Of these Encyclopedists, he notes: "They will not complete it in their lifetimes. I will not even live to see it fairly begun" (p. 27). Indeed, we learn soon after that he is aware his own death is imminent. Nevertheless, the future is a matter of "overpowering concern" to him. When asked why, he says simply: "Call it an identification of myself with that mystical generalization to which we refer by the term, 'humanity'" (p. 28).

In these sentiments, Seldon expresses a moral attitude—a sense of obligation—which contemporary philosophers are also struggling to articulate. One recent such work, aptly titled *Why Worry about Future Generations?* proposes a hint. For its author, Samuel Scheffler, our cultural pursuits, such as science, music, art, and mathematics, have value in part because they extend our actions beyond our individual selves. They have shared histories and trajectories, and cultivating them reflects a love of humanity, and a moral injunction to sustain these activities on that basis. This view echoes Seldon's response to his inquisitors. Yet it is also oddly circular and self-referential. We value future people, and the cultural conditions that will sustain them, because we value ourselves? Because we value what we have achieved and wish them to preserve it? This makes Seldon's "identification" with the future people he ostensibly aims to assist sound largely self-aggrandizing, and his Seldon Plan, frankly, narcissistic.

## Moral Reasoning—Calculating or Calculated?

Two points bear emphasis here. First, Scheffler's work, like that of many contemporary philosophers, deals more with existential threats to humanity than with the challenge Seldon faces. For many current ethicists, obligations to future persons involve stark environmental questions. Should we sacrifice our present interests to stave off environmental collapse? Should we prevent diseases if we are able, to enhance their well-being and that of their children? Seldon does not see the collapse of the First Galactic Empire as an existential threat. While it will reduce the human population galaxy-wide, his concern is to prevent the suffering that would occur before the rise of the Second Empire.

In this effort, Seldon might find a moral impetus for his actions in utilitarianism. Utilitarians identify pleasure as the primary human good, and pain or suffering as a primary evil. As such, we are morally enjoined to maximize pleasure and minimize pain for as many people as possible. One proponent of such moral reasoning was Jeremy Bentham. He suggested that when we are making moral decisions, we should identify our options. Then, for each potential action, we should calculate its total projected utility, the amount of net pleasure it would produce, after subtracting the pain it might also involve. Once we weigh each such proposed action, we can place them on a comparative scale, and select the action with the most total utility. This is sometimes called a 'hedonic calculus'.

Bentham's hedonic calculus identified seven criteria by which to evaluate any potential action. These include the intensity of pleasure it would produce, its duration, its certainty, its immediacy, its fecundity (likelihood to create additional pleasure beyond the initial action), its purity, and the number of people it would benefit (*An Introduction to the Principles of Morals and Legislation*, Chapter IV). We could evaluate Seldon's plan using the same criteria. Seldon requires tens of thousands of Encyclopedists to dedicate their careers, maybe even to risk their lives, to create a better future for people they will never know. Would the pain of those sacrifices be offset by the pleasure produced (or pain avoided) for their beneficiaries? Considering how long-lasting and widespread the benefits would be, weighed against the sacrifices from a much smaller group of people over a much shorter timeframe, the Hedonic Calculus might seem to favor the Seldon plan. The high probability of the Second Empire's rapid rise also supports this conclusion.

At the same time, Seldon himself denies that mathematical methods provide moral guidance. When asked whether his Psycho-history is treasonous, he notes that: "Scientific truth is beyond loyalty or disloyalty." When he details what motivates him, he cites not statistics, but diminished quality of life and suffering, concerns he describes as "idealist" and even "mystical." Moreover, even if he did embrace a utilitarian calculus like Bentham's, that would seem an unlikely moral basis for the Seldon Plan for two reasons. First, on any traditional utilitarian analysis, time-discounting is a significant factor. Most of the criteria applied when weighing up total pleasures and pains strongly favor immediate experiences. They would not generally sanction actions where the pain to some actors, however few, is intense and immediate, while the benefits would not be realized for millennia.

Second, and more pointedly, in calculating future history out as far as Seldon does, the time dilation of the moral analysis grows accordingly. As far as Seldon can tell, speeding up the arrival of the Second Galactic Empire may mitigate vast suffering. But what if the Empire that would arise from the original trajectory—after a Dark Age of barbarism—would provide greater pleasure and less pain overall? What if the total utility of the human future was better served by those future people enduring the suffering he predicts? In that case, a hedonic calculus would reject the Seldon Plan as immoral.

## Doing Deontology Dirty

The very idea that Seldon might have a plan to prevent mass human suffering yet be required to shelve it to achieve an even greater good, might drive him away from utilitarianism and towards a different approach to ethical reasoning, one in which some actions are judged to be right or wrong, independently of the predictable consequences. One version of this approach is called 'deontology'.

In the thinking deontologists, such as Immanuel Kant, no one should ever be treated merely as a means for some else's benefit. All persons deserve equal moral consideration no matter when they live. Humanity itself merits respect. Here, Kant might seem to share Seldon's "mystical" identification with the absolute worth of humanity. For Kant, however, what makes us valuable is our autonomy, our capacity to make informed rational choices without being manipulated or coerced. Any moral action must respect that autonomy

Seldon's plan is an exercise in mass manipulation. During his trial, he notes that Psycho-history can only be understood by a handful of people. His immensely complex plan operates over a huge time span, and only succeeds if people are unaware of its influence. Even the tiny group of Encyclopedists directly involved in executing his plan are manipulated into serving its ends and largely unaware of their true roles. Seldon, moreover, shows absolutely no compunction about using whomever he needs, whenever he needs them, for whatever he needs to attain his goal.

Right from the beginning, when Seldon meets his future biographer, he makes this plain. The young mathematician Gaal Dornick arrives at the capital city of the Empire, Trantor, eager to join Seldon's research team. Dornick is almost immediately arrested, along with Seldon. Seldon confesses to him that he has deliberately provoked the trial, had anticipated Dornick's being taken into custody, and had already calculated the probabilities of Dornick's possible fates, including the likelihood of him being imprisoned or killed.

Seldon has also, as it turns out, manipulated his inquisitors into exiling his team of Encyclopedists, tens of thousands of people, to the planet Terminus at the edge of the galaxy. He needed to do so, he assures Dornick, not only to isolate them from political interference, but also because he was unsure if they would join him voluntarily. As the story unfolds, it becomes clear that every member of his project—indeed, everyone he deals with—is manipulated to engineer his favored future. That future, moreover, is by his design different from that which would emerge if all people involved being were making their own choices.

## Long Hauling Ethics

The *Foundation* saga is a sprawling chess match, a series of events dictated by Seldon. For deontologists like Kant, no end would justify the means—the mass manipulation, the attack on human autonomy—that Seldon uses. Yet maybe Kant is unreasonable, his standards too strict. Seldon describes the collapse of the First Galactic Empire as "a massive thing." As he says: "The Empire will vanish and all its good with it. Its accumulated knowledge will decay and the order it has imposed will vanish . . . A Second Empire will rise, but between it and our civilization will be one thousand generations of suffering humanity. We must fight that" (*Foundation Trilogy*, p. 26). Given what's at stake, maybe Seldon's machinations really are for the greater good. Indeed, given his concern with preserving human civilization, Seldon might sound less like a traditional utilitarian or deontologist and more like a long-termist.

For long-termists, humanity has great potential beyond that of existing individuals as a collective. So morally valuable is that potential that we should spread ourselves across the galaxy, lest a calamity on Earth wipe us all out. We are also urged to develop technologies that both enhance us and improve our quality of life. This view might imply that the lives of far future people, being of higher quality, might be more valuable than those of present people. Indeed, it might suggest that we make significant sacrifices now to increase the quality and the quantity of future lives. For example, we might shift resources away from combatting famine today to advancing longer range goals like space exploration.

Seldon is plainly willing to sacrifice the Encyclopedists' interests for those of far future people. Yet the long-termists' optimistic and expansionary view of the human future, premised on improving both the quality of individual human lives and humanity itself, is a far cry from Seldon's plan. While set in a vast interstellar future, that plan is strikingly conservative. When we meet the initial narrator of the Foundation saga, Gaal Dornick, we see Trantor, "the center of all the Galaxy and the kernel of the human race," through his eyes. This capital city of a sprawling Galactic Empire of twenty-five million planets– its pinnacle, reflecting "12,000 years of imperial progress"—houses forty billion drab administrators (pp. 12–14).

Dornick cannot tell if it's day or night when he arrives and is dazzled by what amounts to a massive underground structure. Its citizens move through mazes of corridors and spend years indoors. Trips "outside" are purchased by ticket and may be supplemented by "sunrooms" which provide artificial light. On his brief look outside: "He could see no horizon other than that of metal against sky, stretching out to almost uniform grayness over all the land-surface of the planet" (p. 14). This grim expanse is heavily fortified, as the Empire endures internal revolutions and trade disruptions. Yet for all its challenges, Seldon rues its inevitable collapse. "Even if the Empire were admitted to be a bad thing (an admission I do not make), the state of anarchy which would follow its fall would be worse. It is that state of anarchy which my project is pledged to fight" (p. 26).

## Empires Past and Future

Here, it is helpful to recall that Asimov models his story on the fall of Rome. In describing the First Galactic Empire, Seldon notes of its inevitable decline: "It is dictated by a rising bureaucracy, a receding initiative, a freezing of caste, a damning of curiosity—a hundred other factors. It has been going on, as I have said, for centuries, and it is too majestic and massive a movement to stop" (p. 26). He worries that the Empire's citizens are nostalgic, envying the lives of their grandfathers. Worse, amid war and anarchy, amid the loss of accumulated knowledge and exploration, looms the stagnation of a Dark Age: "The feeling will pervade the Galaxy that only what a man can grasp for himself at that moment will be of any account" (p. 26). In his fight against this eventuality, Seldon flatly rejects moral presentism. To him, loss of a substantive future heralds personal and social disaster.

At the same time, he aims not to enhance the far future, but to mitigate near-future harm. Seldon predicts disaster from the fall of the First Galactic Empire: thirty thousand years of suffering. But then what? In the case of the Roman Empire, its collapse was followed by a Dark Age. Yet then came a Renaissance and an age of Enlightenment. If that Dark Age had been prevented, would the latter two have followed, or been as productive? In the case of the Galactic Empire, Seldon aims to shorten an analogous Dark Age. But what if the hardship he seeks to prevent would actually seed an even greater Second Empire than the one his machinations may produce?

This is, in fact, a primary criticism of the long-termist approach to ethical issues, that it ignores immediate suffering for a far future, for example, by pouring money into space exploration while people today starve. Surely, the long-termists' critics seem to suggest, we should alleviate suffering now, even if that leaves our successors less well off. Surely, Seldon's plan suggests, Dark Ages should be prevented.

Yet that's the moral challenge of Psycho-history. In engineering, or more accurately, re-engineering thirty thousand years of history, is Seldon improving the human future overall? Or is he improving life in the near term, while dooming even further future people to lesser lives than they might have had otherwise—or worse? To answer that question, we'd need his science to tell us even more than it already does, that is, what comes after the thirty thousand years of barbarism he foresees? A second civilization akin to the First Galactic Empire's? Or a vastly better one then we had before, one Seldon's plan effectively forecloses?

## Civilization and Its Disconnects

Seldon acknowledges that the fall of the First Galactic Empire is inevitable, which raises a broader issue: maybe its cultural resources, the foundations of its current civilization, are inadequate to sustain it. This question, about how civilizations endure, was addressed by the philosopher and mathematician Alfred North Whitehead. In his *Adventure of Ideas,* as sprawling a work of speculative philosophy as Asimov's is of fiction, Whitehead describes any human civilization as an interplay between strong emotions—passions, hopes, motives, drives—and the ideals which incite them. These ideals, like truth, beauty, and goodness, he terms "lures for feeling." Civilizations are collectives, much like the large-scale social groupings Seldon studies. Vast numbers of agents repeatedly select, or in Whitehead's language make real, those ideals by acting upon them to create complex, enduring organic wholes, such as societies, economies, social mores, practices, and systems of thought.

Any civilization is a pattern of realized ideals, chosen repeatedly over time, embedded in institutions and traditions, and enduring so long as those ideals retain their seductive power as lures for feeling. Civilizations thereby maintain their inertia. Eventually, however, these ideals lose their civilizing power as lures, as organizers for feelings. They become exhausted, ineffectual, unable to hold the civilization together. New ideals must then supplant them, sometimes through attrition, sometimes through evolution, sometimes through violent revolution and tragic destruction.

When Seldon describes the First Galactic Empire as bureaucratic, as lacking exploration or curiosity or hope, that sounds much like the cultural ossification Whitehead attributes to European culture as it slipped into its own Dark Age. It had drawn on the prior excellence achieved by Greek and Roman culture and aimed at reproducing it. "But the procedure has its disadvantages. It is backward looking, and it is limited to one type of social excellence" (*Adventures of Ideas*, p. 273). As successful as these civilizations were: "The foundation of all understanding of sociological theory—of all understanding of human life—is that no static maintenance of perfection is possible. . . . Advance or Decadence are the only choices offered to mankind. The pure conservative is fighting against the essence of the universe" (p. 274).

The issue here, for Whitehead, is that the death ossified of civilizations is not only inevitable, but necessary for the seeding of new ones. He does not celebrate the passing of eras of civilization; he regards this, like Seldon seems to, as tragic. Yet once their time has passed, their animating ideals no longer serving as effective lures, they cannot be reanimated. Civilizations, like ideals, have expiration dates. They cannot be retained, or shored up, as Seldon's plan endeavors, because they do not endure through force or manipulation, but ultimately through persuasion. In attempting to engineer a specific future, this would seem to be Seldon's goal, to revive a civilization that has already lost its grip, and to impose that civilization upon a future which—given his projections—would otherwise reject it.

## Barbarians at the Calculators?

In this sense, Seldon's Foundations might function less like centers of culture than like generation ships, with his Encyclopedists as unwitting passengers. Often in this familiar science fiction trope, a group of "sleepers" from an endangered or dying society is catapulted into space and reawakened at some future time to recreate the society from which they came. The survivors, however, frequently find themselves displaced, unable to recreate their ancestors' old ideals under new conditions.

Seldon's successors, charged with a similar project, reflect that dynamic in subsequent parts of Asimov's sweeping saga. Lacking Seldon's direct guidance they flounder, unwitting pioneers and conscripts cast into a future that is in significant ways chosen for them. Ultimately, of course, they find their way back . . . to Trantor. Yet to what end? Are they nostalgic for a time they never knew? Are they content to impose a future upon future people which those people did not—and as Seldon's own predictions show, would not—choose for themselves?

Seldon is a brilliant man. Maybe he knows better than anyone what would ultimately be best for humanity. He sees moral barbarism in allowing human civilization to descend into anarchy. As an historian, however, he would also be aware of the barbarism that has often resulted from the human compulsion to unilaterally impose order upon others for their own good. That too may be a condition of civilization—the premise that the future belongs to the future—and that we should leave it to future people to make of it what they will.

# 17
# Psychohistory's Noble Lie

MARK SILCOX

> HARI: I was engineering the narrative!
> GAAL: That's a fancy way of saying you lied.
>
> —*Foundation,* "Mysteries and Martyrs"

About sixty pages into Asimov's *Foundation*, when the First Vault on Terminus is opened, the recorded voice of Hari Seldon informs a few select members of the planet's elites that the *Encyclopedia Galactica* "is a fraud, and always has been." Salvor Hardin's controversial vision for the future of the colony is thereby vindicated, and the plot tumbles along with little further ado to his adventures navigating a political path between the remnants of the Empire and his planet's barbarous neighbors.

For most of the first season of the TV show, the vault on Terminus hovers in silent menace above the ragtag colony that lies below, narcotizing all who come near and taunting the planet's settlers with the inscrutability of their own future. But when it finally does open near the end of Season One, the digital simulacrum of Hari Seldon that emerges is even more glib than his counterpart in the novel when he informs the settlers of their (hitherto concealed) destiny as political revolutionaries. He practically smirks as he says to them "well, I *might* have lied about that."

Back here in the twenty-first century, we inhabit a social world that is haunted by casual acts of political dishonesty—about the causes of a global pandemic, the results of federal elections, and the private lives of leaders whom we are carefully schooled to admire to the point of reverence. Yet within our own societies any powerful politician, scientist, or public servant caught telling so colossal a lie as Seldon's would surely be reviled by almost all thoughtful citizens. It should puzzle us, then, that in neither version of the *Foundation* story does his confession of deceit about his earlier projections concerning the entire galaxy's future diminish Seldon's stature in the narrative, either as wise prophet or as noble hero. What can explain this difference between how we view acts of political deceit in a work of fiction and the ethical attitudes we adopt towards them in real life?

There are lots of potential answers to this question to be derived from the various things political philosophers have said throughout the centuries about the ethics of deception in politics. The most famous (or perhaps infamous) example of such a discussion is Socrates's defense of the so-called "noble lie" in Plato's *Republic*. But more recent philosophers have tended to address the topic in the context of debates about the significance of *transparency* as a constraint on political power. The idea that governments owe it to their subjects to be as transparent as possible in their uses of political power is often regarded as an utterly non-negotiable condition upon legitimate political authority in the modern world. What our response to Seldon's fictional lie helps make clear is that our willingness to tolerate political deceit turns out to depend upon a more diverse set of factors than orthodox defenders of political transparency are often willing to acknowledge.

Seldon's behavior in these scenes does, in fact, provoke (and to some extent deserves) the reader's sympathy and admiration. It's an interesting question in literary aesthetics how much we can learn from these sorts of reactions toward fictional characters. Sometimes, as readers, we make allowances for behavior we would condemn in real life—for instance, when we cheer for so-called "rough heroes" such as Tony in *The Sopranos,* Gully Foyle in *The Stars My Destination*, or Satan himself in *Paradise Lost*—for no other purpose than to sustain our own enjoyment of a narrative. And sometimes we enjoy fiction (perhaps especially sci-fi) precisely because the circumstances it depicts are so otherworldly or far-fetched, we feel safe in supposing that the ethical or political principles that govern our own lives simply don't have any relevance there. As a near-lifelong fan of Asimov's novels I have always suspected that Seldon's lies to the people of Terminus present a deeper philosophical challenge to readers (and now to viewers) than what happens in either of these other types of cases. We may not be psychohistorians ourselves, or have access to any of the proven results of that fictional discipline. But most of us have at least some strongly-held opinions about the future prospects of our own societies. Might some of these opinions be important enough to us to override some of our other political commitments, perhaps even to an extent that would surprise us?

## Socrates versus Seldon

Was Plato's *Republic*—probably the most influential book about politics to have been written in the west over the past three millennia—also a work of early psychohistory? Certainly, its author shared with Hari Seldon an interest in constructing large-scale political strategies to frustrate the advancement of barbarism and tyranny.

At the heart of Plato's scheme for achieving this is his detailed description of a meritocratic education system designed to train both the soldiers ("auxiliaries") and the rulers ("philosopher kings") of an ideal city-state (a *kallipolis*, in Greek) to protect their society against threats from both without and within. The details of this ancient master-plan are laid out painstakingly by Socrates (the book's main protagonist and Plato's real-life mentor) over the first seven of the *Republic*'s ten books. Quite early on in the discussion, Socrates makes a daring suggestion about how to ensure the stability of such a regime once it has been established:

> Could we, I said, somehow contrive one of those lies that come into being in case of need . . . one noble lie to persuade, in the best case, even the rulers, but if not them, the rest of the city? . . . I'll attempt to persuade first the rulers and then the soldiers, then the rest of the city, that the rearing and education we gave them were like dreams: they only thought they were undergoing all that was happening to them, while, in truth, at that time they were under the earth, being fashioned and reared themselves, and their arms and other tools being crafted. When the job had been completely finished, then the earth, which is their mother, sent them up. And now, as though the land they were in were a mother and a nurse, they must plan for and defend it. (*The Republic of Plato*, pp. 93–94)

An additional component of this elaborate fiction is that each citizen is born from the earth with a specific proportion of gold, silver, bronze, or iron in their soul, which determines the extent of their native capacities and their placement within the *kallipolis*'s political hierarchy. And Socrates's lie also has a theological component: "the god," he says,

> commands the rulers first and foremost to be of nothing such good guardians...as the children, seeing which of these metals is mixed in their souls. (p. 94)

The story citizens are told thereby bears a rather striking resemblance to the founding myths of several real-world nation-states that invoke the divine inspiration of historical figures such as Moses, Theseus, Mohammed, or (as many American schoolchildren still get taught) George Washington.

Recent commentators on Plato's text have tended to regard this part of Socrates's political plan with varying degrees of overt hostility. I.F. Stone, author of the recent bestseller *The Trial of Socrates*, puts it this way:

> the 'noble lie' of the Republic . . . is antidemocratic. Its purpose was to inculcate a sense of ineradicable inferiority in the lower middle classes and 'program' them, as we would now say, for submission to the philosopher kings . . . by 'brain-washing' . . . (*The Trial of Socrates*, p. 166)

The famous mid-century philosopher Karl Popper thought that Plato's doctrine was fundamentally motivated by racism and reactionary conservatism:

> The motive of Plato's wish that the rulers themselves should believe in the propaganda lie is his hope of increasing its wholesome effect, i.e. of strengthening the rule of the master race, and ultimately, of arresting all political change. (*The Open Society and Its Enemies*, Volume I, p. 240)

Popper thought this idea of the "lordly lie" (as he put it) was not only alien to the more enlightened aims of postwar European liberalism, but also "opposed to the democratic and humanitarian tendencies of Plato's time" (p. 141).

What makes the Platonic doctrine so repugnant to both of these authors, and to many of Plato's other readers throughout history (though not all of them) is the idea that political deception should be used to reinforce divisions within an already highly inequitable political hierarchy. But this feature of the noble lie can't play much of a role in explaining why it might seem so much less forgivable than the type of deceit woven into the Seldon plan. Neither Seldon himself nor the other leaders and heroes who advance the interests of the Foundation seem particularly committed to political egalitarianism. Salvor Hardin, to take just one example, is a wise, but frequently autocratic mayor who uses the revelation of Seldon's lie to cement his own political power at the expense of the encyclopedists. The Salvor of the TV show, in her somewhat more ambiguous capacity as "Warden" of Terminus, often adopts a similarly dictatorial attitude toward the other settlers.

A few contemporary political philosophers have tried to justify Plato's doctrine. The American translator and commentator Allan Bloom, for example, contends that "today" it is in fact "generally admitted that every society is based on myths which render acceptable the particular form of justice incorporated in the system." Bloom observes that, because the fictitious hierarchy of "metals" is isomorphic to the actual class hierarchy that Socrates thinks justice requires, "the thoughtful observer will find that the noble lie is a political expression of truths which it itself leads him to consider"—a feature that at least arguably renders it more excusable than other national myths (*The Republic of Plato*, p. 367).

One fundamental difference that distinguishes Socrates's lie from Seldon's is the fact that the former is intended to *preserve* a political regime that has already been put into place, whereas the latter is aimed at *bringing about* a political goal that still lies in the distant future. To even see the point of Seldon's lie (either as one of its victims or as a reader) one must attribute at least some minimal degree of credibility to the science of psychohistory and its capacity to foretell the political future. This difference might actually at first glance seem to weigh *in favor* of Socrates's lie and *against* Seldon's deceptions about the *Encyclopedia Galactica*. After all, surely if there's anything worth lying to protect it's the security and protection of the *kallipolis*, once it has been established. But consider: if the society Socrates envisions really were the very best that human beings were capable of, would defenders of the *status quo* there really *need* a lie to inspire patriotism in their fellow citizens?

Thoughts along these sorts of lines have led philosophers of the modern era to exhibit a fairly consistent commitment to the value of *transparency*, both as a prerequisite for and as an indicator of social and political justice. The most influential version of this doctrine in contemporary political philosophy is John Rawls's "publicity condition" upon the regulation of what he calls a "well-ordered society." According to Rawls, any such ideally-just society must be "effectively regulated by public principles of justice: citizens accept and know that others likewise accept those principles, and this knowledge in turn is publicly recognized" (*Political Liberalism*, p. 66).

The question we have been asking, though, about the extent to which we should allow ourselves to sympathize with Seldon after his deception has been revealed, concerns the slightly trickier issue of how important transparency should be in the less-than-perfectly 'orderly' conditions of the Galactic Interregnum. To what extent can the reasons philosophers have given for favoring political transparency be reconciled with the very specific aims that political lying helps to advance within the Seldon plan?

## Transparency, Expertise, and Autonomy

In his 1791 essay "On Publicity," the moral philosopher Jeremy Bentham provides an inventory of reasons for why government policy and other related business should be enacted in full view of the public. The three "major considerations" he raises are that, through the transparency of their operations, governments are better able:

1. "to constrain the members of the assembly to perform their duty,"
2. "to secure the confidence of the people," and
3. "to enable the governors to know the wishes of the governed," (*Political Tactics*, pp. 29–32)

Bentham's defense of governmental transparency is resolutely *consequentialist*—he focuses, that is to say, exclusively upon the beneficial *outcomes* of government activity he thinks are made more likely when those in power leave themselves open to public scrutiny. This comes across most strikingly in the following passage:

> Consider, in particular, how much public deliberations respecting the laws, the measures, the taxes, the conduct of official persons ought to operate upon the general spirit of a nation in favor of its government . . . It is in this sense that it has been well said that *he who resists, strengthens;* for the government is much more assured of the general success of a measure . . . after it has been discussed by two parties, whilst the whole nation has been spectators. (p. 31)

It is not, he suggests, that a society's rulers in any way *owe* transparency to those living under their authority. It is rather than the additional scrutiny this allows for will simply make them better at their jobs.

Such exclusively results-oriented reasoning has become profoundly unfashionable among political philosophers in the twenty-first century. There are a variety of reasons for this, not all perhaps equally defensible, but in the present context an obvious issue we might raise with Bentham's defense of transparency is that it relies very heavily upon the idea that the public are themselves reliably competent at holding officials accountable. The reader will perhaps not find it too difficult to think of specific instances within our own lifetimes (especially, perhaps, since the birth of the Internet) when the general public failed spectacularly at this very task, in spite of having access to all the information they would have needed to succeed.

Could we offer a defense of transparency in politics that was more robustly resistant to these kinds of considerations? In his 1993 work *Political Liberalism*, Rawls tries to do just this by appealing to the connection between his aforementioned publicity condition upon 'well-ordered' societies and the intrinsic value of human autonomy. "Publicity," he claims

> ensures, so far as practical measures allow, that citizens are in a position to know and to accept the pervasive influences . . . that shape their conception of themselves, their character and ends . . . that citizens should be in this position is a condition of realizing their freedom as fully autonomous, politically speaking. (p. 68)

The important thing about transparency in Rawls's judgment is not that it causes or prevents good or bad policy from being enacted, but rather, that it allows all affected parties to achieve awareness of how the societies they inhabit have influenced the development of their identities as individuals and moral agents. His argument is therefore still at least partly consequentialist, in the sense that its plausibility depends upon the existence of a particular sort of cause-effect relationship between a person's observation of and participation in debates about public policy, and the shape that is taken by their most intimate private thoughts. But it differs importantly from Bentham's argument insofar as it treats no other type of political good *extraneous* to transparency itself as justifying the publicity condition. For this reason, it also presents a more profound challenge to the policies of political deceit pursued by both Hari Seldon and Plato's "philosopher kings."

Just how reliable is the aforementioned cause-effect relationship, though? C. Thi Nguyen raises some serious concerns about the possible side effects of public officials having to be relentlessly honest with the public all the time. Nguyen points out that, at least in situations where "expert domains are made transparent for the purpose of assessment by the public" (p. 5);

the pressure to make the reasoning behind public policy transparent to the public "distorts, to varying degrees, expert action and communication" (p. 9). For example, the simplest way for the US state department to publicly report upon increases and decreases in the amount of sex trafficking throughout the US is by publicizing the number of arrests and convictions of sex traffickers. But this generates the illusion that the best way to curb the practice is *via* policing, rather than the adoption of more systemic but harder-to-measure approaches to crime prevention (such as poverty reduction). Similarly, the most straightforward way for the National Endowment for the Arts to justify theater subsidies to the US Congress is by reporting the box office returns of subsidized productions. But one could just as easily argue that the more tickets a theater company is able to sell, the *less* they actually need public financial assistance.

These problems that arise from attempts to make information from "expert domains" transparent are simple enough to explain: the very *nature* of expertise is that it involves understanding reasons for action not readily comprehensible by the non-specialist. This is not always a deal-breaker, though; Nguyen points out that in plenty of instances there is "successful expert outcome that is identifiable as such by non-experts" (p. 19). Expertise at public health leads to fewer preventable deaths during a pandemic; expertise at building infrastructure leads to bridges and sewers that don't collapse. The types of experts for whom transparency is most problematic are those whose work is conducted on what he calls "cognitive islands"—whose reasoning, that is, can *only* be reliably followed by members of closed, "intimate" groups sharing a common enthusiasm, research program, or repertoire of preferences.

This imagery of isolation and intimacy generates an impression that the problems Nguyen raises for transparency will mostly solve themselves, at least in "well-ordered" liberal democratic societies. In such places, while political transparency is often regarded as non-negotiable (for broadly Rawlsian reasons), citizens also tend to be just as strongly insistent upon the maintenance of a distinction between the *public* and *private* spheres. We expect elected officials and paid public servants to make their reasons for action available to us, but we also teach ourselves not to demand vigorous self-justifications from the inhabitants of small communities of belief and preference (religious groups, political organizations, corporations, media fandoms) as they go about the often-inscrutable business of their lives. And many of us work hard to sustain this attitude, even when the activities of these communities (child-rearing, voting, stockpiling wealth, making artworks) can exert powerful influences upon public life.

But psychohistory as practiced by Seldon and his followers is actually rather difficult to find a place for within this tidy worldview. It is a rigorously demanding form of expertise destined to be fully comprehensible by only a handful of mathematicians. But is it also built with the central purpose of exerting an influence on the cultural development of an entire galaxy. Our tolerance for Seldon's lies must therefore surely require a different explanation from the type of tolerance we extend to members of religious, scientific, and cultural communities, whose reasoning we don't perhaps fully comprehend, on the basis of liberal principle.

Although psychohistory as Asimov depicts it is perhaps a barely imaginable form of human knowledge, its goals and methods nonetheless constitute a project within which nearly all modern people (or, at least, those who have acquired a basic historical education, along with the leisure to reflect thereupon) are somewhat *complicit*. The entertainment of smaller-scale, less mathematically rigorous, but (often) more dramatically vivid theories about the future direction of history is an extremely widely-shared contemporary pastime. From the impassioned belief in so-called "end times" theology to vague notions about the dawn of artificial intelligence, from Marxian theories of inevitable class conflict to sci-fi visions of post-apocalyptic survivalism, our future-fueled imaginative flights have largely robbed us of whatever innocence earlier generations may have possessed when it comes to the prognostication of humanity's long-term destiny.

Not all of us feel the intense commitment to these visions of the future that would make us feel justified in favoring them over relatively uncontroversial principles of social justice, including whatever such doctrines we take to provide the best mandate for political transparency. But mightn't this *change,* if some new method of historical projection came to light that bore some of the marks of objectivity and predictive efficacy that we already see in the mathematical, physical, and biological sciences? And in fact, *shouldn't* our political priorities change in precisely this way if a reliable science of history ever were discovered, like it was by Seldon during those critical years of his life on Trantor?

This seems to me to be the most fascinating possibility that Asimov illuminates with his (heretofore) merely imaginary science of psychohistory, and the best explanation for why we continue to find Hari Seldon appealing in spite of his self-confessed acts of deceit. It is a possibility that runs against many of the dominant sentiments of contemporary liberal political philosophy, whose advocates are inclined to treat the basic principles underlying their vision of "well-ordered" societies as utterly *ahistorical*. For Rawlsians, the preservation of human autonomy requires that as many as possible of the inexorable social forces molding our characters and intentions be knowable to us *right at the present moment*. But to the extent that some of us also aspire (in an admittedly preliminary, haphazard way) to be psychohistorians ourselves, I suspect we would cheerfully swap at least some such opportunities for immediate self-knowledge—even, perhaps, to the point of letting ourselves be deceived by figures of present authority—in favor of the chance to put our shoulders against history's wheel. Or, at least, we might *consider* it, once we felt a bit surer that someone we trusted with authority over us could foresee the direction in which it was rolling. To make such a sacrifice of personal knowledge for the sake of political agency would perhaps, indeed, not be all that different from what Plato might ask from his "philosopher kings."

## Engineering the Narrative

Thinking about psychohistory in the present day can perhaps help us to prepare ourselves for the new and rather fearsome era of political deceit that many contemporary societies seem to have already entered. Many inhabitants of modern nation states feel that they have less to fear from politicians and other figures of public authority simply lying to their faces than they do from the more systematic types of illusion generated by easily manipulable consumer technologies (VR, social media, deepfakes, and so forth) as well as from the injurious preferences and compulsions foisted upon them by advertising and cultural propaganda.

Could the type of lies told to us *via* these less direct, more insidious means ever achieve the type of 'nobility' I have argued we should be tentatively willing to attribute to the deceptions built into the Seldon plan? Perhaps they give us even *more* reason to insist upon political transparency than we had when the only media of deception one had to worry about were the human voice and the printing press. But perhaps, like the loyal citizens of Terminus after the opening of the vault, we should be prepared to treat the value of the truth in politics as at least somewhat negotiable.

# VI

# Foundation and Being

***"All things have a cycle. After destruction, rebirth."***

# 18
# Foundation and Consciousness

JONATHAN P. LANG AND ANDREW M. HAUN

What's a mind, and who has one? Most would agree that human beings have minds: we have subjective experiences, there is 'something-it-is-like' to be us.

Deciding whether non-human entities have minds is more difficult. It seems likely that creatures with human-like brains—namely other mammals—are also conscious. But what about invertebrates like bees or octopuses, whose brains and behavior are so different from ours? What about computers, artificial intelligences, and robots? As an entity becomes less and less like ourselves, our intuitions about its mentality—about its *consciousness*—begin to fail us. It turns out that, very quickly, questions about conscious experience run up against our limited understanding of just what kind of physical underpinnings are *necessary* for mental qualities.

In the science fiction of Isaac Asimov, whether robots can have minds is not an open question: Asimov's robots have minds just as humans do, albeit ones that may differ from ours in terms of sophistication. For instance, Asimov treats robot behavior as a problem not for computer engineers, but for robot *psychologists* such as Susan Calvin (*I, Robot*). The humanity of the robot Andrew Martin is a legal matter hinging on his lack of *mortality*, not on his lack of a mind (*The Bicentennial Man*). *Foundation*'s most sophisticated robot, R. Daneel Olivaw, is suggested to be nearly indistinguishable from a human, and his status as a thinking, feeling creature is never in doubt.

There are other reasons to believe that Asimov's robots have minds. In trying to formulate a theory of consciousness, philosophers and scientists have proposed properties that a system must have in order to be conscious, and Asimovian robots seem to possess at least some of these. Asimov's robots are intelligent and complex. They (sometimes) have bodies like ours, and they communicate with language. They also seem to possess *autonomy,* something that sets them apart from the more familiar robotic systems of our world. For instance, imagine an industrial robot that carries out its program precisely, assembling parts and making the same welds over and over without any deviation in its routine. Such a welder-bot has no autonomy: it's doing what it's designed to do and nothing more, and few would attribute to it mental states (goals, desires, and beliefs) to explain its behavior. The attribution of such states to the ideal Asimovian robot—humanoid in shape, capable of navigating the world, making decisions and adaptively confronting new problems—seems much more appropriate though: its self-generated behavior and decisions naturally suggests that it possesses a mind. If we discovered that the robot were just a puppet though, controlled by a human behind a curtain, it's lack of autonomy would lead us to withdraw our attribution of a mind.

The example involving the mimicking of autonomous behavior brings up an important point about the reliability and completeness of proposed criteria for consciousness. Suppose we could construct a system that *by design* was not conscious—having no subjective experiences whatsoever—but still evinced all the complex behaviors of a human being (including *claiming to be conscious*). This scenario is at least conceivable: it's possible that a system could give all the right signs, and yet there be nothing-it-is-like to be it. Such systems are known as *philosophical zombies* (a term coined by David Chalmers), and they pose a serious problem for explaining which systems do (or do not) have consciousness. If a system having the properties you think are important—behavior, intelligence, complexity—could still be a zombie, such properties seem insufficient for consciousness (and possibly not even necessary). There is considerable disagreement over what physical properties are required for consciousness.

Some people say that basic physics is relatively unimportant, and that the fundamental requirements for a mind concern only the *functions* implemented by a system: if a system behaves and processes information in the same manner as a human brain, it must have a mind. At the other extreme, 'anti-functionalists' argue that what ultimately matters is a system's *physical structure*: if a system is put together in the same way as a human brain, it must have a mind (regardless of what functions it implements). Asimov's stories avoid this debate by withholding detailed, technical explanations of his robots' positronic brains. Are they CPU-based computers, running mental simulations? Or are they synthetic 'neuromorphic' machines that replicate the fine-grained causal structure of a biological brain?

Given its silence on these issues, one might suppose that *Foundation* holds little for readers interested in the metaphysics of consciousness. However, a central theme of the Foundation stories is that minds are things which can *extend* beyond the brain, either by connecting to artifacts in the environment or to other minds.

## The Extended Mind of Golan Trevize

In Chapter Four of *Foundation's Edge* (1982), Golan Trevize obtains an advanced starship—the *Far Star*—to use in his quest. To control the *Far Star*, he lays his hands on a console, which in turn causes his mind to 'extend' throughout the ship. He becomes immediately aware of all its systems and controls, as well as the outside world surrounding the ship. Although initially skeptical of the fact that the interfacing occurred via his *hands* rather than a brain interface, Trevize then reconsiders:

> The hands? But why not the hands? Trevize found himself floating away, almost drowsy, but with no loss of mental acuity. Why not the hands? . . . It was the hands that were the working surface, the hands that felt and manipulated the Universe. Human beings thought with their hands. It was their hands that were the answer of curiosity, that felt and pinched and turned and lifted and hefted. There were animals that had brains of respectable size, but they had no hands and that made all the difference . . . (italics added)

It may seem strange to countenance hands and their activity as part of 'thinking'. Indeed, according to a traditional and still prevalent view of the mind, the mind and its processes are entirely a matter of the brain. Yet, the idea that conscious processes can extend to body parts, as well as processes and tools in the environment, has gained significant traction in cognitive science and philosophy over the past thirty years. This view—the Extended Mind Thesis—states that processes and objects external to the brain can constitute portions of a mind.

Some proponents of the Extended Mind Thesis believe that, while it is *possible* for minds to extend beyond the skull, technology is not yet advanced enough to make this happen.

Others believe that our minds currently do extend. Since future technology is what makes possible the extension of Trevize's mind, the former rather than the latter view may be operative in *Foundation*. But regardless of whether such extension is seen as actual or merely possible, why believe such a radical hypothesis as the Extended Mind in the first place?

## Why Think that a Mind Could Extend?

Imagine a working computer contained within a desktop tower. Suppose that one of the computer's components were removed and placed in another room, but kept connected via a wireless connection. If done properly, redistributing the hardware in this way would make no difference to the system's behavior and the computations it can perform. The only difference is in the computer's spatial footprint, which now extends beyond the tower's casing. Now apply this same reasoning about the computer and tower to the case of *mind and skull*: If some bit of necessary computational processing implemented by the brain can be moved *outside* the skull, and this does not radically alter the brain's functional/computational profile, then we should consider the mind as something that can spatially extend beyond the skull.

Philosophers Andy Clark and David Chalmers codify just this sort of reasoning in the following *Parity Principle*:

> If, as we confront some task, a part of the world functions as a process which, were it done in the head, we would have no hesitation in recognizing it as part of the cognitive process, then that part of the world is (so we claim) part of the cognitive process. ("The Extended Mind," p. 8)

To illustrate how this principle is used to defend the extended mind thesis, Clark and Chalmers invite us to think about the following thought experiment involving two individuals, Otto and Inga, who access navigational information in different ways:

> Both Otto and Inga see a notice for a new exhibition at the Museum of Modern Art (MoMA) and immediately decide to attend. To navigate to the museum, Inga calls forth from her memory a belief about MoMA's location and uses that information to get to the exhibition. Otto's memory is poor though due to Alzheimer's, so he resorts to a different method of accessing the same information: He looks up the address for MoMA in a notebook that he always carries and uses that information to navigate. This notebook doesn't just contain information

> about MoMA's address: It also contains a multitude of other important information that Otto has assented to in the past and recorded in writing. All this information is retrievable by Otto as fast as Inga is capable of calling forth her beliefs. Also, Otto always has his notebook at the ready to retrieve information (just as Inga's beliefs are always available to her for retrieval) and automatically assents to the information therein (just as Inga automatically assents to her beliefs).

If Inga's information retrieval process is a part of her mind (which it surely is), then shouldn't Otto's information retrieval process similarly count as part of *his* mind? If the information Inga retrieves is a belief, then shouldn't the information retrieved from Otto's notebook also count as a belief? Clark and Chalmers argue that since Inga's mental process is functionally identical to Otto's, and the only relevant difference is that Otto's is not inside his brain, the Parity Principle entails that Otto's process must also be mental. In other words, Otto's mind extends into the world.

There are also empirical arguments for the Extended Mind: Research suggests that we do, in some sense, 'think with our hands'. Take the case of gesturing: one study showed that boys tended to gesture more during spatial rotation tasks than girls, which perhaps accounts for the boys' better performance in the tasks. Another study showed that when describing spatial situations, subjects prevented from making hand gestures spoke more slowly and paused more frequently than subjects who were free to gesture. And in a more familiar example, if you've ever played Scrabble you might have used your hands to manipulate the order of the letter tiles, searching for possible words to play. In all these cases, our hands seem a part of the thought process, allowing us to manipulate information in a similar way as we do 'in our heads'.

## Is Trevize Just Another Otto?

While Asimov doesn't give us mechanistic accounts of the mind's substrate or of the *Far Star*'s technology, readers do get a detailed description of Trevize's *experience* as he interfaces with the Far Star:

> . . . as he and the computer held hands, their thinking merged and it no longer mattered whether his eyes were open or closed. Opening them did not improve his vision nor did closing them dim it. Either way, he saw the room with complete clarity—not just in the direction in which he was looking, but all around and above and below. He saw

> every room in the spaceship and he saw outside as well. The sun had risen and its brightness was dimmed in the morning mist, but he could look at it directly without being dazzled, for the computer automatically filtered the light waves. He felt the gentle wind and its temperature, and the sounds of the world about him. He detected the planet's magnetic field and the tiny electrical charges on the wall of the ship. He became aware of the controls of the ship, without even knowing what they were in detail. He knew only that if he wanted to lift the ship, or turn it, or accelerate it, or make use of any of its abilities, the process was the same as that of performing the analogous process to his body. He had but to use his will. (Asimov, 1982, Chapter 4)

Here the situation has some resemblance to that of Otto and his notebook: Information in the environment, accessed by an individual in a fast and automatic fashion, ends up serving the same functional role as a belief in the head. Indeed, one way to characterize Trevize's mind as extending through the ship would be to say that his set of beliefs greatly expands as information from the ship becomes part of his accessible belief store.

Certainly, Trevize has *more* information at his disposal than Otto gets from his notebook, but perhaps that is not an interesting difference: After all, many of us have ready access to vast stores of information via the Internet, and so maybe Trevize's access to Far Star's 'intranet' is similar. Also, while Trevize gains the ability to detect things that humans cannot, perhaps this is merely like humans accessing information from displays (like vehicle dashboards or a cockpit HUD) or through devices that allow us to see things we could not normally (like telescopes or night-vision goggles). So why isn't Trevize's connection to the Far Star the same as accessing information from the internet, or a database, or from a dashboard display? Other than the mode of delivery, what could be different?

Actually, we can see that much is different by attending to how Asimov describes Trevize's inner experience. For instance, consider the case of magnetic fields. Humans are insensitive to magnetic fields, but we *can* measure them with a magnetometer that reports field strength in the form of numbers on a display. But while we may acquire new knowledge by using a magnetometer, the knowledge acquired is via ordinary *visual* experiences: by *looking at the display*. Yet Trevize seems to have some kind of sensory experience of the planet's magnetic field *directly*—he doesn't *see* it as data on a virtual display, rather he *feels* it in a new way that astonishes him. His connection to the Far Star seems qualitatively different from a pilot's use of flight instruments.

In another example, the Far Star–connected Trevize sees throughout the interior of the ship, "not just in the direction in which he was looking, but all around and above and below"—even with his eyes closed. Yet human vision is always from a single observer's perspective—from a pair of eyes located somewhere in space—and it seems inconceivable that it could be otherwise. It can't be that he sees a thousand viewpoints as through a kaleidoscope: the human visual field doesn't have the requisite resolution to support such an experience. Again, it seems that Trevize's experiences have undergone a qualitative change: he doesn't just *know* new things by being connected to the ship, but he has *new kinds of experiences* that were hitherto impossible for him to have.

Trevize's situation is different from Otto's. Otto viewed his notebook to merely extract navigational information, but this was via experiences of the ordinary visual kind. He didn't have new *feelings* corresponding to what it's like to be a page in a notebook, or ink on a page. Trevize doesn't just *extract* information from the ship: He becomes able to enter new experiential states that are unlike anything he has ever experienced, or could ever experience, on his own.

## Is Extended Consciousness Scientifically Plausible?

The extension of conscious experience is not just a matter of philosophical debate. According to a prominent scientific account of consciousness, the Integrated Information Theory, consciousness is a consequence of a certain kind of network complexity. The theory states that if a network is more strongly connected to *itself* than to its *surroundings*, it is a conscious thing of its own. The cerebral cortex happens to fit this bill: it is massively self-connected, while its connections to the outside world—and indeed to the rest of the brain—are weak by comparison. So, according to Integrated Information Theory, consciousness must be localized to the cortex.

One prediction of Integrated Information Theory is that if connections among parts of a conscious system are weakened appropriately, the system should break down into multiple, independent conscious sub-systems. This situation actually arises in the real-life case of split-brain patients. These patients undergo a *callosotomy*, a rare surgery in which the bundle of fibers connecting the two cortical hemispheres—the *corpus callosum*—is severed. According to Integrated Information Theory, this results in *two* separate minds inhabiting one cranium, since each hemisphere is now more strongly connected to itself than to one another. This startling conclusion is actually vindicated by evidence showing that split-brain patients behave as if they are governed by two separate minds.

This principle of strong self-connectedness can be applied to systems generally. Suppose we were to connect the cerebral cortex with some external device in such a way that the connections among the cortex-plus-device supersystem were stronger than the connections within the cortex alone. For more information on such patients' behaviors, Integrated Information Theory would say that now it is the *supersystem*—not the cortex on its own—that is conscious.

Can this principle be applied to the case of Trevize and the Far Star? The implication would be that, through some technological mechanism, Trevize has strongly connected his brain to the ship's systems—which must themselves be strongly self-connected—and thereby extended his consciousness into the ship. However, Integrated Information Theory clearly excludes the hands—and the entire peripheral nervous system—from being part of the substrate of our consciousness: their connections to cortex are too weak in comparison to the brain's internal connections.

So Trevize could not possibly extend his conscious substrate to encompass the ship by mere touch, as there could not be a strong-enough connection between Trevize's brain and the Far Star. However, were a complex, physical connection of the right sort forged directly between Trevize's brain—not through the hands, but through some undescribed device—and the ship's own self-connected network, Trevize's mind might be expected to extend into the ship's systems. In effect, a callosum-like connection between Trevize and the ship would be required to merge them, like our two brain hemispheres, into a densely self-connected whole.

The episode involving Trevize and the *Far Star* reflects a central theme of *Foundation*'s later novels: the connection of minds. So far, we've discussed the possibility of the substrate of consciousness expanding via connections with things like our hands, information-storage devices (such as notebooks), and large-scale processing systems (such as a spaceship). But there's something else that minds might connect to that could cause them to expand: *other minds*.

## The Planetary Mind of Gaia

While it's a central plot device in the early Foundation stories, the theme of connected minds reaches its zenith in the later novels *Foundation's Edge* (1982) and *Foundation and Earth* (1986). In these two books, Asimov explores the notion of a *group consciousness,* a mind that is itself constituted by the individual minds of multiple agents. It's here that readers are introduced to Gaia, the *deus ex planeta* of the Foundation series. Gaia is more than just a planet: It is a thinking, feeling, sentient entity. The substrate of its consciousness is neither solely organic tissue nor the stuff of positronic brains. Instead, Gaia's mind arises from the interaction of all the entities that compose the planet. This includes not just the minds of Gaia's human, animal and robot inhabitants, but also its plants and even the non-living physical components of the planet itself.

Gaia's depiction keeps with the theme of minds extending and connecting. As in the case of Trevize and the *Far Star*, the substrate of Gaia's mind is broadly spatially extended and encompasses aspects of the environment outside of a brain and body. And as with the enigmatic Mule, the minds of Gaia's inhabitants can telepathically connect and influence other minds. Unlike the Mule and Far Star though, Gaia is a spatially extended substrate of connected minds that forms a novel, sovereign consciousness—a *new* mind that emerges as something distinct from the individual consciousnesses that compose it.

Asimov seemed to have a longstanding fascination with the notion of group minds. In the short story *The Last Question* (1959), a supercomputer grows over the eons until it comes to encompass the whole of humanity in its computations. And in *Nemesis* (1989) there is a planet-wide, collective consciousness composed of micro-organisms—which were individually said to lack any consciousness of their own.

## Gaia and Panpsychism

Gaia is a super-mind composed of the minds of its creatures, plants and non-living systems. This assumes that non-living entities (such as rocks, micro-level particles) and plants *could in fact be conscious*. While this assumption in the story world may not give readers pause, many would still see it as a wildly implausible claim about consciousness *in the real world*. Yet *panpsychism*—the position that consciousness is a fundamental and widespread, if not ubiquitous, phenomenon in nature—has long been a matter of serious debate in the philosophy of mind.

The main attraction of panpsychism has typically been the way it meets the challenge of the so-called 'Hard Problem' of consciousness, which can be roughly stated as follows: how could physical stuff, something so categorically and qualitatively unlike consciousness, give rise to consciousness? From a complete physical description of a system (brain or otherwise), we just cannot deduce whether that system is conscious or what its consciousness is like. This is a central and enduring problem in philosophy of mind, but panpsychists have a ready answer to it: The fundamental stuff of our world *is or contains consciousness, and so all things have it*. As elementary particles come together to form compounds and objects with various physical properties, so too do their elementary consciousnesses come together to form larger conscious minds. According to this view, we no longer face the difficult problem of explaining how consciousness could emerge in a physical world from purely physical stuff, because consciousness is already baked into the fundamental fabric of reality.

Panpsychist conceptions of nature have a long philosophical history. In the seventeenth century, the philosopher Baruch Spinoza argued that the natural world was the manifestation of the mind of God, and that any part of the universe was an aspect of that mind. Spinoza's contemporary Gottfried Leibniz had a complementary view of nature, holding that the universe was composed of a vast (or infinite) number of tiny units called *monads*., each endowed with a mind. Physicist-philosopher Gustav Fechner (1801–1887) advanced a picture of nature as a *world mind*. According to Fechner's *cosmopsychism*, the entire universe constitutes a mind of which we are all a part. For Fechner, any dynamical natural system has a mind—humans, animals, plants, ecosystems, the Earth itself, the solar system, and, ultimately, the entire cosmos.

Fechner's world-mind has some strong resemblance to Gaia. However, for Fechner the world-mind was an inevitable consequence of a dynamic and coherent universe. In contrast, Gaia does not seem to be a natural state of affairs: it is a consequence of evolutionary and technological advances that have made possible the telepathic linking of minds. If group minds were naturally occurring, then in *Foundation and Earth* Trevize would not face the question of whether Gaia's consciousness should continue expanding by telepathically folding the Galaxy's other planets and peoples into its group mind: A galactic group mind would rather already exist, in the style of Fechner's *cosmopsyche*.

## Gaia and the Combination Problem

Let's suppose that panpsychism is true. Everything then has some level of subjective experience, and the consciousness of smaller entities combine to form larger consciousnesses. A difficult question then arises: How exactly do micro-minds combine to form composite minds? Science provides rich explanations of how higher-level systems in our world come to have their properties based on their constituents' properties, but it's difficult to envision how micro-experiences could form a more complex one, especially when the latter has aspects that none of the micro-experiences may possess (such as emotions or a sense of self). Also, a fundamental feature of consciousness seems to be its private, subjective nature. But if experience is private, how could conscious subjects be capable of 'mixing' to create the subjective consciousness of a group mind? Without a good account of how this works, we find that we have just swapped the Hard Problem for another equally difficult problem, namely, a *Combination Problem*.

*Foundation* lacks a detailed metaphysical or scientific account of Gaia's genesis, although it does claim that Gaia's mind is realized via telepathic links between minds. While this leaves the Combination Problem unsolved, invoking telepathic links between minds addresses at least one aspect of the problem, namely, that the privacy of subjects' consciousness would always prevents them from blending into a larger, distinct consciousness. If minds can telepathically link, this privacy condition is relaxed, since minds can be directly accessed by others.

The theme of connected minds runs throughout *Foundation*, for example in storylines involving Mule and the Second Foundation. Whereas the "mentalics" of the Mule and the Second Foundation's 'speakers' represent one-way connections from one agent to another, the telepathic connections between Gaians are *reciprocal*. Such mass reciprocal connectivity would in fact be expected of any conscious system, according to Integrated Information Theory and other consciousness theories.

## What Is It Like to Be a Gaian?

Gaia poses another puzzle. What must it be like for the individuals that constitute it? Would they have access to thoughts and feelings of the group mind (and vice versa)? Would their phenomenal experience be qualitatively like our own, or be fundamentally different (and in what way)? Would they even *know* that they were participating in a group mind? If so, how?

Asimov makes it clear that Gaia *does* have access to its constituent minds. Gaia seems to know everything that its constituents know, which means that Gaia has a kind of experiential and epistemic access that most panpsychists wouldn't ever ascribe to group minds (few panpsychists would argue that we have access to the private minds of our micro-constituents). The access apparently also runs in the opposite direction: individual Gaians like the character Bliss seem to have access to the group mind, as well as the minds of other Gaians. But then how individuated *are* these individuals' minds? Are they all just parts of a whole, as your visual and auditory experiences are parts of your singular experience? Surely your visual experiences are not *also* leading their own separate, individuated existence in parallel with yours . . .

Finally, there are also open questions about the *quantity* of minds that make up Gaia. Recall that Asimov postulates only two levels of mind: the group mind, and the individual minds of the physical components and inhabitants of the planet. But why think *only* these two levels exist, and that there are not intermediate group minds that arise *between* these poles? For instance, the minds of any two Gaian inhabitants might form a small group mind themselves, and any pair of small group minds might form slightly larger group minds. This leads to a proliferation of group minds, perhaps each with their own personalities and goals. Asimov never considers this possibility, but neither does he provide enough detail about how Gaia's group mind arises to rule it out. Given that each mind on Gaia is telepathically linked though, why should it be the case that a group mind only emerges, so to speak, at the top?

## Foundation and Philosophy Today

The stories of *Foundation* don't focus on neuroscientific details or physical facts about brains. Nor do they endorse any particular scientific theory of consciousness. Still, with their treatment of minds as things that extend, connect and compose other minds, these stories touch on issues at the heart of philosophy of mind and consciousness science (and this despite a lack of clarity concerning what metaphysical facts are intended to hold in *Foundation*'s universe).

Within one saga we have conscious robots, telepathic manipulation, the merging of minds with starships, and the emergence of a planetary—and perhaps galactic—supermind. So, while its eschewal of technological and scientific details places it outside of the category of *hard* science fiction, *Foundation* remains a timeless work of *psychological* science fiction, still able to engage with core philosophical issues about consciousness.

# 19
# Cleons and Cloning

JOSHUA HETER

The most noteworthy addition to the universe of Asimov's *Foundation* in David S. Goyer's Apple TV+ adaption is the Cleon Dynasty.

According to the newly developed lore, sometime during his reign, Emperor Cleon I concluded that his genetic information to be of such a unique and impeccable quality that it would best serve the Galactic Empire if he (at least, in subsequent iterations of his DNA profile) were to continue to rule in perpetuity. Thus, a system is put in place in which an ever-shuffling lineup of Cleons (in the form of brothers Dawn, Day, Dusk and occasionally Darkness) will rule the galaxy for as long as the dynasty can maintain its grip on the levers of power.

There's something unnerving about even the idea that a ruler here on planet Earth takes himself to have some sort of divine right such that he and his natural lineage should exercise perpetual rule over a geographically limited kingdom. Thus, the hubris required for a ruler to believe that only genetic copies of himself are worthy (or adept enough) to rule over an entire galaxy is truly terrifying. And, there are a great number of philosophical, psychological and political questions that could be raised about this aspect of the Cleons. However, I won't pursue those issues here. There are more interesting questions to be raised about the metaphysics of cloning itself.

## On the Identity of Clones

Philosophers have had a lot to say about cloning at least since the mid-1990s due to the birth of Dolly, a Finnish Dorset Sheep, who was the first ever successfully cloned mammal. Indeed, the scientists at the Roslin Institute of Scotland, who were responsible for Dolly's cloned identity, played a significant role in turning what was once thought to be an issue relegated entirely to the realm of science fiction into a scientific reality.

But what exactly *is* a clone? This, one may argue is a question whose answer is fundamental to all subsequent questions concerning cloning. The most natural answer and one that has received a fair amount of attention is that cloning is about identity. A simple set of criteria might take clones to be the following.

- $C_1$ and $C_2$ are clones if and only if $C_1$ and $C_2$ are both organisms which are identical to one another.

This simple definition raises at least two important issues. The first is that the definition may be accused of kicking the conceptual can down the road, so to speak. Sure, cloning has something (important) to do with identity, but the concept of identity is where the interesting content is to be found. Until a definition of cloning tells us something about that, we really haven't said much about the nature of clones. *Of course*, brothers Dawn, Day, and Dusk are identical, but it's hard to not find sympathy with one who still wishes to ask: but what does that even *mean*?

The second issue raised by this definition, as we will see, is that identity itself may not be sufficient to capture what it is to be a clone. And, depending on how we understand identity, it may not be necessary either.

## Identifying Identity

One of the most fundamental yet mysterious concepts in all philosophical thought is the concept of identity. In some sense, it is just obvious what identity is; we all know what it means to say that two things are identical. Yet, articulating what identity is *precisely* with any theoretical rigor is (as it is with almost any interesting philosophical concept) a real puzzle. This challenge is made only more daunting by the fact that the concept is employed in at least two importantly different ways.

In *Foundation and Empire*, The Mule—a mentalic mutant and powerful warlord—briefly disguises himself as a clown named Magnifico Giganticus as part of a larger plot to undermine the First Foundation. Put simply, The Mule just *is* Magnifico Giganticus. Put just slightly differently, The Mule is *identical to* Giganticus. And of course, what is meant here is that in regard to The Mule and Giganticus, *there aren't two things, there is one thing*: the mutant warlord attempting to expand his empire (who happens to present himself in at least two different ways).

In contrast to this notion of identity, if you purchased this book at a brick and mortar store (presumably, with at least a handful of copies on the shelf), you likely didn't put much thought into which copy you leafed through and brought to the front of the store for purchase. This is of because all the copies were (at least in some sense) identical. However, to say the copy of the book that you purchased is identical to the copy you left on the shelf is certainly not to say that there aren't two things; there is one thing. There *are* two things: the book you purchased and the book which remains at the store. What is meant in this use of identity is that the two copies share all the same (relevant) properties.

Call these distinct notions of identity *numerical identity* and *qualitative identity*. The Mule and Magnifico Giganticus are numerically identical. It is not the case that in their regard there are two things; there is only one thing. However, two different copies of this book are merely qualitatively identical: they are said to share all the same properties—that is of course, if neither copy has a misprint, smudge, or some other blemish or alteration that the other copy does not.

Numerical and qualitative identity aren't entirely unrelated concepts. The Mule and Magnifico Giganticus are not merely numerically identical; they are also qualitatively identical, because *any* two things which are numerically identical must also be qualitatively identical.

There is a case to be made that qualitative identity is merely a species of numerical identity. It could be argued that the set of properties that your copy of the book has just is the same thing as the set of properties had by the book you left at the store. There aren't two things, there is one thing: the set of properties that are instantiated in the two copies of the book. However, such a view comes with a fair amount of its own metaphysical baggage and sorting that out is a challenge for another book. For now, we'll proceed on the assumption that the distinction between numerical and qualitative identity is fully intact.

Now, the point is this. It's obvious that members of the Cleon dynasty (or *any* purported set of clones) are not numerically identical. At any given time there are three or four Cleons kicking around. Spanning the centuries, there is a potentially countless number. Any two members of the Dynasty are seemingly qualitatively identical, and that (along with the fact that they are living organisms) is what makes them clones. Thus, we can update the set of criteria with which we began in regard to the nature of clones.

- $C_1$ and $C_2$ are clones if and only if $C_1$ and $C_2$ are both organisms which are *qualitatively* identical with one another.

So, if there are to be clones at all (insofar as clones must be identical in some sense), they must be *qualitatively* identical. However, as it turns out, there are reasons to think that qualitative identity alone will not be enough to help us pin down what it is to be a clone as there a number of qualities that are not shared by pairs which at least *seem* to be clones.

## On the Non-Identity of Clones

Any two clones (of one another) are not said to be numerically identical; they are merely qualitatively identical. And, so it would *seem*, it is just this latter fact that makes any two organisms clones. However, for any pair of alleged clones, it will not be difficult to push back on this claim as there are a great number of properties that any two alleged clones will not share. One might be so pessimistic as to suggest that if the nature of cloning is to be found in qualitative identity alone among individual organisms, perhaps there are just no such things as clones—even in principle.

As we think about cloning as it relates specifically to the Cleon Dynasty, the first and perhaps most obvious points of individuation between two alleged clones (in this case, any two Cleons) are the differences that come with age. Brother Dawn is a child (or at least, a teenager). Brothers Day and Dusk are adults. Being a child is a distinct property from being an adult. So (at least according to our current working definition of "clone"), Brother Dawn would not be a clone of Brother Day or Dusk. And of course, there are other age-related properties not all of the Brothers share (such as wrinkles, or the ability to grow a beard).

A natural response here would be to attempt to limit the properties relevant to what makes two organisms clones. If Brothers Dawn and Day had been born at the same point in time, one might argue, then the trivial differences that arise from their different birthdays would vanish. And, it is only *those remaining* properties that are relevant as to whether two organisms are clones. However, even if this concession were made, a great deal of differences between any two alleged clones remain. (See the articles on clones listed in the Bibliography.)

A second important difference between any two clones is the set of psychological differences they will no doubt have. Our genetic makeup goes a long way in determining who we are psychologically, but it does not get to write the whole story. To be sure, there are a whole host of factors that influence our eventual psychological makeup which take place entirely in utero. Even if the process of prenatal development could be standardized through some sort of synthetic process (not unlike the one which produces each member of the Cleon Dynasty), producing clones who share literally all the same psychological properties at birth, it would be difficult (if not impossible) to continue that development in the early years of each Cleon's life so that each will have literally all of the same properties as their alleged clone pairs. And of course, seeing as we often take our psychological makeup to be somehow *fundamental* to who were *really* are—certainly more so than any of the age-related properties previously mentioned—this is an especially non-trivial way in which two alleged clones cannot be said to be (even) qualitatively identical.

A third way in which two alleged clones will not be identical is in their perceptual and cognitive differences. To put it somewhat crudely, any two alleged clones will see the world differently both literally and figuratively. Every individual is trapped behind their own subjective experience of the world, and even if two individuals share a single genetic profile *as well as* a baseline psychology (such as their temperament, base desires, or propensity for certain behaviors), they will literally be seeing the world from two different perspectives and occasionally (if not regularly) coming to different conclusions and forming different beliefs about the world and themselves.

Crucially, this type of information processing will begin the moment any sort of standardized, streamlined prenatal development process ends. Even if these types of perceptual and cognitive differences can be minimized to a certain degree (as the caretakers of the Dawn-stage Cleons no doubt try to make happen), this set of perceptual and cognitive differences will nevertheless be another way in which any pair of alleged clones will fail to be qualitatively identical.

The fourth and final point of difference between alleged clones is in their genetic makeup. At this point, you could be forgiven for being frustrated with the discussion thus far. *Of course*, you might exclaim, clones aren't *entirely* qualitatively identical! They don't share literally *all* of their properties; they are merely qualitatively identical in regard to a subset of their properties: all of those properties which make up their *genetic profile*. What makes Dawn, Day, and Dusk clones is that they share DNA. In a way, this is to augment or update our set of criteria for what is to be a clone.

- $C_1$ and $C_2$ are clones if and only if $C_1$ and $C_2$ are both organisms which are *qualitatively* identical with one another at least in regard to the set of properties which makeup their shared genetic profile.

However, as it turns out, the genes of a pair of alleged clones are not enough to ground what it is to be a clone in terms of qualitative identity (even in this limiting sense).

Even if the Galactic Empire developed a process of cloning which birthed new Cleons with a genetic profile that is literally identical with all other Cleons (which would be very different and much more advanced than our own, current technology), this would be only a temporary fix. Our genes change as we age for a host of reasons. Supposing two alleged clones began with a qualitatively identical set of genetic information, it unlikely that each copy will share all the same properties later in life. Their qualitative identity will only be temporary. If what it is to be a clone is to be found in the qualitative identity of genes, are we then to say that two individuals began as clones but then lost that status later in life (because they no longer have a qualitative genetic identity)? That is a fairly odd logical consequence. In regard to the Cleon Dynasty, it's more natural to think of each iteration of Dawn, Day, and Dusk to all be clones at different stages of their lives. But importantly, they are still a set of clones even if at a given time, their genetic profiles do not share literally all the same properties. So it seems, defining clones in terms of a limited qualitative identity won't even do the trick.

## The Process of Cloning

Defining cloning in terms of identity seems natural and intuitive. But there are odd logical consequences to be found if we were to be so rigid as to say that what it means to be a clone is that clones must be literally qualitatively identical (even if only for a subset of their properties). If this were the case, two clones could (and inevitably would) *lose* their clone status (when one clone gains or loses a genetic property that the other does not). Perhaps even more odd, as unlikely as it would be, two organisms which were never clones could *gain* clone status if (through natural or other processes) their genetic profiles were to at least momentarily align. This is not to say that cloning has nothing to do with identity. It very well may, but it probably does not play the type of role we've been considering for it.

The definition I wish to propose is one that is rooted in causality. To put it plainly, a clone is a copy. Or, a clone is an organism that stands in a certain causal relation with a naturally occurring donor organism. Part of the idea here is that Cleon I is not a clone, but every subsequent Cleon that comes after him is. And, Cleon I does not become a clone upon the birth of Cleon II or Cleon III. To put the proposed definition more precisely:

- $C_1$ is a clone if and only if $C_1$'s genetic information exists as a result of a (potentially imperfect) copying process ultimately originating from a naturally-occurring (or initial donor) organism where "copying process" is an *attempt* to achieve qualitative (genetic) identity.

If this is correct, then our initial intuition that the nature of cloning is closely tied to identity was correct, but we shouldn't think that any two pairs of clones (or a clone and its donor organism) must be thought to be literally identical in any sense. And, whether or not this definition is ultimately defensible, it is merely the beginning of the story as there are a host of other metaphysical, ethical, psychological, and political questions that arise from the Cleons and cloning.

# 20
# The Mystery of Math

WALTER BARTA AND GRAHAM LEE

If the predictions made by Isaac Asimov in his *Foundation* series hold true, mathematics will be even more important in the future than it has been in the past. In the form of psychohistory, according to its mathematician creator, Hari Seldon, mathematics will be able to fully describe all natural phenomena, from the "nuclear forces" to the "nervous system" (*Second Foundation*, 1982, II.8).

This total mathematization of nature has been the dream of natural philosophers for generations. One of the first modern scientists, Galileo Galilei, said that "this grand book, the universe . . . It is written in the language of mathematics" (*The Assayer*, pp. 237–38). Such a Galilean claim seems presupposed by a mathematicised science like psychohistory. Following this line of reasoning, mathematician and physicist Isaac Newton developed the mathematics of calculus and also formulated the physics of the Three Laws of Motion. These two innovations complement one another: the physics of the three laws can be most elegantly described in abstract mathematics.

Laws like Newton's, which connect physical phenomena to mathematical equations, form the bedrock of scientific predictions like those of Hari Seldon. Pierre Laplace, a subsequent mathematician and physicist, believed that if some all-knowing creature, like a god (or what has come to be called Laplace's Demon), had the right equation for the universe, it could completely predict all events inside of it (*A Philosophical Essay on Probabilities*, p. 4). Laplace's Demon sounds a lot like Seldon's Psychohistorian, processing human civilizations as sets of zillions of small particles which operate according to calculable mathematical equations.

But, for all its power, what is mathematics? Is mathematics invented or discovered? Is it a human tool or a cosmic pattern? Is mathematics constructed to fit nature or does nature conform to mathematics? Throughout the *Foundation* saga, these questions about the foundations of mathematics spark intense galactic conflict. These controversies in the distant future have their origins in debates between philosophers in the distant past. As a psychohistorian might say, "To understand our future, we have to remember the past and the ones who caused it all" ("The Emperor's Peace"). These questions can be traced back to philosophers in ancient Greece, who studied numbers and theorized about what they are. Before Socrates, who is sometimes considered the founder of Western philosophy, two famous philosophers, Protagoras and Pythagoras, had completely different views on mathematics: relativism versus realism.

Whereas Protagoras thought that mathematics is a human construct, Pythagoras thought that mathematics grants access to truth beyond the world. These views greatly influenced the beliefs of Plato and Aristotle, the two most important philosophical writers of ancient Greece, and subsequently influenced the course of mathematical development into the modern era. In the twentieth century, these conflicts came to a head in the so-called "Foundational Crisis in Mathematics", a fierce debate between philosophers over the nature of numbers, which continues to this day.

## Protagoras and the Measure of a Man

Protagoras was one of the first ancient Greek philosophers to give an account of mathematical truth. According to legend, Protagoras was a genius of geometry. His soon-to-be mentor, Democritus, discovered Protagoras after observing him in the street carrying a bundle of wood blocks so geometrically perfect that it impressed the elder philosopher enough that he hired him, housed him, taught him, and made him into a great philosopher (Gellius, *Attic Nights*). This is not unlike how Hari Seldon pulled Gaal Dornick, his would-be protégé, out of the backwaters of the galaxy to work on the Foundation.

Just like Protagoras's bundle of wood, for millennia humans have been using mathematics for their purposes, especially in the form of technology. One of the cornerstones of the Galactic Empire is its ability to use mathematics instrumentally towards technological ends. As Gaal is told by an imperial liaison, "the Empire will set about solving the problem as we always have. You should believe in the minds that built

Trantor, built the jump drive, that built the Star Bridge" ("The Emperor's Peace"). The enormous accomplishments of the planet of Trantor, the capital of the galactic empire, show just how useful math and science can be. Whether scanning one's biometrics, counting subterranean levels, or gauging years on a jump ship, applied mathematics is everywhere making technology function for human purposes.

Back in ancient Greece, Protagoras went on to become a famous and wealthy sophist, a person who teaches the use of words above the use of facts. Indeed, Protagoras supposedly coined the saying "There are two sides to every argument" and made money teaching both sides. Even in the galactic future there are two sides represented in the Imperial Court of Trantor. For example, Hari Seldon's arguments come into conflict with the Emperor's arguments. This kind of ambivalence is the natural conclusion of Protagoras's general belief in relativism, epitomized in his famous phrase: "Man is the measure of all things" (*Theaetetus*, 152a).

If Protagoras is right, then truths themselves are true only relative to the man measuring them. Hari Seldon's truths are not the Emperor's truths. This applies even to some of the firmest seeming truths of all: truths about numbers. Indeed, in spite of his humble origins as Democritus's disciple, far from becoming a believer, Protagoras became a doubter. According to Aristotle in his *Metaphysics*, Protagoras denied the formal existence of mathematical entities like numbers, suggesting that they do not really exist. For example, Protagoras points out that we may think that we see straight lines between stars in the night sky—between Trantor and Terminus, let's say—but this is nothing more than us superimposing our abstract concepts onto real objects (Aristotle, *Metaphysics*, 998a). We can look around our world for "natural" triangles, squares, or circles, but will do so in vain; we will only ever find approximations of geometrical shapes in nature. Even if we disagree with Protagoras's conclusion, we can see the force of his argument: mathematics is tidy while reality is messy.

Per Protagoras's observation, mathematical conventions themselves may vary relative to different cultures. In the future Galactic Empire, the diversity of mathematical conventions is as vast as the galaxy itself. As Gaal Dornick is right to point out, even the decision to use a base-ten counting system is a convention that is culturally specific and non-universal ("Preparing to Live"). This accords with the Protagorean view, on which even bedrock mathematical truths can have culturally contingent conventions at bottom.

Furthermore, the relativity of truth can benefit the Protagorean's own political purposes. As a teacher of rhetoric, Protagoras could apply his argumentation towards any given political agenda without having to make any special claims to truth. On the Protagorean view, math serves the mathematician. In the future Galactic Empire, the Imperial Court of Trantor takes approximately this pragmatic Protagorean view. The Emperor and his cohort are deeply concerned with mathematics, particularly in its political application. Any math that supports the Empire is embraced; any math that undermines the Empire is rejected. But, of course, such a stance entails that controversial math, like Hari Seldon's psychohistory, may be exiled or outlawed if found useless, inexpedient, or contrary to the Empire's purposes. Indeed, as soon as psychohistory begins to offer predictions at odds with the imperial agenda, the mathematician is arrested for treason and rebellion ("The Emperor's Peace"). As the Emperor himself says, "Art is simply politics' sweeter tongue," and mathematics is apparently one of these arts open for revision ("The Emperor's Peace"). Eventually, the Emperor admits to his own self-aggrandizing view of truth: "We are Empire. History bends to us!" ("The Leap").

Perhaps the most extreme example of a self-serving disposition towards knowledge is the way the planet Synnax outlaws and kills mathematicians and scientists for religious reasons ("The Emperor's Peace"). Through such censorship, the so-called "truths" of the Synnaxian religion can never be questioned. The extremes of the Synnaxian religion show just how self-insulating a relativized system of truth can be. But, even if we are not relativists, we can recognize with Protagoras that mathematics can be used for politics. Even Hari Seldon says that "math is never just numbers. In the wrong hands, it's a weapon. In the right hands, deliverance" ("The Emperor's Peace"). Mathematics has unavoidable practical and political implications.

## Protagorean Critics

Far from accepting a Protagorean view, however, Plato and Aristotle seriously doubted the relativism of mathematical truth, both in a strong sense and a weak sense.

Read in a strong sense, Protagoras seems to be vulnerable to a proliferation of truths: that every claim is equally true. In the dialogue, *Theaetetus*, Plato shows this absurdity by taking the Protagorean conception to its logical conclusion. First, Plato demonstrates that if truth is measured by a man, then each man can arrive at a different truth (171b). Plato can arrive at one truth; Protagoras can arrive at another truth. If everyone can have their own truth, then there can be as many different truths as there are different truth-tellers (152c, 162a). We see this critique play out in *Foundation* when "a thousand imperial mathematicians" are willing to openly contradict Hari Seldon's math, merely for imperial favor ("Barbarians at the Gate"). What Plato initially dislikes about this sort of situation is that the beliefs of fools might be just as true as the beliefs of the wise: that there is neither intelligence nor ignorance at all (170c, 179b). Worse still, this would apply to Protagoras's own beliefs, which would be true just for him (171c). Ironically, Protagoras's book itself was called "Truth", which Plato derides as "his truth", as opposed to "my truth" (152c, 162a). Although some of Hari Seldon's followers seem to trust "his truth" in a Protagorean way, Seldon himself, like Plato, explicitly rejects this relativist attitude, saying, "Math doesn't take sides. It doesn't judge . . . These aren't things I'm anxious to tell people . . . They're not my truths." ("The Emperor's Peace").

Aristotle further formalizes Plato's critique by showing that Protagoras's view leads to a logical contradiction (*Metaphysics*, 1009a, 1047a, 1007b). According to Aristotle's "Law of Noncontradiction," a statement cannot be true and false (1062b). But if everyone can have their own truth, then both an advocate and their opponent can be correct, so that the conclusions of both an argument and its counterargument can be equally "true." This conclusion seems obviously absurd because it implies that something can be both true and false. In the case of mathematics, this would mean that $2 + 2 = 4$ and $2 + 2 \neq 4$. We see this problem manifest itself when imperial handlers give Gaal Dornick an ultimatum: "I'll make the calculus simple for you, Gaal. If you say Hari's a liar, he dies. If you don't, you die" ("The Emperor's Peace"). By demanding that Gaal lie or die, the Empire reveals that their own system has led to a contradiction that must be hidden away and denied to maintain order, while Hari and Gaal are unwilling to compromise truth even at risk to their lives.

Read in a weak sense, Protagoras is perhaps saying something merely trivial. According to Aristotle, rather than making contradictory claims about truth, Protagoras may simply be saying that everything in the outside world is necessarily known or "measured" through our sensory perception, because this is our only access to the outside world. For example, the inhabitants of an ocean planet like Synnax, an ice planet like Terminus, and a metropolitan planet like Trantor might reasonably arrive at different conclusions because their experiences, their windows into the world, are so different. Aristotle agrees that we are constrained by our senses but says that this is something quite obvious and unexceptional (1053a–b). Protagoras thus faces a dilemma: his big idea about truth is either contradictory or trivial.

Even without these critiques, we frequently have counter-Protagorean intuitions, because what seems precisely so special about knowledge, particularly mathematical knowledge, is the independence of its truth from the knower. Mathematicians like Seldon often refer to mathematical principles as neutral truths that "belong to science" ("The Emperor's Peace"). In such a manner, by divorcing himself from his thought, the knower from the knowledge, Seldon levels an anti-Protagorean critique against the Empire and those who would wield mathematical truth for purely political purposes.

## Modern Protagoreans

Regardless of these critiques, following the Protagorean tradition, many modern philosophers believe in types of mathematical formalism: that math is just a series of rule-based language games. The mathematician David Hilbert developed this account of mathematics, later known as "Hilbert's Program", as just a "formula game," a purely linguistic set of rules not unlike grammar. Similarly to Protagoras, Hilbert suggests that we can have as many sets of definitions as sets of definers—though with the additional caveat that they cannot contradict. Inasmuch as mathematics emerges from a set of basic "axioms", or starting assumptions, remarkably different conclusions can be derived from different sets of axioms. Thus, the axioms of mathematics cannot be something out there in the universe but must be something constructed. For example, as a nervous habit Gaal Dornick counts prime numbers, but we might just as easily count Fibonacci numbers, factorial numbers, or any other formal pattern of numbers: no one pattern is unique to the cosmic order of things. The mathematician and physicist, Henri Poincare, put forward a similar view of geometries as "conventions" ("Non-Euclidean Geometries"). Poincare noticed that geometries are just conventional systems that vary depending on the definitions accepted. For example, in Euclidean geometry, on a plane two parallel lines will never intersect; however, in spherical geometry, two parallel lines intersect at the poles of the sphere. Consequently, Foundationists can plot their star-maps according to any given set of self-consistent geometric rules and still find their way across the galaxy. In a similar vein, later modern philosophers, such as Bertrand Russell and Alfred North Whitehead in their *Principia Mathematica*, suggest logicism: that mathematics is entirely derivable from logical rules by extending inferences. Regardless, Protagoreanism and its "truths" have lived far beyond their ancient cultural contexts.

## Pythagoras and the Music of the Spheres

Pythagoras is another of the most famous mathematicians in ancient Greece. His greatest claim to fame is the formula for calculating the lengths of the sides of right triangles, the Pythagorean Theorem, since he is credited as the first thinker to derive the equation, for which it bears his name (*Lives*, 15–16). This theorem is still used to this day and will be used into the distant future, including for such seemingly advanced purposes as calculating trajectories in space travel. Pythagoras's mathematics is said to have been combined into the first and second volumes of Euclid's *Elements*, the most widely used mathematics textbook of all time. He also is alleged to have coined the term "philosophy" itself (9–10). Pythagoras studied musicology and astronomy and developed ideas about both subjects based on mathematical symmetries. He died when, fleeing from invaders, he refused to run across a field of beans—which he believed to be sacred. Thus, in a sense, Pythagoras was martyred for his beliefs, similarly to Hari Seldon.

According to his contemporaries, Pythagoras's own philosophy, which developed into a quasi-religious movement, claimed that numbers emerged from the unity of reality and composed everything in the universe, even space, time, and souls (349). At bottom everything is numbers; mathematics is the fundamental reality. So, to his followers, mathematical theorems were the absolute truths of the universe. In believing that the cosmos is fundamentally numerological, Pythagoras observed numerical patterns in everything. For example, he apparently believed that the number three is in control of the moon because the cube of three is twenty-seven, which is the number of days in the lunar cycle (*Attic Nights*, 1.20). We can see such Pythagorean reasoning guiding future religions as well. The interstellar religion of Luminism believes in the holiness of the number three and worships the "triple blessings" of three goddesses: the maiden, the mother, and the crone ("Death and the Maiden"). This numerological doctrine has its basis in a natural event: the splitting of the moon Surrah into three moons.

Gaal Dornick also encounters the connection between math and other beliefs when translating "Kalle's Ninth Proof of Folding", an ancient mathematical text, which Gaal says is very obscure because "Kalle's writing is poetic. It's beautiful, but it's hard to imagine there's any rigor there. So serious scholars don't read her" ("The Emperor's Peace"). As it was with Pythagoreans, real mathematics is sometimes intermingled with other forms of belief and culture.

Furthermore, like modern scientists and future psychohistorians, Pythagoras advocated the use of mathematics in answering questions about the natural world. For example, he famously used purely mathematical reasoning to estimate the height of Hercules, the famous hero of Greek mythology. Apparently, Pythagoras compared the stadium in which Hercules fought to a stadium used by contemporary Greeks in order to estimate the size of Hercules's foot as compared with the size of the foot of an average contemporary Greek. Then Pythagoras used the ratio of feet to height to determine how tall Hercules was. Although this method may seem imprecise at best and absurd at worst, the use of mathematical reasoning to answer questions about history was a revolutionary thought. Indeed, by using past trends to predict future trends, psychohistorians are ultimately doing the same thing.

In spite of its oddities, the core of Pythagoreanism greatly influenced later philosophy, including Plato and his "theory of the forms". In a dialogue traditionally attributed to Plato, *Timaeus*, the titular Pythagorean entertains the belief that the cosmos is just "participation in number" (*Timaeus*, 39b). All things, including fire, water, earth and air, are ultimately derived from "form and number." Plato himself has been identified with this form of Pythagorean realism about mathematics, the view that numbers are real entities in themselves, so much so that the view is sometimes referred to as mathematical Platonism (*Metaphysics*). Even if we discard many of the more numerological aspects of Pythagoreanism, this mathematical Platonism can be conserved.

In the Galactic Empire, the Foundationist ideology has at least two Pythagorean qualities. First, like Pythagoreans, the Foundationists approach mathematics in a quasi-religious way. Gaal Dornick even describes her math in the terms of prayer: "Once, I prayed in the words of my parents . . . I pray in a different language now. 86,981,803. 86,981,821. 86,981,827. 86,981,848." ("Preparing to Live"). Hari Seldon even goes as far as to describe his psychohistory as "a theorem so abstract, well . . . it might as well have been a prayer" ("Preparing to Live").

Like Pythagoreans, Hari Seldon and the Foundationists put their faith in the independent truth of mathematics.

Second, the Foundation largely operates on a form of mathematical Platonism, with Hari Seldon's psychohistory as its crowning achievement, a revelation of the fundamental mathematical structure of reality. Foundationists, like Pythagoreans, seem to think that they can understand the whole universe by understanding mathematics. Numbers and formulas are not true because wise men say them; wise men say them because they are true. As Seldon insists, "It's just what the math tells me" ("The Emperor's Peace"). The neo-Pythagorean Foundationists can believe in their own plan because they believe that numbers have absolute truth, wherein lies their utility in solving real-world problems. Gaal Dornick proves as much by managing to bypass the "required authorization" of the Starship Raven's navigation system using star charts and vector trigonometry, all from first principles ("Upon Awakening"). Nobody needs to ask authority for the answer when they can calculate it themselves. Furthermore, the Foundationists are notable in their application of mathematical axioms to patterns in nature. The science of psychohistory, like Pythagorean observations of music or orbits, seems to discern and reveal a mathematical basis for the physical world. This power is precisely what makes the Foundation such a threat to the Empire.

## Pythagorean Critics

However, Aristotle did not hold the Pythagorean opinion, that "numbers are the ultimate things in the whole physical universe" to be plausible (*Metaphysics*, 985b). Aristotle believed that the Platonist and the Pythagorean alike are unable to explain how either motion, magnitude, or other physical properties can arise merely out of immaterial numbers. Furthermore, Aristotle did not believe that any account of the connection between mathematical objects and sensible objects could be made. What would come first, the form of numbers or the number of forms?

Aristotle thought that such questions undermined the credibility of Pythagoreanism and mathematical Platonism. Indeed, there is something quite persuasive about Aristotle's view of numbers: although we may observe numbers of things (such as the numbers of stars), we never observe a pure number itself in isolation. Aristotle was closer to holding the belief that mathematics is a "science of quantities"; not real in the Platonic sense. Math makes useful generalizations, but with no independent existence of its own beyond sets of sensible objects. This is not far from how Gaal Dornick puts her own sense of cosmic doubt: "We use math to describe the inexpressible. The things that terrify us most. The vastness of space, the shape of time . . . the weight and worth of a human soul" ("Preparing to Live"). In other words, some of the most important things about our existential condition—space, time, and the soul—still seem irreducible to numbers, their existence remaining as metaphysically mysterious as that of the numbers themselves. Although numbers might assist our understanding of nature, this does not imply that nature itself is numbers at bottom. Staring at a chalkboard full of equations is not the same as staring at a sky full of stars.

## Modern Pythagoreans

Regardless of these criticisms, following in the Pythagorean tradition, many modern philosophers still believe in mathematical Platonism. For instance, the mathematician Kurt Gödel, famous for his "Incompleteness Theorem," believed that human minds intuit immaterial mathematical entities, perhaps like Gaal Dornick's outlier intuitions can detect events before they happen ("Some Basic Theorems"). Still others, like the philosophers Hillary Putnam and Willard Quine, believed that mathematics must be real because it is explanatorily indispensable for descriptions of the natural sciences.

Some modern scientists, like Eugene Wigner, hinting perhaps at psychohistory in the future, have even cited the "unreasonable effectiveness" of mathematics in natural science as proof of either a cosmic order or a cosmic miracle. Regardless, the Pythagorean creed persists in innumerable forms throughout time and space.

To this day, philosophers still widely disagree about the metaphysical properties of mathematics; the so-called "Foundational Crisis of Mathematics" rages on and, much like a Seldon Crisis facing Foundationists, there is no predicting its outcome. Modern philosophers vary on the spectrum between Protagoras and Pythagoras. However, regardless of its foundations, none can doubt the important role of mathematics in the world. The legacy of mathematics, especially its use in the construction of technology and description of nature, can be seen unfolding in modern science. Whether or not humans will ever achieve complete understanding of the rules governing the universe, the thought experiment of psychohistory in *Foundation* allows us to imagine what might happen if they did.

# 21
# A *Foundation*-al Lesson on Free Will and Determinism

JOSEF THOMAS SIMPSON

> There came the Mule. This strange man was not allowed for in the Plan. He was a mutant whose birth could not have been predicted. He had strange and mysterious power . . . that could bend all men to his will.
>
> —*Second Foundation*, 2010, p. 485

Isaac Asimov's *Foundation* series attempts to walk a fine line between implying that human actions are determined and allowing his characters to make impactful, free choices. He carries his readers along this precarious balance through the fictional science of *psychohistory*, a science that, using statistical analysis of massive conglomerates of human populations, predicts, with extremely high probability, how humans will react to events and stimuli.

The fictional science of psychohistory is modeled on the real science of chemistry; in particular, it is modeled on the kinetic theory of gasses. According to that theory, it is impossible to determine what individual atoms moving randomly will do, but nevertheless possible to derive very accurate laws of the motion of gasses using averages of the individuals (Asimov, *Gold*, pp. 185–89). And here we come to the heart of Asimov's attempt to balance free and determined action. Individual human beings behave in highly unpredictable ways while the actions of vast populations can be used to derive laws of how those populations will behave. On its face, this looks like an interesting and clever way simultaneously to have everything we want from an understanding of a predictable universe governed by laws as well as what we want in allowing free and "unpredictable" action of the beings inhabiting that universe.

Couching the predictable behavior of vast populations in terms of probabilities appears to be precisely what opens space to allow free action. If psychohistory can only predict events at high (perhaps extremely high) degrees of probability, then there's always the chance that something (or someone) breaks the probabilities. So much for bandying about accusations of inconsistency against Asimov. He can, it seems, hold that

> The laws of history are as absolute as the laws of physics, and if the probabilities of error are greater, it is only because history does not deal with as many humans as physics does atoms, so that individual variations count for more.

—while simultaneously satisfying the storyteller's need for characters with agency. In other words, the fact that psychohistory operates in probabilities allows Asimov to introduce Salvor Hardin's ingenious solution to the looming threat of Anacreon, twice, Hober Mallow's economic cold war against Korell, and so on.

These heroes of the Foundation appear to make genuine choices, a thought endorsed by the great Hari Seldon himself: "you see, then, that you are faced by hard necessity, and that action is forced on you. The nature of that action—that is, the solution to your dilemma—is, of course, obvious!" (*Foundation*, 2010, p. 69). Seldon does not say which specific action is forced, but only that action (of some kind) is forced. The implication? While the solution is obvious, it does not appear to be strictly determined; it is possible that had Hardin not seen the obvious solution another path would have been taken, a fact he relates to the ambitious Sermak thirty years later:

> The temptation was great to muster what force we could and put up a fight. It's the easiest way out, and the most satisfactory to self-respect—but, nearly invariably, the stupidest. You would have done it; you and your talk of 'attack first', (p. 78)

In this brief exchange, Asimov reiterates that the Seldon plan is not inviolate; choices at critical junctions must be made, and more to the point, may be made incorrectly. And so, the balance between free and determined action is intimated once again.

It is peculiar, then, to jump ahead in the *Foundation* Saga and find the Mule. This character principally serves two functions: one literary and one philosophical. The literary function is to introduce new tension into the now more established Foundation. As a technological and economic powerhouse, the

Foundation is now in a position to easily overcome putative external threats such that previous Seldon crises offer no tension or excitement in the plot. Given the Foundation's status as superpower, anything resembling (or even merely escalating) previous Seldon crises would likely bore the reader and thus the Foundation Saga would die on the vine. Something new, "unprovided for; uncalculated for" (*Second Foundation*, p. 503) is required.

Thus, the Mule is introduced. He is mysterious; for nearly two books the readers do not know his deep motivations, his drives, his methods, his powers, or even what he looks like. The Mule is an ominous presence; a looming threat in the shadows. It is exciting for the reader to try to uncover the mystery.

More relevant for our purposes, however, the Mule serves a philosophical function as well. Since the Mule is unforeseen within the Seldon Plan—since psychohistory could not have predicted the rise of this mutant–his presence is meant to inject randomness and chaos into what the reader until this point sees as a determined historical trajectory. We might wonder why, apart from the literary function, Asimov needs randomness and chaos if his psychohistory, fundamentally probabilistic in essence, allows for the freedom to deviate, and perhaps even baldly flout, the Seldon Plan.

I'm not making any claims about Asimov's actual motives. The Mule may simply and only serve the literary function for Asimov. It is peculiar, however, that the Mule enters the scene when the Foundation is well and truly established and seemingly easily overcomes crisis after crisis. It's as if Asimov saw the Foundation navigate successive crises according to the plan and concluded that psychohistory was, in fact, wholly deterministic rather than merely probabilistic. But on what basis could Asimov—or anyone—draw such a conclusion?

Psychohistory is a science. As such, the claims it makes concern more about our access to reality than to reality itself. In other words, given the circumscribed capacity of human cognition, in many domains we can only interact and engage with the world probabilistically. Are we right now all avatars in an extremely sophisticated computer simulation, as Nick Bostrom has proposed? Is my car currently parked outside where I left it (even though I cannot now see it from my location)? Each of these questions has a definitive answer. Yet, that answer eludes us, speaking in absolutes. For ease of communication (and because humans are quite bad at probabilities, according to Daniel Kahneman), we do, however, tend to speak in absolutes: Where's your car? It's in section 33, row 4. It is both possible and plausible that our car was towed or stolen without our knowing it. The reasons and evidence we have for very many of our beliefs are not absolutely conclusive; we could be wrong, even when the probabilities are in our favor.

There is another reason we avoid probabilities in our discourse: psychological custom and habit. As David Hume maintained, "whenever the repetition of any particular act or operation produces a propensity to renew the same act or operation . . . we always say, that this propensity is the effect of *Custom*." Why do I maintain that my car is in section 33, row 4 even when I know it is possible that it could have been towed or stolen? Quite simply, because in my mind the probabilities have stacked up over years of my parking, leaving my car, and returning to find it exactly where I left it. This propensity is not conscious. We automatically form these associations and their accompanying beliefs. This may explain why, even though psychohistory is explicitly articulated in terms of probabilities, Asimov introduces the Mule. As the Foundation reliably (and with seeming ease) overcomes Seldon crisis after Seldon crisis, the probabilities begin to solidify into absolutes. An aberration is needed to jolt the plan, to give the appearance that it can be unmoored.

## He Bent the Plan Seriously, but Not Fatally

It's no coincidence that the Mule is a mutant. For what is a mutant but an individual with a mutation, a *random* genetic aberration. The introduction of the Mule, it seems, gives Asimov the ability to allow the Foundation (and foundationers) to make free choices once again, to have the possibility of (perhaps unknowingly) deviating from the Seldon Plan. As the First Speaker of the Second Foundation intimates, the Mule "was unprovided for; uncalculated for. He bent the Plan seriously, but not fatally" (*Second Foundation*, p. 503).

The introduction of the Mule mirrors an ancient discussion on free will. According to ancient atomists, the two fundamental entities in existence are atoms and the void. Everything that is—objects, events—is the result of atoms moving through the void. Atoms fall toward the center of the cosmos, perpetually. Democritus maintains this path is determined by a swirling vortex and on this path atoms collide to form aggregates like people, planets, and animals. Aristotle demurs. The main problem is that according to such a model, atoms would have to have always been in motion, stretching back infinitely. This means that Democritus does not provide an actual explanation of the movement of atoms, but merely assumes they have always been in motion.

In response, Epicurus attempts a corrective; atoms have both weight and a natural motion towards the center of the cosmos ("Letter to Herodotus," 43:3). In providing this explanation, Epicurus introduces a new problem. If atoms naturally fall downward in straight lines, how do these atoms collide in order to create the furniture of the universe? This account of atomic motion appears to be wholly deterministic. Lucretius captures the problem nicely:

> Moreover, if all motion is always linked, and new motion arises out of old in a fixed order, and atoms do not by swerving make some beginning of motion to break the decrees of fate, so that cause should not follow cause from infinity, from where does this free volition exist for animals throughout the world? ("De Rerum Natura," 2.251–10)

And so Epicurus introduces *the swerve*. The "solution" to the deterministic behavior of atoms in the void is to say that every so often some of the atoms swerve slightly. This, in turn, causes collisions and chain reactions.

It may seem at this point that Epicurus has traded determinism for randomness and that this will not do as an explanation of free will. An indeterminate and random contraction of the muscles in my arm, leading to my slapping my boss in the face, is just as much out of my control as one that occurs due to the determined behavior of atoms. The temptation to write Epicurus off on this basis is powerful, but we must resist it all the same.

Epicurus does not introduce the occasional swerve of atoms to explain free will. Rather, the swerve is meant to clear the obstacle of determinism. If, due to this occasional swerve of atoms, the collisions of the same cannot be wholly predicted, then the determinate trajectory of atoms is broken. Nevertheless, despite not explicitly suggesting the swerve as the causal explanation of free will, Epicurus has arguably two difficulties to overcome.

Recall that according to Epicurus everything is made of atoms in the void (even human souls). In which case, our free actions are the result of collisions of atoms in our brain (or mind). So either, our actions are caused by the determinate falling of "brain" atoms or they are caused by random swerving "brain" atoms. Neither option appears up to the task of explaining free will. The former intimates that our actions are not "up to us" because they are the result of whichever atoms happen to be the ones constituting my brain, falling in a wholly predictable and determinate pattern. The latter intimates that our actions are not "up to us" because they are the result of random swerving atoms in our brain. In either case, our actions do not appear to be "up to us."

By analogy, we can pose the same challenge to the introduction of the Mule in the *Foundation* saga. The trillions of people throughout the empire are the analogs to atoms in the void. The Mule is one of those "atoms" that swerves. So either, the actions of the massive conglomerates in the empire are caused by the determinate trajectory of the universe as demonstrated by pyschohistory or they are caused by random "movements" and "collisions" of those "atoms". Again, neither option is up to the task of explaining the free choices and actions of the characters in the *Foundation* saga. The former intimates that the character's choices are caused by the psychohistorical laws discovered by Seldon and thus not "up to" the individual characters. The latter intimates both that individual actions of the characters is random and that psychohistorical laws are a mere fiction since psychohistory cannot predict when and if an "atom" will swerve. In putting the problem this way we have stumbled upon the free will dilemma. We can formulate the dilemma like this:

1. Either causal determinism is true, or it is false.
2. If it is true, then I am compelled to act as I do, and do not have free will.
3. If it is false, then how I act is random, and do not have free will.

Therefore,

4. I do not have free will.

## Asimov's Alternative Possibilities

The introduction of the Mule has two purposes: literary and philosophical. The philosophical purpose has principally to do with human agency and free will. Further, if Asimov introduced the Mule as a kind of analog of the Epicurean swerve, we've also seen strong reasons to question whether that saves free will from the scylla of determinism and the charybdis of randomness. It remains now to be seen if Asimov needed the Mule to save free will.

Traditionally, theories of free will have attempted to satisfy two conditions: a control condition and an alternative possibility condition. According to the control condition, we want to say that an action is free only if the source of the control of the action is the agent herself. The intuition is that actions are free only if they are "up to us"; if we are not coerced. According to the alternative possibility condition, we want to say that an action is free only if the agent could have done otherwise than she in fact did. The intuition is that actions are free only if the agent could have taken a different action than the one she in fact took. Together, these two conditions are the pillars of a theory of free will.

The free will dilemma formulated above and these two putative conditions on free will are related in the following ways. Causally determined actions appear to violate both conditions. If my action is determined to happen, then it seems that it is neither under my control—violating the control condition—nor possible for me to choose an alternative action—violating the alternative possibilities condition. And, if my action is the result of true randomness, then it seems that it is not under my control—violating the control condition.

On the assumption that Asimov wanted to give his characters the agency to make free choices—rather than assuming all actions are strictly determined, say—the accounts of free will available would have to either reject premise 2. or 3. of the free will dilemma. Compatibilists reject premise 2. and endorse the idea that free will and determinism are compatible. In other words, the truth of determinism would not undermine free will. Libertarian incompatibilists reject premise 3. and endorse either that randomness does not undermine free will or that a rejection of determinism does not strictly entail randomness; there is a middle way, perhaps. In other words, determinism and free will are incompatible *and* determinism is false. Since the Mule is seemingly introduced as a corrective to the increasingly inflexible determinism of psychohistory, we will only focus on compatibilism.

## Pritcher Fought the Mule. Until, That Is, He Was Converted

Classical compatibilists argue that determinism is no threat to free will by analyzing the fundamental concepts of 'freedom' and 'determinism'. Once we understand these concepts, they argue, we will see that the putative conflict is illusory. Moreover, a proper analysis will also yield a different understanding of the intuitive conditions that seem to constrain viable accounts of free will.

When we ask whether an individual acted freely, we want to know if they were able to do what they wanted to do without sufficient constraint. Toran and Batya Darell were free to vacation on Kalgan just in case they wanted to go to Kalgan and were not impeded from doing so. They could have chosen Trantor or Anacreon or any number of other worlds because there was nothing stopping them (they were not incarcerated–physically restrained—they did not have their ship impounded—lack of opportunity—they were not forced at gunpoint, say—coerced—or in comas--lack of ability). Freedom, then, should be understood as nothing more than doing what we want to do in the absence of constraint.

Not only is freedom undermined by constraint, detractors argue, but freedom is also undermined by the inability to do otherwise. And this, they urge, would precisely be the case if determinism were true. Determinism implies there are no different possible paths in the future—thus violating the alternative possibilities condition on free will. The intuitive idea is that determinism implies that past events together will the laws of physics entail the present. If so, then it seems that determinism implies that individuals do not have genuine choices; that since the present and the laws of physics together entail the future any decision between two or more choices is wholly illusory. The problem is that opponents of compatibilism claim that genuine freedom means that at any decision point there must be genuinely open possibilities. The mantra "Same past, different future" is the rallying cry.

When Hardin chooses to initiate a nuclear cold war with the outer planets, he has the choice to offer atomic technology to all of the outer planets, some of them, or do something else. Incompatibilists urge that if everything was exactly the same–molecule for molecule and event for event identical–up to the point of decision, Hardin could have chosen something else, perhaps muster forces and attack Anacreon. On its face, this seems like exactly what it means to have genuinely open possibilities. And, if genuinely open possibilities are a condition of free will, then, it seems as if free will requires same past, different future. But classical compatibilists demur. Hardin, in choosing to offer atomic technology to all of the outer planets, had a specific set of reasons and motivations—"the solution to the first crisis was obvious" (*Foundation*, p. 70). If everything was identical up to the point of decision, then those very reasons and motivations that caused Hardin to make the choice he did would, in fact, be causally impotent. Those reasons and motivations, it turns out, are not the explanation for his choice. This is strange. What is more, the new alternative choice appears completely arbitrary and random. If literally everything was exactly the same up to the choice and in one possibility Hardin chooses to initiate a cold war while in another possibility he doesn't, then it seems that his choice has no causal explanation whatsoever.

Now, if free will is just having the ability and power to do what one wants to do absent constraint and that genuinely open possibilities cannot explain why one option is chosen over another, then in what sense does freedom require the ability to otherwise; in what sense is choice a part of the story at all? In order to account for the alternative possibilities condition on free will, classical compatibilists offer a hypothetical analysis of the ability to do otherwise.

Determinism implies that the choices we make and the actions we take are the result of the past together with the laws of physics. So, same past, *same* future. At first, this seems like a rejection of the condition of alternative possibilities. However, if we recall the classical compatibilist account of freedom, we can rethink what we mean by alternative possibilities. Freedom is the ability to do what you want to do without constraint. The choices you make are explained by your beliefs, desires, intentions, motivations, and reasons. Why does Hardin initiate the cold war? Put simply, Hardin does this because he *believes* it is the best way to protect the Foundation and he is *motivated* to take action because no one else is. But, had he had different motivations, beliefs, and reasons, he would have chosen something else. Classical compatibilists argue that the ability to do otherwise is hypothetical. Hardin would have done otherwise, *if* he had wanted to. Put differently, an individual is free just in case she does what she wants *and* she would have done otherwise if she had wanted to *and* nothing would have constrained her from doing so.

Yet, Han Pritcher offers a compelling objection to classical compatibilism. What happens when all of one's motivations, desires, etc. are unknowingly and deeply manipulated? After the Mule converts him, Han still satisfies the classical compatibilist demands. He only does what he wants to do, viz., serve the Mule. The problem is that due to the Mule's mental conversion, Han is unable to *want* anything different. He solely desires to serve the Mule and cannot even entertain the thought of going against him. The hypothetical analysis of alternative possibilities must expand to include wants and desires as well. 'Pritcher is free only if he could have done otherwise' means that Pritcher would have done otherwise if he had wanted to. And this means that he could have wanted to want to do otherwise. Which means that had he wanted to want to do otherwise he would have wanted to want to want to do otherwise, ad infinitum. This vicious regress made salient by examples such as Pritcher's have led many philosophers to reexamine the conditions of free will.

## Lady Callia Was Something of a Puzzle

The difficulty with classical compatibilism arises from the hypothetical account of alternative possibilities. But what if the alternative possibilities condition was nothing more than a confusion. In 1969, Harry Frankfurt argued that the ability to do otherwise is, in fact, not a condition of free will. The reason we think it is a condition is because in very many cases (perhaps nearly all), proscribing alternative possibilities undermines *source control.* Hence, of the two "original" pillars of free will, the only one that is an actual condition on free will is source control; the action or choice needs to be up to the agent.

Frankfurt's argument is based on an example similar to the following. Suppose the Mule wants Pritcher to assassinate a warlord. Now due to Pritcher's conversion by the Mule, if just before Pritcher decides not to assassinate this warlord, the conversion kicks in (before he is even conscious of forming the intention not to assassinate him) and Pritcher then decides to—forms the intention to—assassinate the warlord. In this case, we would explain the assassination by appealing to the conversion. However, let's suppose that Pritcher decides to assassinate the warlord. In this case, two things are true. First, the assassination was completely up to Pritcher (the conversion does not kick in because Pritcher is not going against what the Mule wants). Second, Pritcher did not have the ability not to decide to assassinate the warlord. It seems, then, that Pritcher both freely chose and did not have the ability to choose otherwise. In other words, he was determined to assassinate the warlord and still freely chose to do it.

Nevertheless, Pritcher is not the exemplar of free agents. We know his more significant choices are the results of the desires and beliefs he has because he has been converted by the Mule (even if, for many of his mundane actions, the conversion plays no role). What we need is a way to understand freedom of the will that takes source control as the fundamental condition while also satisfying intuitions about mental mani- pulation undermining that freedom. For this we must turn to so-called New Compatibilists.

New Compatibilists, persuaded by Frankfurt's argument, want to ground free will in an individual's deep self, in their character, values, and capacity to engage in practical reason. Gary Watson distinguishes between an individual's desires and values. The latter are those things that our practical reasoning judges best. And it is when we act in light of our values rather than appetitive desires that we are free.

> The *valuational system* of an agent is that set of considerations which, when combined with his factual beliefs (and probability estimates), yields judgements of the form: the thing for me to do in these circumstances, all things considered, is *a*. (Gary Watson, "Free Agency," p. 346)

But even here, Pritcher satisfies this account as well. His practical reason judges that serving the Mule is best. In which case, Watson's account gives the wrong verdict. Since our values can be manipulated through no fault of our own, the judgments we make based on those values are corrupted. What's missing here is a more basic or fundamental aspect of our character or intellectual ability. To see this we need only ask whether Pritcher would be able to be moved by objectively factual information contrary to the Mule's will (even if the Mule himself tells Pritcher). As this exchange between the Mule and Pritcher makes clear:

> "Then," said Pritcher. still insistent, "why not remove my own Conversion, if you think that will improve me. I can scarcely be mistrusted, now."
>
> "That never, Pritcher. While you are within arm's reach, or blaster reach, of myself, you will remain firmly held in Conversion. If I were to release you this minute, I would be dead the next."
>
> The general's nostrils flared. "I am hurt that you should think so."
>
> "I don't mean to hurt you, but it is impossible for you to realize what your feelings would be if free to form themselves along the lines of your natural motivation. The human mind resents control. The ordinary human hypnotist cannot hypnotize a person against his will for that reason. I can, because I'm not a hypnotist, and, believe me, Pritcher, the resentment that you cannot show and do not even know you possess is something I wouldn't want to face." (*Second Foundation*, p. 422)

How, then, could we build on Watson's view to rule out Pritcher while also maintaining a significant role for practical reasoning?

For this, I suggest we look to another New Compatibilist, Susan Wolf. Distinctive about Wolf's view is the central role of being able to recognize the True and Good. According to Wolf, the inability to recognize or be moved by what is True and Good undermines freedom. If we put this together with Watson's account, we have the following account of free will:

> An individual acts/chooses freely just in case (a) the source of the action or choice is the agent herself, (b) the action or choice is motivated by the individual's practical reasoning from endorsed values, and (c) the agent has the ability to recognize and be moved by reasons for action grounded in the True and the Good.

The most nebulous condition is (c) and is made more clear by illustration.

Consider the Lady Callia and Lord Stettin. When we first meet Callia and Stettin, we can be forgiven for thinking that Callia is a bit dim and Stettin nothing more than an overbearing warlord. We soon learn that Callia is from the Second Foundation, a hidden faction whose members have all developed the ability to "convert" others as the Mule could do. We learn further that Stettin is under her manipulation. The contrast vis-a-vis the characterization of free will above is instructive. As a Second Foundationer, Callia values the mission of the Second Foundation—to ensure the First Foundation remains on course in the Seldon Plan. As such, her actions, both in her manipulations of Stettin and in her aiding in the escape of Arkady from Kalgan are motivated by her judgment that doing so furthers (or, at least, doesn't hinder) the Second Foundation's mission. Hence, she freely makes these choices.

Alternatively, Stettin, while clearly more subtly manipulated than Pritcher, cannot align his choices with the True and the Good, because his values are not really his own; they are the artifact of Callia's mental powers. When Homir Munn wants an audience with Stettin and access to the Mule's Palace, Stettin's initial reaction is to refuse, but after a brief exchange with Callia, his disposition toward Munn, Arkady, and their request changes. He's unable to deny Callia's desire to entertain Arkady. His decision does not reflect his values, in this instance and we later find out it is because of Callia's mental intervention.

We now have a workable account of free will, compatible with determinism, that gives the correct verdict of both Pritcher and Stettin. What is left is to see if this account would have allowed Asimov to give agency to his characters without relying on the "swerve" of the Mule. To be sure, the Mule as a literary device is engaging and interesting. One wonders, though, if the story about the philosophical need for the Mule suggested earlier was driving the literary need, or vice versa.

## The Fall of the Empire . . . Is a Massive Thing . . . and Not Easily Fought

As a storyteller, Asimov was motivated to create interesting characters who make meaningful and impactful decisions in the world they inhabit while maintaining a consistency and plausibility. As is often the case in grand and sweeping stories such as the *Foundation* saga, new characters emerge providing new challenges and injecting new tensions. Equally often, these new characters offer a reminder or corrective of the consistency or plausibility of the story. It is a master storyteller's gift to do this subtly. In this way, the Mule seems to fulfill this role beautifully. But if the introduction is a corrective, it is easy for the reader to assume the corrective is needed. In this way, as we have seen, it is not clear that Mule was needed at all since the consistency and plausibility he appears to correct is what appears increasingly to be a fully deterministic universe.

Asimov was not a philosopher and so probably not familiar with the many and varied theories of free will that would have allowed him to grant agency to his characters within a deterministic setting. We have seen that there are such theories; that agency is not undermined by determinism. But then we may never have had the Mule, a character who, without firing a shot, infiltrated and took control of the seemingly impenetrable Foundation. The saga may have turned out to be nothing more than a serialized telling of the "Seldon Crisis of the week." Perhaps his motivation had nothing to do with free will. Perhaps the Mule is nothing more than a Checkhov's gun to introduce the powers of the Second Foundation. In which case, the Mule doesn't mirror the Epicurean swerve. Nevertheless, his presence and abilities and the impact they have on the characters still offers a *Foundation*-al lesson on free will and determinism.

# Bibliography


Allen, Roger MacBride. 1993. *Isaac Asimov's Caliban*. Ace.

Aquinas, St. Thomas *Summa Theologica, Prima Pars*. gutenberg.org <www.gutenberg.org/cache/epub/17611/pg17611-images.html>.

Aristotle, 2016. *Metaphysics*. Hackett.

Augustine of Hippo, *The City of God: Volume One* <www.gutenberg.org/files/45304/45304-h/45304-h.htm>.

Asimov, Isaac. 1941. Nightfall. *Astounding Science Fiction* (September).

———. 1942. Foundation. *Astounding Science-Fiction* (May). Re-titled "The Encyclopedists," incorporated as Part II of *Foundation* (1951).

———. 1950. Runaround. In *I, Robot*. New York: Doubleday.

———. 1950. The Evitable Conflict. *Astounding Science Fiction*.

———. 1950. *I, Robot*. Gnome.

———. 1951. *Foundation*. Gnome.

———. 1952. *The Currents of Space*. Doubleday.

———. 1952. *Foundation and Empire*. Gnome.

———. 1956. The Last Question. *Science Fiction Quarterly*.

———. 1967, *Asimov's Guide to the Bible: Volume One, The Old Testament*. Wings.

———. 1969. *Asimov's Guide to the Bible: Volume Two, The New Testament*. Wings.

———. 1976. *The Bicentennial Man and Other Stories*. Doubleday.

———. 1981. *Asimov on Science Fiction*. Doubleday.

———. 1981. *Asimov's Guide to the Bible: The Old and New Testaments*. Wings.

———. 1982. *The Foundation Trilogy: Foundation, Foundation and Empire, Second Foundation*. Bantam.

———. 1982. *Foundation's Edge*. Doubleday.

———. 1983. The Role of the Heretic. In Asimov, *The Roving Mind*. Prometheus.

———. 1986. *Foundation and Earth*. Doubleday.

———. 1988. *Prelude to Foundation*. Doubleday.

———. 1989. *Nemesis*. Doubleday.

———. 1993. *Forward the Foundation*. Doubleday.

———. 1995. *Gold: The Final Science Fiction Collection*. Harper Prism.

———. 2004. *Prelude to Foundation*. Bantam.

———. 2010. *Foundation: Foundation and Empire; Second Foundation*. Everyman's Library.

———. 2012. *Foundation Trilogy*. Random House.

Baier, Annette C. 2011. *The Pursuits of Philosophy*. Harvard University Press.

Benn, S.I. 1988. *A Theory of Freedom*. Cambridge University Press.

Bentham, Jeremy. 1999. *Political Tactics*. Clarendon.

Bentham, Jeremy. 2007 [1789]. *An Introduction to the Principles of Morals and Legislation*. Dover.

Bogdanov, Aleksandr. 1977. *La Science, l'Art, et la Classe Ouvrière*. Paris: François Maspero.

Bostrom, Nick, 2003. Are We Living in a Computer Simulation? *Philosophical Quarterly* 53.

———. 2016 [2014]. *Superintelligence: Paths, Dangers, Strategies*. Oxford University Press.

Brown, Richard, and Kevin S. Decker. 2009. *Terminator and Philosophy: I'll be Back, Therefore I Am*. Wiley.

Burrow, J.W. 1985. *Gibbon*. Oxford University Press.

Calvin, John. *The Institutes of the Christian Religion: Volume One* <www.gutenberg.org/files/45001/45001-h/45001-h.htm>.

Carnap, Rudolf. 1966. The Elimination of Metaphysics through Logical Analysis of Language, In A.J. Ayer, ed. *Logical Positivism*. The Free Press.

Castelvecchi, Davide. 2016. Can We Open the Black Box of AI? *Nature News* 538.

Chalmers, David J. 1996. *The Conscious Mind: In Search of a Fundamental Theory*. Oxford University Press.

Clark, Andy, and David Chalmers. 1998. The Extended Mind. *Analysis* 58:1.

Confucius. 1979. *The Analects*. Penguin.

Darwall, Stephen. 2006. The Value of Autonomy and Autonomy of the Will. *Ethics* 116:2.

Descartes, René. 1996. *The Philosophical Writings of Descartes*. Two volumes. Cambridge University Press.

———. 1997. *Meditations on First Philosophy*. Hackett.

Eaton, A.W. 2012. Robust Immoralism. *Journal of Aesthetics and Art Criticism* 70:3.

Ehrlich, Stacy B., Susan C. Levine, and Susan Goldin-Meadow. 2006. The Importance of Gesture in Children's Spatial Reasoning. *Developmental Psychology* 42:6.

Engels, Friedrich. 1975. *Anti-Dühring: Dialektik Der Natur*. Berlin: Dietz Verlag.

Epicurus. 2003. *Letter to Herodotus 43–3*. In A.A. Long and D.N. Sedley, eds. *The Hellenistic Philosophers*. Cambridge University Press.

Epstein, Brian. Social Ontology. In *The Stanford Encyclopedia of Philosophy* <https://plato.stanford.edu/archives/win2021/entries/social-ontology>.

Evers, Kathinka. 1999. The Identity of Clones. *Journal of Medicine and Philosophy* 24:1.

Fechner, Gustav. 1966. *Elements of Psychophysics*. Holt, Rinehart.

Fischer, John Martin. 2011. Indeterminism and Control: An Approach to the Problem of Luck. In Michael Freeman, ed., *Law and Neuroscience*. Oxford University Press.

Frankfurt, Harry, 1971. Freedom of the Will and the Concept of a Person. *Journal of Philosophy* 68. Reprinted in Gary Watson, ed. *Free Will*. Oxford Readings in Philosophy, 2003.

Fukuyama, Francis. 1992. *The End of History and The Last Man*. Free Press.

Galilei, Galileo. 2022. *The Assayer*. <www.princeton.edu/~hos/h291/assayer.htm>.

Gazzaniga, M. 2005. Forty-Five Years of Split-Brain Research and Still Going Strong. *Nature Reviews Neuroscience* 6:8.

Gellius, Aulus. 1927. *Attic Nights*. Harvard University Press.

Gibbon, Edward. 1990. *Memoirs of My Life*. Penguin.

———. 1995–2000. *The Decline and Fall of the Roman Empire*. Six volumes. Penguin.

———. 2014. Gibbon's *Essay on the Study of Literature*: A New English Translation. Translated by Robert Mankin. *Republics of Letters* 3:3.

Gödel, Kurt. 1951. Some Basic Theorems on the Foundations of Mathematics and Their Implications. In Gödel's *Collected Works, Volume III*. Oxford University Press.

Grue, Lars, and Arvid Heibergh, 2006. Notes on the History of Normality: Reflections on the Work of Quetelet and Galton. *Scandinavian Journal of Disability Research* 8:4.

Gunn, James. 2005. *Isaac Asimov: The Foundations of Science Fiction*. Revised Edition. Scarecrow.

Hacking, Ian. 1983. Nineteenth Century Cracks in the Concept of Determinism. *Journal of the History of Ideas* 44:3.

Han Fei. 2003. *Han Feizi: Basic Writings*. Translated by Burton Watson. Columbia University Press.

Hart, Vi, and Nicky Case. 2014. The Parable of the Polygons <https://ncase.me/polygons>.

Hayes, Wayne B. 2007. Is the Outer Solar System Chaotic? *Nature Physics* 3:10.

Hegel, George Wilhelm Fredrich. 1977. *The Phenomenology of Spirit*. Oxford University Press.

Hilbert, David. 1950. *Foundations of Geometry*. Open Court.

Hofstadter, Douglas R., and Daniel C. Dennett. 2000 [1981]. *The Mind's I: Fantasies and Reflections on Self and Soul*. Basic Books.

Hume, David. 1975 [1748]. *Enquiries concerning Human Understanding and concerning the Principles of Morals*. Oxford University Press.

Hume, David. 2011 [1739] *A Treatise of Human Nature: Being an Attempt to Introduce the Experimental Method Reasoning into Moral Subjects*, Oxford University Press.

Huntington, Samuel P. 2007 [1996]. *The Clash of Civilizations and the Remaking of World Order*. Simon and Schuster.

Ingersoll, Earl G., and Isaac Asimov. 1987. A Conversation with Isaac Asimov. *Science Fiction Studies* 14:1 (March).

James, William. 1956. The Dilemma of Determinism. In *The Will to Believe and Other Essays in Popular Philosophy*. Harvard University Press.

Joseph, Lawrence E. 1990. *Gaia: The Growth of an Idea*. St. Martin's Press.

Kahn, Leonard. 2013. Rule Consequentialism and Disasters. *Philosophical Studies* 162:2.

Kahneman, Daniel. 2013. *Thinking, Fast and Slow*. Farrar, Straus, and Giroux.

Kane, Robert. 1998. *The Significance of Free Will.* Oxford University Press.

Kierkegaard, Søren. 1992. *Concluding Unscientific Postscript to Philosophical Fragments*. Princeton University Press.

———. 1983. *Fear and Trembling / Repetition*. Princeton University Press.

Kinsella, Michael T., and Catherine Monk. 2009. Impact of Maternal Stress, Depression, and Anxiety on Fetal Neurobehavioral Development. *Clinical Obstetrics and Gynecology* 52:3.

Kotz, Samuel and Eugene Seneta. 1990. Lenin as a Statistician: A Non-Soviet View. *Journal of the Royal Statistical Society: Series A (Statistics in Society)* 153:1.

Krugman, Paul. 2021. 'Dune' Is the Movie We Always Wanted. *New York Times* (October 26th) <www.nytimes.com/2021/10/26/opinion/dune-movie-foundation-series.html>.

Kuhn, Thomas Samuel. 1996. *The Structure of Scientific Revolutions*. Third edition. University of Chicago Press, 1996).

Kunda, Ziva. 1990. The Case for Motivated Reasoning. *Psychological Bulletin* 108:3.

Laertius, Diogenes. 2022. *Lives and Opinions of the Eminent Philosophers*. gutenberg.org <www.gutenberg.org/files/57342/57342-h/57342-h.htm>.

Lakatos, Imre. 1978. *Philosophical Papers, Volume 1: The Methodology of Scientific Research Programmes*. Cambridge University Press.

Lao Tzu. 1963. *Tao Te Ching*. Translated by D.C. Lau. Penguin.

Laplace, Pierre-Simon. 1951. *A Philosophical Essay on Probabilities*. Dover.

Liu Cixin. 2014. *The Three-Body Problem*. Tor.

Locke, John. 1991. *An Essay concerning Human Understanding*. Oxford University Press.

Long, A.A., and D.N. Sedley, eds. 1987. *The Hellenistic Philosophers, Volume I*. Cambridge University Press.

Lovelock, James. 1979. *Gaia: A New Look at Life on Earth*. Oxford University Press.

———. 1988. *The Ages of Gaia*. Norton.

———. 1991. *Gaia: The Practical Science of Planetary Medicine*. Gaia Books.

———. 2006. *The Revenge of Gaia*. Penguin.

Lucretius. 2007. *The Nature of Things*. Penguin.

Marx, Karl. 2021 [1848]. *Communist Manifesto*. Marxists. <www.marxists.org/archive/marx/works/1848/communist-manifesto/index.htm>.

———. 2022. Introduction: A Contribution to the Critique of Hegel's Philosophy of Right. Marxists. <www.marxists.org/archive/marx/works/1843/critique-hpr/intro.htm>.

Mill, John Stuart. 2002 [1861]. *Utilitarianism*. Hackett.

———. 2015. *On Liberty and Other Essays*. Broadview.

Neiman, Susan. 2001. What Is the Problem of Evil? In Maria Pia Lara, ed. *Rethinking Evil: Contemporary Perspectives*. University of California Press.

———. 2002. *Evil in Modern Thought: An Alternate History of Philosophy*. Princeton University Press.

Alec Nevala-Lee. [2018]. *Astounding: John W. Campbell, Isaac Asimov, Robert A. Heinlein, L. Ron Hubbard, and the Golden Age of Science Fiction*. Dey Street.

Newton, Sir Isaac. 1846 [1729]. *The Mathematical Principles of Natural Philosophy*. Daniel Adee.

Nguyen, C. Thi . 2022. Transparency Is Surveillance. *Philosophy and Phenomenological Research* 105:2.

Nozick, Robert. 1969. Newcomb's Problem and Two Principles of Choice. In Nicholas Rescher, ed. *Essays in Honor of Carl G. Hempel*. Springer.

O'Connor, Timothy, 1995. Agent Causation. In Timothy O'Connor, ed. *Agents, Causes, and Events: Essays on Indeterminism and Free Will*. Oxford University Press.

Orwell, George. 1949. *Nineteen Eighty-Four: A Novel*. Secker and Warburg.

O'Sullivan, John. 1845. Annexation. *The United States Magazine and Democratic Review* 17. New York.

Parry, Marc. 2013. Quantitative History Makes a Comeback. *Chronicle of Higher Education* (February 25th) <www.chronicle.com/article/quantitative-history-makes-a-comeback>.

Pettit, Philip 1989. Consequentialism and Respect for Persons. *Ethics* 100:1.

Piper, Adrian M.S. 1978. Utility, Publicity, and Manipulation. *Ethics* 88:3.

Plato. 1997. *Plato: The Complete Works*. Hackett.

Plato. 2022. *Theaetetus*. gutenberg.org <www.gutenberg.org/files/1726/1726-h/1726-h.htm>.

Plato. 1991. *The Republic of Plato*. Basic Books.

Poincaré, Henri. 1905. Non-Euclidean Geometries. In *Science and Hypothesis*. Walter Scott.

Popper, Karl Raimund. 1963. *The Open Society and Its Enemies*. Two volumes. Princeton University Press.

———. 2002 [1935]. *The Logic of Scientific Discovery*. Routledge.

Purves, Dale, and R. Beau Lotto. 2003. *Why We See What We Do: An Empirical Theory of Vision*. Sinaeur.

Putnam, H. 1979. What Is Mathematical Truth? In *Mathematics Matter and Method: Philosophical Papers, Volume 1*. Cambridge University Press.

Priest, Graham. Koji Tanaka, and Zach Weber. 2022. Paraconsistent Logic. In *The Stanford Encyclopedia of Philosophy* <https://plato.stanford.edu/archives/spr2022/entries/logic-paraconsistent>.

Rauscher, Frances H., Robert M. Krauss, and Yihsiu Chen. 1996. Gesture, Speech, and Lexical Access: The Role of Lexical Movements in Speech Production. *Psychological Science* 7:4.

Rawls, John 1971. *A Theory of Justice*. Harvard University Press.

———. 1993. *Political Liberalism*. Columbia University Press.

Reichenbach, Hans. 2021 [1937]. *Experience and Prediction*. Hassell Street.

Rescher, Nicholas. 1960. Choice without Preference. A Study of the History and of the Logic of the Problem of 'Buridan's ass'. *Kant-Studien*.

Russell, Bertrand. 1903. *The Principles of Mathematics*. Cambridge University Press.

———. 1972 [1945]. *The History of Western Philosophy*. Simon and Schuster.

Scheffler, Samuel. 2018. *Why Worry About Future Generations?* Oxford University Press.

Searle, John R. 1992. The Rediscovery of the Mind. Bradford.

———. 1997. *The Mystery of Consciousness*. New York Review of Books.

Selin, Helaine, ed. 2012. *Astronomy Across Cultures: The History of Non-Western Astronomy*. Springer.

Spinney, Laura. 2012. History as Science. *Nature* 488 (August).

Stone, I.F. 1988. *The Trial of Socrates*. Little, Brown.

Tononi, G., M. Boly, M. Massimini, and C. Koch. 2016. Integrated Information Theory: From Consciousness to Its Physical Substrate. *Nature Reviews Neuroscience* 17:7.

Trevor-Roper, Hugh. 1993. Introduction. In Edward Gibbon, *The Decline and Fall of the Roman Empire*. Everyman.

Tucker, Aviezer. 2001. The Future of the Philosophy of Historiography. *History and Theory* 40 (February).

Turchin, Peter. 2007. *War and Peace and War: The Rise and Fall of Empires*. Penguin Books.

———. Peter. 2008. Transforming history into science: Arise 'Cliodynamics'. *Science and Technology* <www.sott.net/article/161508-Transforming-history-into-science-Arise-cliodynamics>.

Watson, Gary. 1975. Free Agency. *Journal of Philosophy* 72. Reprinted in Gary Watson, ed. *Free Will*. Oxford University Press, 2011.

Wenmackers, Sylvia. 2021. Path Correction. *Nature Futures* (13th October).

Whitehead, Alfred North. 1933. *Adventures of Ideas*. Free Press.

Wigner, Eugene. 1960. The Unreasonable Effectiveness of Mathematics in the Natural Sciences. *Communications in Pure and Applied Mathematics* 13:1 (February).

Williams, Bernard. 1973. A Critique of Utilitarianism. In J.J.C. Smart and Bernard Williams, eds. *Utilitarianism: For and Against*. Cambridge University Press.

Winthrop, John. 1892. A Model of Christian Charity. In Edmund Clarence Stedman and Ellen Mackay Hutchinson, eds. *A Library of American Literature: Early Colonial Literature, 1607–1675*. New York.

Wolf, Susan. 2011 [1989]. Sanity and the Metaphysics of Responsibility. In Gary Watson, ed. *Free Will*. Oxford University Press.

Zhuangzi. 2020. *Zhuangzi: The Complete Writings*. Translated by Brook Ziporyn. Hackett.

# The Encyclopedists

**Luis Felipe Bartolo Alegre** was a philosopher from the Peruvian sector of planet Earth. Although interested in almost every topic, he has mostly written articles and presented talks on topics such as philosophy of language, theory of science, argumentation theory, and logic. He was also one of the main promoters of the Galactic Society for Symbolic Logic.

**Walter Barta** is about 6 feet tall with shoes on, 200 pounds with shoes off, 20 years old (in the hexadecimal system), has approximately 2 siblings and has memorized 5 primes. He works 40 hours per week as a graduate researcher in a digital humanities laboratory at the University of Houston trying to reduce humans down to numbers, though finding them 99% uncooperative.

**Lisa Bellantoni** is an Associate Professor of Philosophy at Albright College. A wannabe psychohistorian, her research focuses on the ethical aspects of emerging technologies, particularly artificial intelligence, human enhancement, and space exploration. When the Second Galactic Empire rises up, she hopes it offers assigned parking.

**Cora Buhlert** was born and bred in Bremen, North Germany, where she still lives today—after time spent in London, Singapore, Rotterdam and Mississippi—and holds an MA degree in English from the University of Bremen. Cora has been a fan of speculative fiction for as long as she can remember. Discovering *Foundation* in an airport bookstore at the age of sixteen not only made a lengthy delay much more pleasant, but also blew her mind. Though Cora writes in various genres, science fiction, fantasy, and horror will always be her first loves. Cora is a three-time Hugo finalist for Best Fan Writer and the winner of the 2021 Space Cowboy Award. When Cora is not writing, she works as a translator and teacher. Visit her on the web at www.corabuhlert.com or follow her on Twitter under @CoraBuhlert.

**Daniel Fried** is an Associate Professor at the University of Alberta, where he specializes in Chinese literature and philosophy. He is also co-host (with Jon Blumenfeld and Joseph Kolacinski) of the Star's End podcast, on which he can be heard regularly ranting about how the Encyclopedists are the true heroes of Foundation.

**Nathaniel Goldberg** was born sometime in the pre-Galactic Era. Nathaniel is said to have taught philosophy on the "origin world," which Lameth (following Green) places in the Alpha Centauri, Sol, or 61 Cygni system. Nathaniel is also said to have written three books, including *Superhero Thought Experiments: Comic Book Philosophy*.

Best known for its amazing name, psychophysics is the *original* psychoscience: we can be certain that the robopsychology and psychohistory of the distant future will be built upon the endeavors of psychophysicists like Dr. **Andrew Haun**, a scientist at the University of Wisconsin-Madison.

**Joshua Heter** is an Associate Professor of Philosophy at Jefferson College in Hillsboro, Missouri. He is (both numerically and qualitatively) identical with the person who co-edited *The Man in the High Castle and Philosophy*, *Westworld and Philosophy*, *Better Call Saul and Philosophy*, and *Punk Rock and Philosophy*.

**John P. Irish** teaches American Studies, Humanities, and Philosophy classes at Carroll Sr. High School in Southlake, Texas. He received a Doctorate of Liberal Studies in Humanities from Southern Methodist University; although, in his future life he hopes to receive a Doctorate in Psychohistory from Streeling University. He lives in Bridgeport, Texas with his wife and their children—Tom, Annie, Teddy, and Lucy (otherwise known as their pets).

**Leonard Kahn** is the Associate Dean of the College of Arts & Sciences at Loyola University New Orleans. He is considering taking a sabbatical at Streeling University on Trantor in order to brush up on his psychohistory, predictably enough

**Jonathan P. Lang** received his PhD in Philosophy from the University of Wisconsin-Madison and is now a member of the UW-Madison Center for Sleep and Consciousness. When he's not thinking about philosophical issues in *Foundation*, he's thinking about foundational issues in philosophy, namely, those related to explanation, causation, and the nature of consciousness.

**Graham Lee** has an MA in Philosophy from the University of Houston. He is considering taking the professional leap of faith into further graduate study in philosophy, despite the notoriously difficult academic job market, hoping to one day overcome this sub-galactic system in doing so.

**Leib Litman** is a Professor of Psychology at Lander College, New York, where he teaches courses in psychology and neuroscience. He has been collecting Isaac Asimov books since he was a kid. Leib and Isaac Asimov have a lot in common. They are both from Russia, grew up in Brooklyn, and became college professors. But there are also differences. Compared to 550 books that Asimov wrote, Leib wrote only one so far. Will Leib catch up? Only the future will tell!

**Elad Magomedov** supposedly lived in the year 34 After Musk. According to some historians he was a gardener at the Institute of Philosophy in Leuven, Belgium; other scholars claim he was a professional fighter for the festival known as the MMA.

From the *Encyclopedia Galactica*, 116th Edition, 1020 F.E.: **Daniel Malloy** is a rumored inhabitant of the mysterious "Earth", the supposed original home planet of *Homo sapiens* in the days preceding the Galactic Empire. According to legend, Malloy could be found at an institution called "Aims Community College." "College" is an archaic word for an educational and research institute, so some authorities believe that Malloy was a research subject. Others consider it more likely that Malloy was employed at Aims to teach and write about philosophy.

**Trip McCrossin** teaches in the Philosophy Department at Rutgers University, where he works on the nature, history, and legacy of the Enlightenment, in philosophy and popular culture, and where the occasional history-of-philosophy student will mumble that he's not so much a psychohistorian as a psycho historian.

**Petar Nurkić** is a Ph.D. candidate in philosophy at the Faculty of the Philosophy University of Belgrade and a Research Associate at the Institute for Philosophy at the same university. His area of expertise is epistemology, philosophy of science, and history of philosophy. In 2019 he published an article on AI morality inspired by Isaac Asimov's work. Since then, he has published many short texts trying to popularize philosophical accounts of dealing with machines. He is a bit of a workaholic and always late on deadlines. Forgive him, please, 'cause he will not forgive himself.

**Christopher Petersen** is an Instructor of Philosophy at Southern University and A&M College. He has a BA in Biblical Studies/Biblical Languages, half of a MA in Theological Studies from Candler School of Theology at Emory University (after which he joined the Army), a MA in History from Middle Tennessee State University, a MA in Philosophy from Louisiana State University, and is now a PhD candidate in Philosophy at Florida State University. As you can see, he's had a hard time figuring out what he wants to do. Perhaps if he had been able to use the method of psychohistory, he could have anticipated each of these "Intellectual Crises" and acted accordingly.

**Mark Silcox** has worked as a security guard, a short order cook, a freelance writer in the video game industry, and as Chair of Humanities and Philosophy at the University of Central Oklahoma. He has published five books and over twenty-five science fiction and horror short stories. He has also made many prophetic recordings for the guidance of world leaders centuries after his death.

**Josef Thomas Simpson** is from the Los Angeles region of the Origin Planet, but currently resides in Maryland near the capitol, Washington, DC. During his young life in Los Angeles, two clineman (swerves) radically altered his life. The first was a random event that led him to community college (he had previously thought he was not going to pursue higher education). The second was being introduced to philosophy. That swerve led to transferring to a university, then on to earn two master's degrees and a PhD in philosophy. He currently aids underperforming students in gaining the skills to succeed in collegiate academics and also lectures in philosophy.

**Joshua Tepley** is an Associate Professor of Philosophy at Saint Anselm College. He has a BA in Philosophy from Bucknell University and a PhD in Philosophy from the University of Notre Dame. His research interests include free will, personal identity, ontology (the study of being), and the intersection between philosophy and science fiction. He's a huge fan of Isaac Asimov and recommends the stories "Nightfall," "The Last Question," and "The Bicentennial Man."

The *Encyclopedia Galactica* mentions **Sylvia Wenmackers** as a Professor of Philosophy of Science at KU Leuven, Belgium. As a teenager, she wanted to read the entire local library, starting from A. Soon enough, she was hooked on Isaac Asimov's robot stories and his *Foundation* series. Science fiction motivated her to study Physics. Paradoxes and thought experiments about Physics lured her out of the lab and into the philosopher's armchair.

**Mark Zelcer** is Assistant Professor at Queensborough Community College, CUNY, where he teaches philosophy, psychohistory, and related courses. He writes about the philosophy of mathematics and ancient Earth political philosophy. He and Leib Litman collected hundreds of books written by Isaac Asimov and plan on reading them when they are available as holographic book-films.

# Index

ALSO FROM OPEN UNIVERSE

# Neon Genesis Evangelion and Philosophy

## *That Syncing Feeling*

VOLUME 2 IN THE OPEN UNIVERSE SERIES,
POP CULTURE AND PHILOSOPHY®

**Edited by**
**Christian Cotton and Andrew M. Winters**

On the surface, it's a story about badass teens who pilot colossal intelligent rockets to defend Earth from destruction by pitiless Angels. Looking deeper, *Neon Genesis Evangelion* is a profound examination of depression, despair, resilience, and purpose, in the teeth of life's ineluctable futility.

*"To any real otaku, this is a great book, but as someone who more than delves into artificial intelligence, any chance to talk about giant machines that seem to have minds of their own is a chance I will surely take!"*

—ROBERT ARP, Instructor in Artificial Intelligence, US Army, and editor of *1001 Ideas that Changed the Way We Think* (2013)

*"Is* Neon Genesis Evangelion *a cure for the despair and loneliness that is our sickness unto death? If you're like Shinji, then* Neon Genesis Evangelion and Philosophy *is here to show you why. From the fragility of truth to the power of wishful thinking, the authors pilot their philosophical EVAs to battle the ignorance that keeps us apart, while enlightening readers on how to break down their own walls of fear and loneliness."*

—COURTLAND LEWIS, author of *The Real Meaning of Doctor Who* (2021)

**CHRISTIAN COTTON** is an independent scholar and freelance author. He has taught philosophy at Piedmont College and the University of Georgia. He remains unsure exactly what Shinji's deal is.

**ANDREW M. WINTERS** teaches philosophy and religious studies at Yavapai College. He wonders whether we're experiencing the Third Impact or whether humanity is going through its own adolescence.

ISBN 978-1-63770-004-4 (paperback)
ISBN 978-1-63770-005-1 (ebook)